THE EXTERMINATION OF CHRISTIANITY

---|---

A TYRANNY OF CONSENSUS

by

Paul C. Schenck
with Robert Schenck

HUNTINGTON HOUSE PUBLISHERS

Huntington House Publishers
P.O. Box 53788
Lafayette, Louisiana 70505

Library of Congress Card Catalog Number 93-78794
ISBN 1-56384-051-0

Excerpts from
A History of Marxist-Leninist Atheism and Soviet Anti-Religious Policies &
History of Soviet Atheism in Theory and practice and the Believer and the Believer
and Soviet Anti-Religious Campaigns and Persecutions Vol. 1 & Vol. 2
by Dimitry Pospielovsky
Copyright © 1988 St. Martin's Press is reprinted by permission of St.
Martin's Press Inc. & MacMillian Accounts & Administration Limited.

Excerpts from
Hollywood vs America: Popular Culture and the War on Traditional Values
by Michael Medved
Copyright © 1992
reprinted by permission of Harper/Collins, Inc.

Excerpts from
Illiberal Education: The Politics of Race and Sex on Campus
by Dinesh D'Souza
Copyright © 1991
reprinted by permission of the Free Press, Inc.

Excerpts from
The Rise and Fall of the Third Reich
by William L. Shirer
Copyright © 1959, 1960 by William L. Shirer
Copyright © 1987, 1988 Renewed by William L. Shirer
reprinted by permission of Simon & Schuster, Inc.

Dedication

---|---

To Rebecca,
With whom I have shared half my life,
My best friend, wife, and magnificent mother of our
children.
She has sacrificed much, given even more, and has never
given up.

And to our children,
Who make us feel so powerful.
Seven on earth,
And one in heaven.

And to God
Who is able to keep us from falling,
And to present us faultless,
Before the presence of His glory with exceeding joy,
To God our Savior,
Who alone is wise,
Be glory and majesty,
Dominion and power
Both now and forever.
Amen.

Contents

— | —

Acknowledgments		vii
Introduction	America's Second Civil War	ix
Chapter One	A Tyranny of Consensus	22
Chapter Two	The New Intolerance	42
Chapter Three	A Christian Kristallnacht	70
Chapter Four	Prime Time Prejudice	89
Chapter Five	Big Screen Bigotry	108
Chapter Six	Injustice in the Courtroom	118
Chapter Seven	Ignorance in Academia	139
Chapter Eight	Five Steps to Disaster	169
Chapter Nine	Securing the Sacred	189

Chapter Ten   Heaven Help Us   **206**

Epilogue   **219**

Notes   **234**

Acknowledgments

— | —

This volume would not have been possible without the assistance of numerous colleagues, staff, and dear friends. My research assistant, Reverend Greg Regis, spent countless hours reading and summarizing, running for information and then running for more. He spent the hours I could not at the libraries. My secretary, Kitty Zilliox, who has never tired in over a decade of service, worked around the clock, even while recovering from major surgery, to prepare the manuscript for the publisher. Karen Swallow Prior read the manuscript, made numerous important recommendations, and helped rewrite the more difficult material. Hers was truly a labor of love. Reverend Sameh Samir Sadik provided invaluable assistance at Regent University in Virginia Beach, where I did most of the writing. Members of our staff, June Chittenden, Amy Tartick, and Phyllis Alvarez, read the manuscript, checked the sources and made important suggestions. Phyllis's husband, Rene Alvarez, was a lifeline to the computers, and he also proofread. He gave hours and hours, which otherwise would have been devoted to sleeping, preparing the drafts. Stephen Sementilli and his wife, Ann, went way beyond the call of duty, working long days and nights, proofreading, entering changes, checking sources, and making suggestions. My friends, Jeff and Michelle Spencer and James and Beverly Duane, read the manuscript and made numerous valuable suggestions. Pastor Dwight Saunders, at one time my attorney and now a fellow pastor, and Reverend Charles Nestor, who has been my friend all my adult life, also read the manuscript and made suggestions. Sandra

Koerber, who has, since we met, helped me in a great variety of endeavors, read the manuscript, made important suggestions, and did some rewriting. Ann Galie, Donna Ketchum, Linda Marshall, Charlie McGuire, Sandy Mott, Janice Powell, Mary Ruberto, Anna Schanley, Tom Spence, and Terri Summers helped with the proofreading and word processing. A special word of thanks must go to the Elders of New Covenant Tabernacle Church, John Ferguson, John Kennedy, David Martin, James Mize, Domenick Nati, John Terreri, and George Walsh, and the congregation for making possible the writing sabbatical without which this book would never have been completed. I am indebted to my fellow activist, Randall Terry, for linking me up with Huntington House Publishers, and special thanks to the editors Mark Anthony and Renee Cazayoux for their assistance and for giving a new writer a chance. Special thanks to my brother, Reverend Robert Schenck, who helped shape the work, added important data, assisted with most of the chapters, and wrote the epilogue. And thanks to my parents, Henry and Marjorie Schenck, my father-in-law, James Wald, and our whole family for their constant encouragement and their matchless investment, which made possible the equity of love and support that went into this work.

Introduction

――――――――― | ―――――――――

America's Second Civil War

We are in the middle of the greatest ideological struggle in America's history. This dramatic assertion is also a very discomforting one. It seems to me that it must be easier to live some time before such a struggle, or some time after it. For instance, I should think that it would have been more comfortable to live in 1850, before the Civil War, or in 1880, after it.

We who belong to the current generation have no such luxury. We are living in the midst of a very great conflict, indeed, a "combat" of personal and public convictions. It is no secret that this conflict has been brewing for some time— erupting at intervals on the campaign trail, in the legislatures, in the schools, in the courts, and in the streets. These eruptions have resulted in wins, losses, and stalemates for both sides. They have ranged from tame debates to rancorous antagonism to violent confrontation and even murder.

I am referring to the clash between two competing philosophies or ways of living. One is what has been referred to by the Rev. Martin Luther King, Jr., in his "Letter from Birmingham Jail," as the "Judeo-Christian Heritage." This phrase summarizes a world view based on belief in a personal Creator-God who is revealed in Scripture, attested to in the order of creation, referred to by statesmen, scholars, and philosophers, invoked in the great documents like the Declaration of Independence, and revered by the vast majority of American citizens. This Judeo-Christian heritage hands down to each successive generation common tenets of faith and practice, which include standards of morality, carefully constructed definitions of relationships between the sexes, within families, and in society, and certain principles of government. These are held to be applicable and binding on every "tribe, and tongue, and people and nation." In contemporary terms, that means regardless of their race, sex, age, or nationality. In short, it is a belief in moral absolutes that pervades and impinges on every aspect of human life and civilization.

The other competitor is what I have come to call the false consensus (false in the way that we use the Greek form *pseudo*). It is an amalgamation of various philosophies and theories, some dating back over 250 years to the Enlightenment, that period when men like Voltaire and Rousseau elevated "Reason" above God. They conducted a terrible revolution in France by employing militant atheism to overthrow the Church. Those anti-religious passions survive today through the philosophical writings of that period. Other components of this consensus date back less than a generation, to the time when the British rock group Jethro Tull proclaimed on the jacket of their gold-selling album, "In the beginning, man created god." In the early 1960s a group of theologians declared the "death of God," that is, the God of the Judeo-Christian tradition. Since that time, the divine throne has been up for grabs—mostly being seized by trendy superstars like Madonna and Michael Jackson.

Some have referred to the false consensus by its parts: secularism, materialism, and humanism, among others. These terms refer to world views that deny the existence of a personal Creator-God; or at least they deny any capacity for any knowledge about his nature and existence, as well as his active involvement in people's lives. They further deny any transcendental origin or meaning to life, as well as moral absolutes; they contend that truth, morals, and values are relative, fluid, and evolutionary. Humanism, which is a very small part of the false consensus, maintains that humanity is the measure of all things. There is more determinism in the false consensus than humanism. Determinism teaches that humans are the unwitting subjects of external natural forces more powerful than their own cognition. According to the consensus, the forces of economics, the subconscious, and evolution ultimately determine the mores by which we live.

An examination of these philosophies shows why Judeo-Christian culture is threatened. Yet, the prevalence of these philosophical systems is not enough to explain the dominance of the false consensus.

Francis Schaeffer made the following observation in his *A Christian Manifesto* over a decade ago:

> The basic problem of the Christians in this country in the last eighty years or so, in regard to society and in regard to government, is that they have seen things in bits and pieces instead of totals.[1]

This still appears to be a problem. The false consensus, to really be understood, has to be seen as a whole. It is not a conspiracy in the technical sense of the term. There is no shadowy cabal meeting behind closed doors in smoke-filled rooms, plotting to expunge every vestige of faith from the face of the earth. In fact, there is more competition among the purveyors of the false consensus than there is communication. To offer a "conspiracy theory" would be a waste of time, chasing after mirages, figments of the imagination. I find no evidence whatsoever of an organized, deliberate, human conspiracy against religion. Yet there is an abundance of evidence that a consensus against religion, and Christianity in particular, does exist in Hollywood, in academia, and in the courtroom. This evidence is so overwhelming that it behooves conscientious Christians and other religionists to try to understand why it has become so pervasive in the last generation. That is the purpose of this book: to expose the false consensus, the anti-religious campaign that is so pervasive in contemporary American culture.

When they are divorced from everyday living, the two competitors, secularism and Judeo-Christian religion, seem to do well, coexisting side-by-side in the community, the university, and even in the same person's mind and heart.

But when the rudimentary principles of these two belief systems are applied to the critical issues of family and society, of life and death, they clash, and no middle ground remains where they can rest undisturbed by one another.

The American public is in serious conflict over issues of private behavior and public policy. The American people literally stand on the battlefield of the soul; the controversy rages all around and soon will escalate into a full-scale social, political, and spiritual conflict. The most critical juncture at which these two worldviews collide is the subject of morality; in particular, sexuality, and specifically, marriage and family, heterosexuality, homosexuality, and abortion. The false consensus on abortion has inadvertently brought into the debate another set of issues: suicide, euthanasia, and the sanctity of human life. By insisting that abortion is merely a private matter of what a woman does with her own body, pro-abortionists have de facto conceded that suicide, and similarly, being voluntarily killed, can only be a matter of what someone else does with his own body. On every hand, militant secularism is bullying the Church, hemming her in, and corralling her so she can be lassoed and tamed. But in the world, the Christian is the perennial maverick. "Who is he who overcomes the world?" St. John inquires. "He who believes Jesus is the Son of God."[2]

Those who fail to comprehend the depth of passionate conviction held by the contenders on both sides of this controversy will ultimately be swept aside and left behind. Because of an unwillingness or inability to grasp the importance of those convictions, our nation may have to suffer another national schism, with the commensurate devastation. Spiritual passions run very deep. Fidelity to religious convictions about worship, sexuality, marriage and family, and the sanctity of life exceeds commitment to personal autonomy, physical pleasure, and material prosperity.

Secularism[3] insists that deeply held religious beliefs must be suppressed in order to maintain a so-called pluralistic and diverse country. This assertion is untenable. Nothing is more influential in the forming of a citizen than his cherished convictions. These have virtually everything to do with how he defines himself in his roles and responsibilities, how he relates to others in his personal and public life in relationship to his community. To tell a person that he must dismiss his convictions, divest himself of his beliefs, or disguise the practice of his faith is in effect to deny his personhood and exclude him from any meaningful participation in society.

It must not escape the contemporary American that this republic was founded by persons seeking religious freedom and that it is the product of a great and bold experiment balancing liberty and responsibility upon the fulcrum of the Judeo-Christian ethic. That the founders and sustainers of this democracy were and continue to be overwhelmingly religious, and particularly Christian, puts the lie to the secularist inference that fervent religious faith is a danger to democracy. In the history of civilization, no nation on earth has been able to achieve and sustain our standards of liberty and justice except through strong religious faith. A secular nation hostile to Christians and to Christianity will ultimately be a nation hostile to itself. Yes, self-destruction!

The election of Bill Clinton as president of the United States in November 1992 was hailed by many secularists as a triumph over the so-called religious right. The term itself has taken on a pejorative sense and has been widely and consistently used to denigrate and defame persons of conscientious Christian faith who will not divorce their beliefs from their social and political responsibilities. Clinton and his running mate, Al Gore, were touted as a part of the new generation of youthful politicians, unfettered by the restrictiveness of the previous generation. They were the "MTV" candidates—fresh, vital and, in the president's case, even a little bit naughty. They represented the antithesis of the stodgy, prudish, puritanical religionists of the Republican administration and their emphases on personal responsibility and traditional definitions of proper sexuality, marriage, and family.

With the inauguration of Clinton, the sexual revolution and its concomitant immoralities moved up to Pennsylvania Avenue. On the weekend of 24-25 April 1992, Clinton fled the White House as thousands of homosexuals and lesbians descended on the nation's capital in a flagitious orgy. In return for cash and votes, Clinton made campaign promises to support the homosexual legislative agenda. He had let the genie out of the bottle and, in spite of an overwhelmingly negative public response, was beholden to the gay activists. As a result, a clear agenda of social change has been implemented against conscientious Christians in America. In the words of one lesbian leader, "We're out of the outhouse, into the White House, and President Clinton is leading the way!"

In addition to homosexuality, the Clinton administration supports the free distribution of birth control to public school students, taxpayer-funded abortion on demand, and the use of the brains and bodies of pre-born children in scientific experimentation. In spite of his campaign promises to focus on the economy, the president's first two weeks in office included five executive orders increasing the number of abortions and calling for one order permitting homosexuals to serve in the military. These symbolic actions clearly expose the undeniably revolutionary sexual agenda that formed the covert platform of his campaign and that continues to drive the agenda of his administration.

Bill and Hillary Clinton are young as presidents and first ladies go. They are quintessential "baby boomers," the generation born between 1946 and 1964 so widely celebrated in contemporary culture. The parents of this tidal wave of toddlers knew firsthand what it meant to put others first, paying the price for others, yet going without. Not only had they endured World War II, with its larger than life demands, but they had also known the deprivations of the Great Depression. The parents of the boomers were determined to provide better for their children.

As a result, these boom kids were far better off than any generation before them. They were coddled and comforted and well provided for. And there were more of them, too. So many that as they emerged from their diapers and playpens, they began to overrun and overwhelm everything in their path. Their needs and desires literally shaped the world around them. They created new markets, new products, and a new worldview.

Growing up, many of them learned to see a telephone, a television, and a T-Bird as rights to be grasped, not privileges to be earned by following a work ethic based on the clearly defined responsibilities of faith, family, and community. Like spoiled children, many boomers became accustomed to the world's revolving around them and its doting and fetching and wiping up after them, too.

As they entered puberty, the boomers imposed a mass adolescence on America. One mark of coming of age is the testing of authority, and boomers did it with a vengeance. Protests against the war in Viet Nam, immersion in the drug culture, and the sexual revolution—through these expressions, the boomers tested and stretched the limits. This liberation became thematic as the first class of boomers came of age in the sixties. Like ordinary youngsters coming of age, many boomers shimmied out on the limb, found the dangerous reach, and drew back to appropriate parameters. But for others it was to become a liberation gone awry. For some the end of the limb was too confining; it wasn't enough to venture away from the trunk and then return. Once out on the limb, they sought to redefine the tree altogether, and they exchanged the maturity and strength of the trunk for the danger and thrill of the farthest reaching branches.

There had been a national revival of religion in the post-World War II era, which on the Protestant side gave rise to modern evangelicalism, perhaps best exemplified in the rise of Billy Graham. On the Catholic side, the Church hierarchy strengthened moral theology as it countered modern trends. The Christian resurgence began to wane, however, just as the boomers began coming of age. Many boomers focused the massive offensive weaponry of their adolescent rebellion on the biggest target they could find: their parents' faith.

Philosophically, many of them doubted and ultimately renounced the Judeo-Christian traditions of their parents and their churches. The boomers were the most massive group ever of young Americans to go to college. There they were exposed to a plethora of secular and non-Christian philosophies, which they avidly explored, experimented with, and assimilated. They eventually embraced, to a large extent, a hastily concocted amalgam of Marxist and Freudian determinism and Darwinian evolutionism. But ultimately, it boiled down to a callow hedonism. This rejection of Christianity was fueled by a pervasive cynicism toward organized religion that was born of youthful rebellion and later sustained by disappointments with the churches.

The boomers often repudiated the traditional moral definitions of relationships that restricted sexual intercourse to within marriage; they experimented with innumerably varied coital couplings. Later they would have the juvenility to wonder where all the babies, diseases, and abortions came from!

In short order, the materialism of the eighties overcame the earlier socialism of the sixties, and many rejected moderation for excess. Even among liberals, happiness was increasingly equated with economic prosperity to the extent that death was considered preferable to poverty. Poverty, home-lessness, and the health care crisis threatened boomers with the prospect that they too could become poor or homeless or hopelessly sick. In a convoluted altruism, boomers advocated for government solutions in a desperate attempt to preclude, to the greatest possible extent, the potentiality of their suffering anything less than total satisfaction.

To be fair, some boomers are now waking up to some of their errors. Social analysts now talk about a "neo-traditionalism" that seeks the stability of the past while keeping up with the innovations of the present. From the mid to the late eighties, in an attempt to find direction for their own lives and help in raising their children, boomers returned to the churches and synagogues they had walked out on during their rebellious years. Unsatisfied with what appeared to them as ambiguous "moral platitudes," their reunion was only brief, and by the early nineties many were again exiting the churches.

The boomers, though, did retain a form of religion, mostly self-defined. For instance, we have a renewed disapproval of unwed motherhood, but on economic rather than moral grounds. Certain forms of pornography are decried, not because they are prurient, but because they are misogynistic. We have the advancement of the causes associated with children, not because we are entrusted by God with their care, but because children satisfy us and sometimes make us happy. For too many boomers, "wanted children" are more like decorations: enough of them add a nice touch to the family photo, or balance off the backseat of the Saab. Too many are clutter, dishevelling, and make a poor presentation!

This is why, although we currently recognize birth out of wedlock, sexually transmitted diseases, AIDS, crime, and violence as terrible social problems desperately requiring solutions, we are at the same time re udiating Judeo-Christian morality, with its stress on chastity, fidelity, self-control, and responsibility. Instead our solutions are abortions, Norplant, condoms, and the acceptance of homosexuality.

The Clinton administration's insistence on federally sponsored, publicly funded abortion-on-demand and its support of the Freedom of Choice Act, as well as scientific experimentation on the pre-born, has nothing to do with compassion and everything to do with selfish satisfaction. The Freedom of Choice Act contains virtually no references to the transcendent, intrinsic value and dignity of the nascent child, nor the rights of nascent life, which Christians hold as a paramount moral principle. It says nothing about the enduring responsibility society has toward women, expectant mothers, women in crisis, and their children, not to mention the responsibilities of men and fathers to these same groups. It is this licentiousness and obsession with personal autonomy, together with the absence of moral standards, against which conscientious Christians so vociferously object. The president, however, like so many of the boomer establishment, has turned a deaf ear, even to the protestations of his own Baptist denomination, and prefers to denounce Christian dissent as religious fanaticism.

There is perhaps no element of this new world view that is more reprehensible and offensive to the Christian conscience than the promotion of the use of nascent children in scientific experimentation. This is the most pernicious innovation of our contemporary secularist, technocratic society. The technology, vocabulary, and propaganda of so-called fetal tissue transplantation is ominously similar to and in many cases identical with that of the jargon of the Nazi doctors who conducted experiments on concentration camp victims.

In a uniquely truthful and reflective article on fetal research, *Newsweek* magazine reported on a team of Finnish and American scientists that decapitated a dozen prematurely born infants that were "aborted live" [sic] and "kept the heads alive artificially for study." The article included another study in which "aborted fetuses" were kept alive in saline solution to determine whether they could absorb oxygen. "Science does not advance in a moral vacuum," the writers intoned. "Time and again it intrudes on the concerns of conscience."[4]

But it was conscience-be-damned for President Clinton, who on his second day in office issued an executive order making the federal government a sponsor of this macabre and barbaric venture. In a gratuitous jab at people of conscience, Clinton claimed he was liberating "science and medicine from politics"—as if there were no ethical considerations at all involved in the harvesting of healthy human fetuses to implant their cells in ailing adults. In this instance, the president used his political pen to paint conscientious Christians as hard-hearted moralists who are willing to see others suffer while they stick uncompromisingly to their antiquated ideas.

In sloughing off the grave ethical implications of such experimentation, Clinton revealed that he is under the spell of the false consensus: There are no transcendent moral absolutes, only politics. The Judeo-Christian tradition begins with an agreed upon set of mores that determine what the politics will be. The false consensus has it the other way around; politics determines the mores.

Because of their commitment to chastity, fidelity, and heterosexuality, Christians are commonly depicted in the entertainment/news media as bigots. At abortion protests and homosexual marches, this chant can be heard: "Racist, sexist, anti-gay, born-again bigots, go away!" This epithet expresses what so many secularists believe: that opposition to immoral, sexual practices is equivalent to racial prejudice, misogyny, and gay-bashing. Discrimination has become a nasty word in our contemporary culture. It is nasty when it is used to deny equality of housing, pay, or other liberties to citizens because of their sex, skin color, or nationality. But to use the term so wisely employed by the chairman of the joint chiefs of staff, the "benign aspects" of a person's identity (skin color, gender, disability or impairment, national or ethnic origin) are not at all equivalent to his sexual practices. The legitimate requirement that all people be treated with equal justice does not mean that aberrant sexual practices should be accepted or legalized. The push is now on, however, to demand that all Americans accept and affirm homosexual practices. By insisting or insinuating that all Americans accept what is scripturally condemned and morally offensive, the proponents of homosexuality consign conscientious Christians to an internal cultural exile. By the same token, teaching students in school that homosexual behavior is normal drives a wedge between Christian parents and their children. Children who read *Heather Has Two Mommies* or *Daddy's Roommate* from pre-school up will be left with the distinct impression that their parents are narrow-minded bigots whose prejudices against gays should be rejected and replaced by a more urbane and tolerant secularist, relativistic morality.

The culture of the false consensus, that is, of the elite minority in media, academia, and the liberal law establishment, has completely divested itself of Judeo-Christian morality and replaced it with a nouveau secularist relativism. Even though the vast majority of Americans still hold, to some extent, to traditional beliefs, the cultural elite make the majority feel like the minority by projecting their own set of mores. The false consensus operates by false peer pressure. Television, for instance, consists of a relatively small number of producers (it takes about 120 people to create a half-hour segment) communicating their beliefs to millions of viewers. Yet the effect is transposed. The cultural elitists create the aura of majority by virtue of the ubiquity of their medium, and the viewers are "minoritized" by virtue of their isolation and anonymity.

Because of their commitment to biblical morality, Christians are routinely stereotyped in popular entertainment and in the news media. Hollywood depicts practicing Christians (and to a lesser extent observant Jews) as hypocrites, lunatic fanatics, rapists, mass murderers, and cannibals. In television shows believers are not treated any better. Prime time television continues to cast Christians as miscreants, fun-hating puritans, sexually dysfunctional misogynists, and dangerous fanatics. Broadcast and print journalism demonstrate a clearly documented bias against persons of Judeo-Christian religious heritage. News services have made wildly exaggerated claims about religious leaders and protesters and critics of the popular culture. These misrepresentations have created a negative view of people of faith in the minds of many Americans and have contributed to widespread disdain for religious practices, especially for the Christian clergy.

The three great culture makers, the entertainment and news media, academia, and the liberal law establishment, evince a moral consensus drastically different from the one held by most Americans, and they unwittingly cooperate to create an environment deliberately hostile to persons of religious faith. As conscientious Christians are increasingly treated as undesirables and are forced out of mainstream America through the effective use of stereotypes, hyperbole, and misrepresentation, the consequence for millions of citizens who hold to traditional religious beliefs and practices will be defamation, discrimination, and ostracism.

The academy (the universities, colleges, and public schools) are a close second to the media in playing the adversary to traditional religion. Over the last thirty years, the ivory towers of academia have specialized in desecrating the Judeo-Christian philosophy and replacing it with varied strains of Marxist, Darwinian, and Freudian determinism. The result is that Christians are presented in the classroom as bourgeois oppressors, superstitious primitives, and sexually frustrated neurotics.

Like Darwinism, secularism has achieved a doctrinaire status in the academy. To understand this, it is important to review its origins. Secularism began its ascent during the Enlightenment, became a persecutory crusade during the French Revolution, and was propelled toward the twentieth century by Darwinism. At its inception, secularism was philosophically atheistic, intellectually opposed to supernaturalism, and passionately opposed to the church. These three characteristics have often paired secularism with Marxism. Far from being "neutral," secularism has always been determined to effect the demise of religious faith. In this regard, secularism and Marxism are confluent tributaries. Contrary to popular understanding, secularism is not the absence of religion, but rather the antagonist of religion.[3]

In recent times, the courts have begun to reflect the secularist false consensus as they have used their extensive powers to limit and, in some cases, to deny Christians their basic civil and constitutional rights. Judges have prohibited the possession and distribution of Bibles and religious tracts, "witness," and prayer in public buildings, parks, and street corners. The curtailment and outright denial of these civil liberties go almost unnoticed by a media already disdainful of believers and cynical about the legitimacy of the First Amendment when it comes to the public practice of fervent Christian faith. The public, mostly ignorant of these injustices, has fallen, to some extent, under the secularist spell. When one group of Christians was barred from praying in a municipal building, a middle-aged woman nearby was heard by one bystander to say, "They can't do that! Pray in public? That's illegal!"

All of this should sound off alarms, not just in churches, synagogues, and mosques, but in newspaper columns, newsrooms, civil rights organizations, civil liberties groups, and among citizens who cherish the Bill of Rights and reject the intolerance of anti-religious bigotry. But, alas, the alarm remains silent, and the incidents of defamation continue to increase. Soon, anyone who identifies himself with the Judeo-Christian way of seeing will wind up as a persona non grata in secular America. While it currently seems unthinkable and unlikely that religious liberty could be lost altogether in America, a social, political, and cultural environment that is intolerant and hostile to religious faith will in effect nullify the First Amendment and its protections, with the result that religious freedom will have a shallow, hollow ring "from shore to shore."

ONE

A Tyranny of Consensus

One afternoon in the spring of 1991, I received a telephone call in my church study from James Comerford, a member of the board of education for the 48,511-student Buffalo public school system.

My secretary buzzed the intercom and told me that the school board president was on the line and had a personal matter he wished to discuss with me. I was happy to take the call.

"Reverend Schenck?" he asked in what I recognized as his distinctive mellow tone. (I had met Mr. Comerford once at a reception for the city's mayor.)

"Yes, Mr. Comerford, good to hear from you. What can I do for you?"

"The board of education is appointing a committee to review the health curriculum of the school system. Each board member can nominate two individuals to serve on the committee, and I'd like to nominate you to serve on the committee. Would you accept?"

I didn't hesitate. This seemed to me to be a great opportunity to participate in a critically important process with serious implications for the students enrolled in New York State's second largest school system.

"Absolutely," I replied enthusiastically. "It's an important civic responsibility. I'd be glad to help."

The conversation lasted no more than ten minutes. He told me I'd hear from him within a month. It was about three weeks later when I received a form letter from the superintendent of schools, Dr. Albert Thompson, inviting me to an orientation session at one of the city's magnet schools.

The meeting was disorganized. It was not clear what the goal or purpose of the committee was. There were over eighty people present, and the group was divided into categories according to subject and grades. We were asked to choose which grade levels we would like to work within but not which subjects we would like to treat. (A health curriculum was being presented, a separate AIDS curriculum, and a human development curriculum.) I chose the fifth grade group because I felt that the problems associated with sexuality—teen pregnancies, abortions, sexually transmitted diseases—were too far advanced in later grades for a curriculum to make a real difference. I believed that if we addressed the problems early enough, we could make genuine progress.

The caucus was literally directionless and amounted to a brief talk from the superintendent and a private reading of the present curricula, which appeared to be a mish-mash of poorly organized and presented materials. The meeting was completed within an hour-and-a-half, and we were dismissed with an indication that a follow-up meeting would occur in two weeks. That meeting was never convened. Instead, a smaller committee of twenty, of which I was selected as a member, was convened in the board chambers at City Hall. Dr. Thompson told us at that meeting that the previous group was temporarily suspended, pending our review and the drafting of a recommendation for the revision of the present health and human development curriculum. Our new committee was redubbed the "Health Education Curriculum Policy Review Committee."

I was eager to begin although I had a definite impression that my presence on the committee was a source of consternation to some of the others, and I sensed that it would become a public controversy. I was well known in western New York as a pro-life activist and a critic of many liberal policies on moral and social issues, such as contraceptives in schools and the promotion of homosexuality in public education.

I was right. As soon as it was known that I had been appointed to the committee, the *Buffalo News*—the only major newspaper in town and avowedly liberal and pro-choice in its editorial position—criticized Mr. Comerford for appointing a "fundamentalist, anti-abortion minister from the suburbs" to a city school district committee. The undertone of the editorial was that I was the closest thing to a racist bigot the newspaper could imagine. Furthermore, they inferred duplicity in my appointment, since Mr. Comerford had misspelled my name on the nominating ballot (an error so common I no longer notice it), in their opinion an attempt to disguise my identity!

Attempts were made by the opponents of my nomination to the board to have my appointment rescinded, but they failed. I attended the first meeting without incident. We would meet every week thereafter for nearly eight months, with few exceptions. The meetings lasted for about two hours. The first few meetings seemed to proceed smoothly. Dialogue was meaningful, and eventually some real substance was addressed. I recommended that we hold off on any recommendations until we could hear from the state education department about the curricula that it considered to be proven most effective in reducing the rates of pregnancy, sexually transmitted disease, and abortions among students in public schools.

A request was made for a resource person from the state education department, and instead we got a representative of the state health department. I asked her, "Do you have any studies that identify a truly effective curriculum being utilized in a public school system in New York State that has reduced the rate of teen pregnancy and STDs?"

The representative, a small-framed, middle-aged professional woman with short-cropped black hair streaked with grey, and wearing a casual top and slacks, slid back into the curvature of her chair, slung her head from side to side, winced, and glanced furtively toward the table top.

"Well," she sighed hesitatingly, as if to prepare us for the worst, "people sometimes get mad when I tell them this, but we do have a curricula being utilized in a school system that was ranked third in the state in teen pregnancies and STDs that now is number thirty-three in the state after six-and-a-half years."

I prepared for what I was convinced would prove to be the ammunition for the condom distributors on the committee—and for what would prove to be the opponent of my position on abstinence and chastity. But I was up to it; I just decided that this was going to be a big stumbling block to try to overcome.

"Well," I prodded. "Please describe it for us."

"Well," she exhaled, "it is an abstinence-based [wince], parent-driven [defensive body posture as if to fend off rotten tomatoes], non-contraceptive model of sexuality education."

She rolled her eyes, lips settled flat and drawn out as if to say, "Yup, it's hard to believe, but it's true."

I was incredulous. What I thought would be my most formidable enemy turned out to be my ally. I was indignant.

"Why do you wince? If that's the truth, then that's what we want to know."

"Well," she began with her now standard preparatory prefix, "most people get very upset when I tell them that."

Her dirty work done, she finished with an offer of an address where the curriculum could be obtained, and she departed.

But that was not the most bizarre event of that meeting. After the woman left the room, a discussion ensued, led by myself and a professor from the University Medical School and director of a city health clinic (where abortion referrals were made) as to whether such a "controversial curriculum" was really worth its success in stemming teen-age sexual activity. The conclusion was, it wasn't. On to the next curriculum. The life and health of the children were exchanged for a mess of political correctness!

We continued to hobble along. I avoided as much controversy as I could at the outset of the committee's work for three reasons: first, to try to disprove some of the members' image of me; second, to give them all a fair chance; and third, to save my ammo for the end, which I had already anticipated would be an ideological conflagration.

As the committee proceeded, the opposition seemed to

be following a very similar game plan. Conflict over ideas
and convictions continued to mount and become increasingly more intense. At another point in the ongoing discussions, I had urged the committee to address not just the
intellectual and physical needs of the students but the students' "souls" as well. (I stressed that I was using the term
soul in the classical, and not the spiritual sense.) The reaction
to my employment of the word *soul* was visceral.

"Souls!" shrieked a committee member. "That sounds
like you're talking about God, and we can't mention God!"

"We can't mention God," I reiterated. "But we can
mention anal intercourse, oral sex, erections, and menstrua-
tion—amazing," I said.

It *is* amazing to consider just what we have come to in
public education. Previously unmentionable private aspects
of exclusively adult behavior with grave consequences for
children—consequences incontrovertibly demonstrated in one
study after another—are now as common as multiplication
tables and vowels—but God, acknowledged and worshipped
by over 90 percent of the American public, cannot even be
mentioned in the corridors or classrooms of the public school!
But it is not just Scripture or theology that is taboo. The
moral precepts derived in part from Scripture and from
western traditions are also out.

For a brief time I was unofficially serving as de facto
chaplain at the "Judges' and Police Executives Conference"
in western New York. It was just after my appointment to the
curriculum committee, and a two-part, front-page story on
my views had run in a rival suburban newspaper. A city court
judge approached me at the dinner meeting and asked, "Are
you the minister that is against distributing condoms in
school?"

"Yes," I told her.

"Then what do you think is the answer [to teen-age
pregnancy], abstinence?" she asked ruefully. I affirmed.

"Abstinence until what?" She was baiting me, and I knew
it.

"Until marriage," I supplied.

"Monogamous?"

I was eager to get where we were going. "Yes."

"But that's a religious doctrine, and religious doctrines don't belong in public education." We had finally arrived! "What if I don't believe that somebody should have just one sex partner?" Was she really proposing that the classroom was the place to dispose of monogamous marriage?

"Surely, your Honor, you don't believe that marriage is the exclusive possession of Judaism or Christianity? Monogamous marriage has been practiced since the dawn of civilization and has a long tenure in Western culture." I knew I was on thin ice.

"That's just it." She was certain she had uncovered my Achilles heel. "Western. What about Eastern or African cultures?"

"Are you suggesting that we teach polygamy and women as chattel?" I asked sarcastically.

The subject of abortion was addressed by the health committee. Everybody, including myself, tried to avoid a conflict and really worked at a consensus. It was decided that abortion would simply be defined for students, and the definition chosen by the committee unanimously was "Abortion is the termination of a pregnancy, which can be natural or induced, which results in the destruction of the fetus." That, combined with fetal development as part of the human development curriculum, I felt would clearly communicate to the students, in noninflammatory language, what really happens to the child that is aborted. The rest would have to be left to the intelligence of the student and the interpretation of the instructor. I was satisfied that this was the closest we would ever get to the truth about the murderous nature of abortion.

The definition passed. I was amazed that it was accepted unanimously without the usual pro-abortion protestations and offers of clever euphemisms to cover up the crime. I was uneasy. I expected it to fall apart. It did—at the very next meeting.

Absent at the previous week's meeting was a young pediatrician who was, unbeknown to me and the other members of the committee, the wife of the public clinic director. When she whisked into the room late (which she customarily did, usually spending a third of the meeting on the telephone and the other third filibustering as the only font of intelligence in the room) and read the definition, she dismissed it as erroneous, fraudulent, and misleading. "Abortion," she insisted with the disgust of a school marm admonishing a failing student, "is simply the termination of a pregnancy." Her edict delivered, and acknowledging the consent of the committee to her remonstrance, after ascertaining that the definition would be recast to conform to her verbiage—she prepared to leave. A busy physician need not negotiate a diagnosis.

"With all due respect," I offered, "simply because the doctor says so, is it necessarily true? After all, she is a pediatrician, not an Ob-Gyn." Whoa! She exploded. Her eyes were set in rage, and glowering at me, she expressed indignation and offense.

"I don't question what kind of clergy you are! I haven't asked you about your education or training, have I?" she retorted, implying that I was a mail order preacher, freshly emerged from the "previously owned" lot.

I attempted to ignore her ire, lest we become embroiled in an argument and an exchange of insults.

I turned to the co-chairs and offered, "I think we need to ask for other opinions. Perhaps we could return next week with definitions drawn from doctors who are trained in pre-natal medicine." After the shouting, it was decided we would return to the question.

For one administrative reason or another, the topic was delayed for two weeks. On the third week, we returned. I was confident that my allies on the committee would handle the subject well and with success, so I had determined not to go to the meeting, which was becoming tedious and a source of stress. I was notified, however, that the pediatrician was coming to the meeting with the express purpose of defeating the definition.

I knew what I would do. Some time previously, we had been given the remains of four aborted children for burial, after a pathologist working for an independent laboratory had been ordered to dispose of them in a commercial garbage disposal system. Stricken in conscience, but fearful for his career, the pathologist had secretly been conveying the bodies to clergymen who would agree to arrange for burials. We had agreed, as we had on other occasions, to bury the remains. It was however, the first time I had engaged the voluntary services of a funeral director—a sympathizer with the pro-life movement—to arrange for the burials. He had taken possession of the bodies but was forced to return them when he discovered that they required death certificates for burial. In New York state, every child aborted after the eleventh week of development is required to have a death certificate filled out by the abortionist. This is a terrible irony in a state known for its liberal abortion laws.

The babies' remains were packed in plastic tupper-ware type containers and carefully stored in the washroom in my pastoral office. I went into the washroom, put on a pair of heavy rubber surgical gloves, and opened one of the round, green-grey containers. When the airtight seal had broken, a very light spray of formalin, with its biting odor, wisped into my nostrils. Reaching into the grey, littered liquid, I began to pull out a torso with the spinal column exposed, a frail, toothpick-sized, shattered clavicle on one end, shriveled penis, scrotum and buttocks on the other end. I was careful and reverent as I searched for all the extant members—a perfectly formed but severed arm, shoulder to fingertips; another arm, mutilated and tethered together by sinuous material; a leg from the thigh to the toes; another leg, butchered like the arm; the head was unnaturally elongated—smashed by forceps at the end of a muscular hand that should have delivered this baby, not destroyed him.

With all the pieces in place, I wrapped the shredded little corpse in wet paper towels and gently placed it in a secure corner of my book bag.

When I arrived at the department of curriculum development office where our committee met, I went immediately into the bathroom. It was a single, unisex toilet, and so I locked the door, placed my briefcase onto the sink, and stared for a moment into the mirror. Could I do this? Should I do this? Would there be legal consequences if I were to produce this dead child before the committee? Could I be dismissed? I was so sick and tired of the rhetoric, the euphemisms, the clever denials of the pro-aborts on the committee—and for that matter, at large—that I determined they should see the victim of their cavalier policy and of their crafty deception. I positioned the little boy's eviscerated cadaver so that I could readily access it without fumbling. I muttered a prayer for forgiveness as I exited the bathroom and headed the short distance down the hall to the committee room.

The meeting was a fog. Perhaps if I had not chosen such a dramatic and potentially illegal demonstration I would have been able to engage in a meaningful way in the discussion, and maybe even changed their minds. I don't know. I'll never know. I was convinced that the propaganda would win out, that the display of this tiny victim would be more a corroborating witness to their condemnation than even a change agent. The end of the meeting finally approached. The abortion definition was rescinded, and the doctor's new, improved, sanitized propaganda statement was adopted against the protests of the minority. When the final vote approached, I rose. My hands trembling as I reached into my case, I nervously announced, "The fact that abortion results in the destruction of the fetus is undeniable—I'll show you the victim of an abortion procedure." At that I placed the wet towel casket on the committee table. Shock and disgust replaced smug defiance on the faces of my opponents. They denounced me for my "stunt" and castigated me for "carrying someone's fetus around like that!" The room emptied as members scattered for cover as if I had unpinned a hand grenade. I was unhappy and unsatisfied with my production. I was ambivalent about its effectiveness. It didn't change the committee's decision.

After that, whether due to embarrassment or disgust (or both), I decided that the rest of the committee work was essentially a lost cause. I was growing weary of the battle and disappointed at my lack of success. I convinced myself that going on was futile, and I decided to absent myself from all but the last two meetings. Meanwhile, however, I had decided and discussed the possibility of authoring a minority report. I know I would have the support of at least three other members of the committee, and I thought we'd have a shot at one of the co-chairs.

I notified Mr. Comerford by phone that I would submit a draft of a minority report. He was grateful and felt it would be effective in balancing the recommendations of the majority report.

The last meeting was with the board of education in a public meeting in the chambers. I had hastily prepared a draft of the minority report, but I was unable to make copies for distribution before the meeting. I knew it would be less effective, but I decided to read the draft and offer corrected copies to the president at a later date.

When I arrived at City Hall, I was told we would caucus in a side room for about an hour before the public meeting. When we went into the caucus room, I announced that I would be reading a draft of a minority report.

"Oh no you're not," declared one of the co-chairs.

"I was told by the president that this was an open mike meeting and that every committee member who wished to could speak."

"Yeah," was her reply. "But you can't speak!"

"Why?" I did my best to feign naivete.

"Because we have a consensus here." "Yeahs" and "amens" broke out.

"But consensus means a general agreement. The minority doesn't agree. We dissent. So there isn't a consensus."

"It doesn't matter—we have a consensus," she insisted, and the choir chimed in. As we went out the door (everyone, including myself, unwilling to continue the argument), some members denounced me. "How could you do this, a member of the cloth?" one asked, inferring that all "members of the cloth" know that their place is to be submissive, non-controversial, and acquiescent.

Entering the board chambers, I was surprised to see the gallery packed. All the media was there—television cameras, microphones, newspaper reporters. As we took our seats, a representative of a community activist group sat immediately to my right and a Planned Parenthood board member to my left. Behind me was a nurse from the county medical center that seemed very familiar with the abortion practices at that hospital.

The co-chairs were introduced, and they read the majority report. There seemed to be an anxious anticipation in the air. It was as if the cameras and stenopads were poised for the insurrection. When the co-chairs had completed the majority report, Mr. Comerford, now the president, announced that I would be presenting a minority report. I went to rise to the microphone when I felt a tug from behind me, grabbing my clerical collar. The woman behind me pulled me backward into my seat and whispered, "Don't you say anything!" I tried to rise again. This time, an arm grasped my right forearm, and another hand pulled me backward again by my collar into my seat.

The third time thwarted them. I faked a forward advance, eluded their grasps and rose to the microphone. The pencils oscillated, the cameras whirred, the microphones lunged forward. I read what was essentially a brief synopsis of the report, and then I sat down. The room was charged. Indignation, indolence, and rage were exuded by the crowd. The clinic director rushed to the mike and denounced me as a "terrorist" and a saboteur. Others rose with various recriminations.

In the end my minority report, signed only by a Mrs. Glaser, Mr. Provenzano, and myself, overshadowed the majority report. It was effective in staving off the acceptance of the majority report during the tenure of the board but eventually succumbed after the following election. The minority report was completely forgotten, the contrived "consensus" won out, and the public impression afterward was that the "consensus" contained sensible recommendations that they did not know would allow students to be instructed in the usage and obtainment of contraceptives, abortion information, "alternative families" (a.k.a., same sex marriages), and on how to perform safe oral sex.

This is an all too typical example of how secularist moral relativism is foisted on the public. The members of the committee were not representative of the community. The numbers were strongly weighted toward what might be represented as liberal or eccentric positions on moral and ethical issues. Certainly the most outspoken and influential members were predominantly backers of birth control dissemination, abortion referrals, and a positive presentation of homosexuality. At one point during the deliberations, the clinic director lauded an experimental program in Rochester, New York, that allowed birth control prescriptions to be written in the school health office without requiring parental notification or permission! It was not just parental concerns that were under represented but the parents of the students themselves—there were only four actual parents of city school students on the committee. For all its celebration of the liberation and rights movements of the past, the "New Left" is swiftly adopting with little debate a policy of censorship and suppression of ideas and beliefs that is incongruous with left-wing ideologies and practices.

By the New Left I mean those groups that have assimilated the values of the sixties, including the sexual revolution, radical feminism, homosexuality, abortion, and socialistic structures such as public education and the communal control of resources, as well as a tacit atheism as national dogma. At many points, the New Left and militant secularism agree. The anti-religious thrust of militant secularism is assisting the New Left's emphasis on sexual practices, gender roles, and political and educational policies that promote the licentious tenets of the sexual revolution.

I do not mean to impugn or reject all the components of left-wing ideology. In fact, there are some tenets of the Left that at least appear to be quite compatible with Christian teaching—those, for instance, that favor negotiation over armed conflict. Neither am I challenging an equality of respect and dignity for women and men, which is usually a position identified with the political Left. In many ways biblical Christianity asserts the equality of women and men in the eyes of God. In an ancient culture that restricted the religious rights and privileges of women, the New Testament clearly asserted that in Christ "there is neither male nor female." Women in the Bible often occupied offices that are identified with males: Jewish women served as heads of state, commanders of armies, prophets, visionaries, teachers, and counselors; Christian women served in apostolate and were ordained as deacons in the churches.

Racial equality is also compatible with the teachings of Christ. The Old Testament requires that the Israelites must provide equal justice and must not discriminate between a fellow countryman and a "stranger," nor any member of another race.[2] Indeed, the whole concept of separate "races" is an idea foreign to the Bible. Only in extremely rare cases is the color of skin or other physical characteristics of peoples ever mentioned in the Bible. When such references are made, they are only incidental. While nationalism plays a significant role in biblical politics and history, race does not.

By referring to the New Left, I do not mean that the issues of racism, sexism (which I prefer to call "gender arrogance"), and pacifism are incompatible and contradictory to Christian conviction. They are areas of social concern in which Christians have been engaged actively. And there is much, much more that the church must do to resolve the continuing injustices and controversies involved in these struggles. Why do I believe the New Left should be vigorously challenged?

The New Left has its roots in a philosophical and political ideology that derives from the amalgamation of Marxist and Freudian determinism, and the cultural and moral relativism of the 1960s which had its roots in existentialism and nihilism. Practically, the New Left expresses this mixture as a materialistic, utilitarian hedonism. In a phrase, it is all that is worst about the non-Christian philosophies that have been rampant on college campuses in the last thirty years.

The New Left, true to its Marxist concept of "class-struggle," is attempting to co-opt the American "under-class" by blaming the "haves" of the eighties for the poverty and disintegration of urban and minority communities; and it is bamboozling the "middle class" by appealing to working people's interests in such things as the economy, college education, schools, and health care. Meanwhile, it is advancing an agenda that is dramatically redefining morality and militantly opposing religious beliefs. The New Left is religiously atheistic, philosophically utilitarian, politically socialistic, and morally libertarian. It is, in a word, anti-Christian.

In its attempt to expedite the capture of the American middle class, the New Left has, along with secularism, turned to a policy of censorship and intimidation of dissenters who would stand in the way of their progress. Drawing on the resources (much of it provided at public expense) of state universities, and combining them with legal funds such as the National Organization of Women Legal Fund, the New Left has established a pattern of using state and federal courts to harass, intimidate, threaten, and punish individuals, movements, and institutions that differ with its party line.

The New Left has also been very successful in using the media to publicly scorn religious beliefs about morality, marriage, the family, and religion. The agenda advanced through public television, for instance, has been overwhelmingly leftist and anti-religious in tone for the past twenty years.

Perhaps the most insidious and most dangerous component of the New Left platform is its influence and usage of American public education. The universities, colleges, and public schools have served the New Left in an extraordinary fashion. Relying on the legal decisions of the courts that effectively banned religion from public education, and with it the traditional values over which it was principal steward, the New Left quickly rushed in to fill the vacuum. Relativism, materialism, humanism, utilitarianism, social Darwinism, atheism, and a host of other "isms" began replacing the traditional Judeo-Christian world view, which had predominated in American education since its inception. No other criterion was necessary for evaluating the appropriateness of these ideologies for the classroom other than that they were "non-religious." Even if a doctrine, theory, or philosophy was blatantly anti-Christian, it did not matter—as long as it was not defined as a religious belief, it was permitted and promoted in the name of "secular" education.

Over the last twenty-five years or so, this symbiosis of secularism and the New Left has been able, through the use of the media, academia, and law, to create the impression of an overwhelming consensus among Americans that approves of, if not embraces, the tenets of the New Left and the sexual revolution. If anybody or any institution attempts to question this "consensus," to challenge its thesis or, dissent from its dogma, it is subject to ridicule, scorn, and outright censorship. The news media often falls back on hackneyed stereotypes of "ignoramus fundamentalists" or dangerous fanatics to discredit conscientious Christian dissenters who dare challenge the contrived consensus.

If the dissenters are too recalcitrant, they may find themselves defendants in a federal lawsuit or in contempt of a federal temporary restraining order or sent to jail without due process for summary contempt of a judge's order. Such an atmosphere of intimidation has served the New Left well in making speedy progress toward establishing a new social order, a "cultural consensus" devoid of any vestige of the traditional, Judeo-Christian world view. The same consensus was reached by the health education committee.

How did this consensus come about? The committee was a diverse one, whose members spanned age, sex, race, and, I would suppose, economic strata. For instance, it included a seventeen-year-old female sophomore with a Spanish surname and a late forty-something Italian-American white male; an average educated, divorced black male and a black, female Ph.D.; a thirty-something pediatrician and an activist clergyman. How could such a diverse group achieve a consensus on the most controversial issues being faced in American society today, a consensus thus far unachieved in any other context?

The fact is, it was not a true consensus but a contrived one. It is the consensus only of the secularist-New Left coalition, an eclectic concoction of political and philosophical theories, which emanated from the radical, cultural revolution of the 1960s, and sought to overthrow the traditions, conventions, and morals of Judeo-Christian America. Though this consensus is far afield from the heart and soul of the average American, black or white, Hispanic, Asian, male or female—it has been given the illusory status of a majority, or at least the validity of the only respectable, intelligent, acceptable, and practical position on the immensely important social issues that vex and divide us as a nation and a people. This validity was conferred upon this foreign *Weltanschauung* by a consortium of what I have come to call the three great culture makers: the entertainment/news establishment, academia, and law.

There is no question that Americans believe in and worship God in overwhelming numbers. According to a recent poll conducted by the Barna Research Group Ltd. and reported in the 5 April 1993 edition of *Time*, 54 percent (of Americans aged eighteen to twenty-six) said that religion is "very important to me." That number soared to 65 percent in the twenty-seven to forty-five bracket, and a whopping 79 percent for those in the ages forty-six to sixty-four range. As to those who were asked to agree that the Bible was the "totally accurate" Word of God, a surprising 65 percent of the eighteen to twenty-six year-olds answered in the affirmative. Seventy-three percent of twenty-seven to forty-five year-olds and 80 percent of the forty-six to sixty-four year-olds agreed that the Bible was the "totally accurate" Word of God. As far as those who attended worship services the previous week? Thirty-six percent of the eighteen to twenty-six year-olds, 40 percent of the twenty-seven to forty-five year-olds and 60 percent of the forty-six to sixty-four year-olds went to church.

Yet recent studies show that members of the news/entertainment media are largely irreligious when compared to the American people.

We will assess the effect of this disparity between the religiosity of the American people and the irreligiosity of the cultural revolutionaries who are working their will upon the American public through the cultural venues of entertainment, education, and law throughout this book.

The irreligious elite, having assumed the helm of culture-making in America, have used the enormously powerful venue of motion pictures, television, news reporting and commentary, the classroom, and the courtroom to impose their false consensus—drawn largely from the hedonistic notions of libertinism so popular among the radical left-wing of the sixties—upon the general public.

For example, the family has been described as the "first church," and Christians learn from the Scriptures the importance of the family as a reflection of our relationship with

God. A husband should love his wife "as Christ loved the Church and gave himself up for her," a wife should "submit to her husband as to the Lord," children should "honor" their mothers and their fathers, and fathers should not exasperate their children.[3] The Christian "must manage his own family well," for "if anyone does not know how to manage his own family, how can he take care of God's church?"[4]

However, through coercive sexuality education programs, effective parenting seminars, and anti-parent legislation both for schools and "health care," the New Left is seeking to undermine and effectively cut off the family from nurturing the convictions and attitudes of young people. If the New Left can, for instance, persuade young people that two or three or six homosexuals living together and raising children is as legitimate a definition of "family" as mother-father-sister-brother is, then they know they will have set the stage for the ultimate abandonment of the traditional Judeo-Christian standard of morality. If the family is destroyed, then the nation will cease to be the soil for Christian growth and will finally be "up for grabs," a condition the New Left has planned effectively to exploit through the tyranny of consensus. As we consider the implications of this dichotomy, we will see that the revolutionaries will be unable to accomplish their goal of a total transformation of American society without using their power to crush Christian opposition to their program.

This they are prepared to do, indeed, are already doing to some extent, by the employment of stereotype in entertainment, the imposition of censorship in education, and the use of civil and criminal law to mete out punishment to dissenters from their consensus.

This has had the result of impugning traditional Christian beliefs about life, love, marriage, sex and children, the sanctity of human life, homosexuality, suicide, and euthanasia. It is critical to recognize that these are all subjects that involve what is sacred to the believers in God and the Bible. The Holy Scriptures are filled with revelation, instruction, and guidance on these topics. Since serious, conscientious Christians are deeply concerned with that revelation, as well as their relationships and responsibilities toward others, they are not prone to be silent on these topics, nor to ignore what they see as flagrant violations of the higher, moral Law. As the culture-makers heap relentless acrimony on Christian morality, it soon turns to insulting, maligning, and stereotyping Christians themselves. Not content with contradicting the beliefs of orthodox Christians, the Hollywood elite, the education establishment, and the courts have turned to the defamation of Christians in their all-out attack on the Judeo-Christian tradition. The overwhelmingly irreligious media, in tandem with the intelligentsia, and supported by the often whimsical courts, gang up on what one judge called "the disgusting practice of public prayer" and malign, intimidate, browbeat, threaten, litigate against, and failing those measures, in isolated, but increasingly more common incidences, use physical force to subdue uncooperative God-fearers.

The tyranny of consensus is being exercised broadly in our secularized society. Children are led to believe that reading the Bible and praying at school are illegal—in at least one incident high-school students were arrested for praying around the flag pole after school! College students are taught that biblical faith is incompatible with modern knowledge. One time when I was guest lecturing at a local college campus, the sociology students were told by the host professor that biblical faith was antithetical to the United States Constitution! Movies, television, and contemporary music hold religious beliefs and Christians up to continuous ridicule and depict them as hypocrites, Fascist moralists, and even as rapists, murderers, and cannibals! Federal judges have issued injunctions with penalties of imprisonment and huge fines for public prayer, Bible reading, and the distribution of religious literature.

This atmosphere of ridicule, intimidation, discrimination, and defamation exerts a diabolical tyranny over the inalienable right to a religious life. The spirit of the Declaration of Independence, the Bill of Rights, and especially the First Amendment, which states unequivocally that "Congress shall make no law respecting an establishment of religion, or prohibiting the free exercise thereof," is being seriously jeopardized by this mounting assault. Christians, who have throughout the history of the United States acted as a conscientious and positive influence for righteousness and justice (Note the role Christians have played in the abolition of slavery, in a woman's right to vote, in civil rights, and in the pro-life movement.), are being forced out of the mainstream of American life and denied civil rights by the proponents of the secularist consensus.

Jay Alan Sekulow, constitutional lawyer and chief counsel for the American Center for Law and Justice, (ACLJ) in an interview with *The Paper*, the campus publication of Regent University in Chesapeake, Virginia, commented on the Supreme Court case *Lamb's Chapel v. Center Moriches School District*, in which the Rev. John Steigerwald of Lamb's Chapel on Long Island, New York, applied for permission to use a public school facility to show a film series about family issues. The request was denied because the school district considered the film religious in nature. Stating that a ruling in favor of the school district "would authorize censorship on the religious speaker . . . censorship targeted directly at Christians (that) could be utilized to muzzle the church . . . (and) marginalize our input from a biblical perspective," Sekulow went on to say that what the school district did in denying access to school facilities to a Christian group while allowing other groups use of the same facilities is too typical of what those who hold the extreme separationist position believe: that public property, and specifically governmental institutions, should be off limits to religious, and, in particular, Christian expression.

Indeed, some have even suggested that the so-called establishment clause in the First Amendment indicates that there should be a "suspicious hostility"[5] between government and religion. According to Keith Fournier, of the ACLJ, content-based discrimination[6] clearly is being practiced by America's cultural institutions.

The travesty here is that the secularists have been able to co-opt the courts in their drive to suppress religious ideas and to eventually knock out their competition. In the five-year period between 1988 and 1992, many federal judges allowed themselves to be used as patron saints of the abortion industry in America by writing restraining orders and injunctions prohibiting conscientious Christian protesters the rights of assembly, speech, religious exercise, and expression. During that period, before the Supreme Court ruled in *Bray v. Alexandria Women's Clinic*, Christians were hauled into courts, fined tens of thousands of dollars, had their assets frozen, and were imprisoned for violating court orders against kneeling in prayer, singing hymns, distributing Bibles and religious tracts, and preaching in public. This period saw the most egregious denials of civil and human rights since the civil rights struggle of the previous generation.

It is critical that conscientious Christians and all people of conscience practically resist the New Left's attempt to foist on America a contrived consensus before it is too late. The battle will soon move from the public sector to within the family itself. The doctrine of political correctness on the university campus will soon become, if it has not already, the unretractable dogma of the American high school. Students will be expected to conform to the new definitions of morality, family, and atheism or suffer academically, socially, and personally. This will have serious implications for the Christian family, sowing dissension and strife within the family unit, contributing to the further degradation of the family, and potentially destroying it. Serious Christians must wake up now and take notice that the combined forces of secularism and the New Left ideology have created an environment that is increasingly hostile to their beliefs and practices. The stage has been set to effectively marginalize, vilify, and criminalize conscientious Christian faith. If the deliberate defamation of Christians is not exposed for what it is—antireligious bigotry and discrimination—all people of religious faith, whatever their creed, will in the end be the losers. And the soul of the nation will, for all intents and purposes, have gone to hell.

TWO

The New Intolerance

———————— | ————————

There can be no doubt that the claim that an insidious prejudice and intolerance toward Christians currently exists in American culture will take many citizens, Christians and non-Christians alike, by surprise. Perhaps the claim will even sound unbelievable, exaggerated, embellished, untrue. After all, religious faith, religious institutions, and religious people all appear to be quite well and very safe—indeed, perhaps better than they've been in years!

Churches continue to be organized and grow. Conservative denominations, such as the Southern Baptist, Nazarene, Assemblies of God, and Church of God, mark double and triple digit increases in their memberships. The Roman Catholic Church, so widely perceived to be moribund in the U.S., shows a respectable growth of 23 percent for the thirty-four-year period ending in 1989. Among Jews, numerical statistics are difficult to ascertain, but a significant number of young Jews are returning to traditional observance.

A recent cover story published by *Time* magazine announces exuberantly that "a quiet revolution is taking place . . . Increasing numbers of baby boomers who left the fold years ago are turning religious again . . . many are traveling from church to church or faith to faith, sampling creeds, shopping for a custom made God. The generation that forgot God," *Time* says, has remembered.

With this kind of religious revival going on in America, how can anyone make a claim that religion or religious people are in trouble, much less that they are in jeopardy of their liberty or their lives? Surely such an allegation already stands disproved by the clear facts: America is a permanent refuge, a guaranteed safe haven for religious faith and expression.

Or is it? The history of Nazi Germany puts the lie to the assertion that a culture that plays host to a flourishing religious community vouchsafes religious freedom. Before World War II, Germany was the virtually unmatched fertile soil for religious worship, theology, sacred music, and evangelism. It was the birthplace of Luther and the Reformation, and German is still today a requisite theological language for *ordinandi* and theologians around the world. Yiddish, the colloquial language of a millennium of Jewish theologians, rabbis, intellectuals, artists, and Zionists, is short for Yiddish daytsh, "Jewish German," a High German language written in Hebrew letters. Who would think that a country that gave the Jews a language, a unique culture called Ashkenazi still preserved in Israel and by worldwide Jewry today, as well as some of its greatest rabbis, its finest thinkers, writers, and political theorists, would in the span of an average lifetime become its crematorium?

Who would ever conceive that the nation that produced Martin Luther, the Reformation, and the very term *evangelishchite*, as well as the Amish, Mennonite, and other anabaptist pietists, and the missionary Moravian brethren, would turn into the very incarnation of satanic evil, outstripping its Christian missionary successes with genocidal murder on an unprecedented scale?

Hitler persecuted the churches while he relished in choosing a loyal Nazi as a bishop. Political support for religion is not equivalent to a sincere commitment to religious freedom. Despots throughout history have courted religious constituents for their own purposes.

"All that is necessary for evil to prevail is for good men to do nothing" is the oft quoted maxim of Sir Edmund Burke. The scandalous and infinitely sad chronicle of the rise and fall of the Third Reich is a demonstration of the ability of a culture to quickly turn viciously, furiously, even "uncharacteristically," on what is best within it. The innate capacity of sinful humanity for destruction is unfathomable.

The banality of evil was explored in Hannah Arendt's

landmark study of the complicity of ordinary Germans in the holocaust of the Jews.[1] Arendt's thesis was that the genocide of the Jews was not the result of an unsurpassed level of moral depravity in the German people, but rather it was the result of a quite ordinary moral indifference that is universally characteristic of human beings.

Arendt's examination of Adolf Eichmann led her to conclude that the Holocaust could not have occurred without the complicity of innumerable ordinary people who were not morally depraved, but were "detached," socially, psychologically, and ethically from what was being done to the Jews.

In fact, Eichmann and other S.S. officers implicated in actually implementing and executing the Holocaust—men like Rudolf Hoess, notorious commandant of Auschwitz; Franz Stangl of Treblinka; and Albert Speer, Hitler's architect of the "Final Solution"—each claimed in their war crimes trials that they were merely doing their jobs. Eichmann described his oversight of the deportations of millions of Jews to the death camps by saying, "I sat at my desk and did my work."[2]

In the book *How Holocausts Happen: The United States in Central America,* the author Douglas Popora concludes that:

> [I]t does not require sadistic, or insane people to carry out genocidal activities. Ordinary people will perform those functions just as well. But for genocide to occur, more is needed than just government bureaucrats willing to obey an order. A genocidal government must have the compliance of its public as well, for if the public outcry is sufficient, the government will be unable to carry on. Conversely, it is the absence of such criticism that allows genocide to take place. In the end, genocide is a crime an entire society commits.[3]

History has shown that persecution has been committed similarly. In fact, persecution has served as a precursor to genocide.

When the world was throwing communism out, the universities were going garbage picking. Much of the strategy and tactics of the secularist forces is concocted in the

universities and taken directly from the old communist handbook. Atheism and anti-religious bias, censorship, and the
harassment of dissenters are all indicative of Marxism. Karl
Marx himself was an atheist and had nothing but contempt
for Christianity, which he called "an opium of the people"
and "a cultus of abstract man," perfectly suited for "bourgeois society," a pejorative designation.

According to William S. Sahakian,

> Marxists reject religious doctrines about spiritual val-
> ues, the soul, immortality, and God, asserting that
> religion is an illusion and that the illusory happiness
> based on it must be condemned. "Religion is the sign
> of the oppressed creature, the heart of the heartless
> world, just as it is the spirit of a spiritless situation. It
> is the opium of the people." God does not create
> man; rather, man creates invalid religion with its
> mythical god. Religion functions as a police force, as
> a bourgeois technique to dissuade the masses from
> revolting by promising them a better, happier exist-
> ence after death than their exploiters allow them to
> enjoy during their lifetime on earth.[4]

Popular Christian apologists Josh McDowell and Don
Stewart maintain that

> Marx saw two compelling reasons to abolish religion
> and promote atheism: first, his materialism denied
> the existence of the supernatural; and second, the
> very structure of organized religion had, through the
> ages, condoned and supported the bourgeois sup-
> pression of the proletariate. . . . We must make this
> clear: abolishment of religion is an integral part of
> Marx's dialectical materialism.[5]

Gaining most of its momentum as a backlash against the
excesses of Sen. Joseph McCarthy's (1946-1957) Committee
on UnAmerican Activities, Marxism became vogue and eventually very influential on college campuses in the 1950s and
continued to proliferate in the radical years of the sixties
and seventies. This has been well documented. One survey
showed that almost 60 percent of college and university
professors described themselves as Marxist, Communist, or
leaning to the Left, politically.

In his celebrated work that exposed the foibles and contradictions of political correctness in academia, *Illiberal Education: The Politics of Race and Sex on Campus*, Dinesh D'Souza revealed the agenda shared by so many classroom revolutionaries. Quoting Frederick Jameson, a Marxist theorist at Duke University, the professor describes his mission as "to create a Marxist culture in this country, to make Marxism an unavoidable presence in the American social, cultural and intellectual life, in short, to form a Marxist intelligentsia for the struggles of the future."[6]

John Leo, writing in *U.S. News & World Report* (18 January 1993), commented on the Modern Language Association of America's latest annual convention held at the New York Hilton Hotel. According to the article, "Some 11,000 college teachers of language and literature gather each year" at the conference. Of the presenters and participants in the convention, Leo summarizes that "the vacationing ideologues here are suffering from a swarm of radical isms, but the central one, totally dead in the real world, is Marxism. It is a vulgar Marxism, adapted by British radicals, and it goes like this . . . everything we do or say works to support our ideological interests. So literary studies are properly a branch of leftist politics and nothing more."

It is not credible to maintain that the economical and philosophical elements of communism should prevail, even thrive, in a large segment of academia without its more malevolent aspects, including censorship, ostracism, and punishment of dissidents, being excused, tolerated, or even accepted and implemented. The repressive political correctness enforced upon college campuses today is a manifestation of this darkest side of Marxist ideology and practice.

Many of today's high-school teachers, college and university professors, lawyers, judges, and legislators who gained office in the seventies and eighties were influenced by Marxism in the 1960s through the professors on campus. Some were even its disciples. As one judge put it to me, "I went to a liberal law school in the late sixties; these were my people who helped put me into office." The Democratic party also embraced a wing of far Left ideologues in those decades.

This may help explain the disdain for religion and, in particular, orthodox Christianity, which is expressed by so many within the professions of education and law.

As a result of the pervasiveness of Marxist ideology in academics, communist practices of "silencing" opposition subtly crept into the growing left-wing American intelligentsia. Just as Lenin had introduced the concept of a ruling elite of professional revolutionaries that would lead the workers of the world into communism, so the New Left today advances a platform clearly built on a ruling elite of intellectuals and professionals, e.g., professors, lawyers, and medical researchers, that will lead the American "middle class" and "underclass" into the false consensus. If the ordinary American does not consent to the secularist-New Left consensus, if many academics are to have their way, then the dissenter would be subjected to ridicule, ostracism, expulsion, civil and even criminal penalties, including jail. Today, even without the "communist style" practices of censorship and intimidation by the New Left of academia, if academic, political, legal, or medical professionals dissent from the consensus, they might have their credibility or reputation questioned, be pushed out of professional societies such as the bar or medical associations, or be threatened with legal action. A clear example of this is the celebrated confirmation hearings of Supreme Court Justice Clarence Thomas, a dissenter from the false consensus who was subjected to a national inquisition that was designed to put any other would-be justices on notice that dissent would not go unpunished.

Another example of this is the large number of lawyers who felt compelled to resign from the American Bar Association when the organization broke a long-standing tradition of remaining neutral on controversial social and political issues and voted at its annual meeting in 1992 to support unrestricted abortion-on-demand. Thousands of conscientious objectors to the practice of abortion, the vast majority of them Christians who objected on moral and religious grounds, had no other recourse than to disassociate themselves from the largest, most prestigious legal association in America.

One day I received a cryptic message in my church office

that a noted surgeon in my town had called for me. He left his name and number but asked that I not use my own name when I returned the call. Instead, a code name was supplied. Curious, I followed the instructions and returned the call. He thanked me for my cooperation and then told me that he and his wife had been, until recently, pro-choice on the abortion question. Until, that is, they had tried to start their own family and encountered fertility problems. Coming to terms with how much they desired to have a child, and their apparent inability to conceive one, they began to realize how sacred and precious every human life—from conception—is. Now, he declared to me with an almost triumphant tone, "We have come to see things your way." Of course, I cannot take credit for the pro-life position, but I knew what he meant. He went on to tell me that an area abortionist had been invited to address a medical society to which he belonged, and he wanted me to know this and perhaps organize a picket. I agreed to make an attempt to do so. "Please, if anyone should ask you how you got this information, please don't refer to me or tell anyone I was the source." I agreed and assured him that the information was safely confidential. But then I told him that one day he would have to speak up and let his dissent be made known to his colleagues.

This kind of intimidation and peer pressure may be expected among adolescents or even novices in particular trades or professions; after all, we all seek acceptance and belonging. But even an implied threat among seasoned professionals—and that among men and women of science, against those who do not acquiesce to the politically correct position on important issues—is unconscionable.

Another major influence in the academy and the training of students who came of age in the sixties and seventies was the psychological theories of Sigmund Freud. Freud, like Marx, was an atheist, and his writings were filled with derogatory remarks about religion—Judaism and Christianity in particular. In fact, Freud believed that religious faith was a manifestation of mental illness.

Freud wrote of religion in *Civilization and Its Discontents*:

"The whole thing is so patently infantile, so incongruous with reality, that to one whose attitude to humanity is friendly it is painful to think that the great majority of mortals will never be able to rise above its view of life." Again, in *New Introductory Lectures on Psycho-Analysis, XXXV*, he decreed, "While the different religions wrangle with one another as to which of them is in possession of the truth, in our view the truth of religion may be altogether disregarded." Finally, in the same volume Freud announced:

> Religion is an attempt to get control over the sensory world, . . . by means of the wish-world, which we have developed as a result of biological and psychological necessities. But it cannot achieve its end. Its doctrines carry with them the stamp of the times in which they originated, the ignorant childhood of the human race. Its consolations deserve no trust . . . and it is dangerous to link up obedience to [ethical standards] with religious belief. If one attempts to assign to religion its place in man's evolution, it seems not so much to be a lasting acquisition as a parallel to the neurosis which the civilized individual must pass through on his way from childhood to maturity.[7]

With such contempt touted as the most sublime and advanced insight into the human psyche ever produced, is it any wonder that students should develop prejudices about religion and stereotypes of religious people? Freud and his disciples represented religious faith as a sickness, a mental illness—a danger to normal human development. This may well explain why many college-educated people view Christian faith in such a negative light. They have literally been taught that religious people are mentally and emotionally ill!

Such a view is intrinsically intolerant. How can a community of healthy, intelligent people tolerate such a malignancy? In this view, Christianity must either be treated, eradicated, or at the very least "managed." This then explains the motivations behind so many of the intellectual elite who treat Christians so condescendingly. And if the Christianity begins to spread, they feel forced to apply the appropriate remedies, including ostracism, if necessary, as a form of involuntary confinement!

The most well known and universally acknowledged component of the new "consensus" is Darwin's theory of evolution. According to Jeremy Rifkin in *Algeny*:

> The fact is, there is one proposition that has been largely spared from the constant carping that surrounds most intellectual questions. It seems that Darwin's theory of evolution has been granted a reprieve of sorts. For decades it has enjoyed a rather privileged position within the academic community. Many would be quick to defend its special status.[8]

Rifkin later summarizes Karl Stern on the theory of evolution.

> At a certain moment in time, the temperature of the earth was such that it became most favorable for the aggregation of carbon atoms and oxygen with the nitrogen-hydrogen combination, and that from random occurrences of large clusters molecules occurred which were most favorably structured for the coming about of life, and from that point it went on through vast stretches of time, until through processes of natural selection a being finally occurred which is capable of choosing love over hate, and justice over injustice, of writing poetry like that of Dante, composing music like that of Mozart, and making drawings like that of Leonardo.[9]

In short, the immense complexity of the world, the incomprehensible genius of the human mind, and the subtlety of the human spirit are each the product of accident and chance, and no intelligence conceived of it nor implemented it, and no supra-intelligence is guiding it toward its end. Life is nothing more than an accidental collision of stuff that continues accidently toward greater complexity and improvement.

There is no question that Darwinism has enjoyed a special status among the intelligentsia. According to the false consensus, to question the theory of evolution is considered as absurd as questioning that the world is round or that the earth revolves around the sun. Evolution long ago lost its post as a theory of origins and was catalogued along with facts. Today, few scientists and educators, not to mention ordinary and ordinarily educated people, would dare question the "fact" of evolution. Anyone who would deny the accidental advent of biological life in the face of overwhelming evidence must be an idiot, a fool, or a charlatan. The only problem with this line of thinking is that the evidence is far from overwhelming. The fact is that there is no evidence at all.

According to an article that appeared in the *New York Times* on 30 March 1993, "Reseachers say they have been unable to detect any overall evolutionary drive toward greater complexity, at least over periods of tens and even hundreds of millions of years."

In addition to the theories of Marx and Freud, the pervasiveness of atheism, agnosticism, and skepticism in the academy contributed to the growing disdain for religious faith. Writings that were standard fare in the curricula of the colleges and universities of the fifties, sixties, and seventies included Hegel, Feuerbach, Comte, Nietzsche, Jasper, Sartre, Bayle, Spinoza, Fichte, and Hume, atheists one and all. Students who had left typical American family configurations, mother-father-sister-brother-grandparents and their collective faith, and had, as the first generation to do so in record numbers, entered college and read these classic philosophies were enraptured by the depth and breadth of their perceptions of the human spirit. The intellectual exercise and the breathtaking insight of these thinkers and observers mesmerized the novitiates and systematically poisoned their Christian faith.

Many of the students became jaded and tossed out any consideration of the veracity of a theistic, much less a Christian, explanation of the world. In the place of the traditional, biblical definition of life, an existentialist, nihilistic, and hedonistic world view was planted.[10]

If all of this ideology—the Marxist type, the Freudian theory of psychoanalysis with its pathological model of religion, as well as that of the atheists, the agnostics, the nihilists, and the hedonists—had remained in the ivory towers of academia, the damage would most certainly have been contained and probably would have ultimately been nullified in the larger society beyond the campus. But the problem is that they did not remain "contained" but were spread through the training of teachers that eventually went into the high schools, middle schools, and elementary schools of America. These essentially anti-Christian philosophies were spread by journalists and reporters who interpreted events through the lenses of non-Christian and anti-religious glasses. The venue of films and television brought them to the general population. We'll look at this in greater detail in a later chapter, but suffice it to say now that Hollywood became enamored with the awesome sagacity of academia and, with a disdain for nuance and ambiguity, popularized dangerous over-simplifications and downright distortions of political, economical and psychological theories in well-made and hugely influential films that ultimately carried the political, philosophical and psychological disapprobation for religion to the American people.

The philosophical and ideological revolution in America spread a virulent iconoclasm throughout the major components of popular culture: the entertainment-news media, academia, and law; and anti-religious sentiment was fast setting in among a preponderance of professionals. While religion continued unabated and, on the surface, apparently unaffected, a malicious undercurrent had begun among the makers and shapers of American culture that would ultimately erupt in an all-out assault on religious persons in America.

The pervasiveness of these opposing forces to Christianity put Christians on the defensive. In almost every setting, they were being forced to justify their allegiance to a Deity who had been "dismissed" by the philosophers, "disproved" by the scientists, and "debunked" by the journalists. Many Christians, if not most of them, were intimidated by the smug, self-confidence of the opposition. Believers then retreated from public discourse about religion. Fatigued and beleaguered, the "Body of Christ" went into a sort of hibernation. Their opting for a personal, private piety played right into the hands of the anti-religionists whose aim was to eradicate religious faith from the public square.

The scarcity of robust Christian faith made it easier for the secularists to sweep religion out of the halls of popular entertainment, public education, and legislation. With Christianity effectively suppressed, the work of secular revolutionaries was expedited. A Nietzschean nightmare of a world permanently devoid of deity, and reliant only on a detached, self-devising humanity, was well on the way to realization, unhindered by pesky Christianity.

As secularism racked up victories one after the other, and as the sexual revolution trounced traditional morality, and as the hedonistic counterculture trumpeted individualism, drug-induced "self-realization" and self-expression unfettered by bourgeois responsibilities, an unexpected, almost spontaneous event occurred, seriously impeding the otherwise unencumbered ascent of the unreligious: Revival!

In a mere seven-year span, *Time* magazine would declare "God is Dead" and herald the "Year of the Evangelical" on its horologe of American life.

As the sixties drew to a close, a religious counter-revolution was set into motion among two distinct but related groups. The first group was the older, traditional evangelical Christians—namely the Baptists, some Presbyterians, Reformed Christians, Evangelical Free, and other denominations and movements that represented the growing and maturing National Association of Evangelicals, which was begun in 1948 as a modern coalition of Bible-believing, "born-again" Christians who were technically and culturally more progressive than the fundamentalists.

Increasingly more sophisticated and influential—as well as technologically equipped, the evangelicals were represented by articulate and impressive spokesmen like the evangelist Billy Graham, publications like *Campus Life* and *Christianity Today*, and colleges and graduate schools such as Wheaton in Illinois and Gordon-Conwell in Massachusetts. These personalities and institutions brought a new degree of respectability to biblical faith that had been lost in the first half of the twentieth century. Quietly building their ranks through immensely popular "crusades" among youth (such as Youth for Christ) and families (the Billy Graham crusades, "Hour of Decision" broadcasts, and innumerable other venues), the evangelical churches, especially, but not exclusively, of the midwestern U.S. began to burgeon, giving rise to what eventually came to be referred to as the multiple-thousand member "super-churches." Christian broadcasting also emerged in this period, giving Christianity a new platform in America through radio and television.

At about the same time, the traditional, historic churches—both Protestant and Catholic—became hosts to the most powerful religious movement in modern American history: the charismatic renewal. Initiated in the late fifties and early sixties, and dubbed "neo-pentecostalism," charismatic Christianity, like her evangelical siblings, embraced a "personal" encounter and relationship to Jesus Christ—but in place of the quiet, almost invisible piety of the past, she gave expression to faith through the public, extraordinary and supernatural manifestations of the Holy Spirit. Among these manifestations were the glossolalia, or gift of tongues, miracles, and healings. Because the charismatic renewal emphasized the "baptism of the Spirit," it was adaptable to both evangelical faith, which stressed the "born-again" experience of salvation, and Catholic faith, which taught that salvation came through the sacraments and obedience to the teachings of the church. To put it simply, both Catholic Christians, saved by baptism and sacramental obedience, and evangelical Christians, "born again" and saved by faith, were candidates for the baptism of the Spirit. The missing link between these two expressions of Christian faith was the Pentecostals.

The Pentecostal denominations that formed in North America during the first three decades of the twentieth century include some of the fastest growing church bodies in the world today: the Assemblies of God, which soared in membership from just under 500,000 in the late 1950s to over ten million worldwide by the mid-eighties. Others, which have experienced slower but significant growth, are the Church of God, the Church of God in Christ (reportedly the largest Pentecostal body in the world), which is predominantly African-American, and the International Church of the Foursquare Gospel. An estimated 10 percent of the membership of these churches, with the exception of the Church of God in Christ, is Hispanic.

While mostly ignored, Pentecostal/charismatic Christians were permeating the churches and renewing and revitalizing Christianity at just the time that secularism was about to celebrate its triumph over that incarnationalist superstition.

One more aspect of the religious revival of the later sixties and seventies should be observed: the so-called "Jesus movement" among members of the counterculture. Itself a "counter-revolution" against the drugs and sex of the hippie culture, the Jesus movement swept thousands of youth into an unconventional, street culture-based, conservative Christianity. Innovative, contemporary evangelism that left unchallenged the long hair, distinctive dress, and music of the younger generation successfully led to the conversion of formerly drug-abusing young people. Coffee houses, "underground" Christian publications, and communes, along with the highly successful drug-rehab program Teen Challenge founded in 1958 by the Assemblies of God minister David Wilkerson, brought about a historic revival of religion in America. Many of these Christian youths ultimately found their way into progressive Baptist and Pentecostal churches, helping to build the super-churches of the seventies and eighties. As the "Jesus People," as they came to be known, grew older, many became the pastors, leaders, teachers, evangelists, and missionaries of those churches. In large part the Jesus People are responsible for the emergence of a contemporary form of Christian expression, especially in music, which further promoted the gospel and led to the conversions of a subsequent generation of young Americans.

This unprecedented, latter twentieth-century revival of religion effectively challenged secularism in the public square. But while Christianity reached the heart of millions in America, secularism was claiming its institutions. Believers met in record numbers, filling stadiums in gigantic "crusades" and charismatic "conferences," fanning out over cowpastures at "Jesus festivals," overflowing church fellowship halls and the basements of homes for prayer meetings, packing out rented storefront coffee houses playing gospel folk tunes and scarfing down "munchies" while discussing biblical eschatology and prophecy, and building what would become mammoth evangelistic ventures like the Christian Broadcasting Network (CBN) of Virginia Beach.

Meanwhile, the anti-Christian forces of the secularist-New Left coalition were working their way into the non-religious cultural establishments of entertainment, education, and government. The lasciviousness, immorality, and materialism of Hollywood made show business an uninviting and less-than-attractive option for saints. The spiritually arid and unsatisfying world of the intelligentsia and the seeming endlessness of academic searching, along with its agnosticism, equally led to the Christian avoidance of education as a profession. Similarly, the apparent corruption and powermongering inherent in much of politics served to dissuade the earnest new converts from choosing government as one's "tent-making." As a result, a great divide began to occur between people of faith and their secularist opponents. As members of the American community, the new Christians would ultimately have to share in the same institutions as their non-religious countrymen. But by the time they got there, they would find that all the seats had been taken by the secularists, who, although a minority, had carefully and successfully strategized the takeover of these critical and influential bastions of cultural influence.

Conflict was inevitable. Since the confrontation was ideological—one of beliefs and concomitant practices—the controversy would take the form primarily of words. Christian evangelists, emboldened by the large crowds and huge audiences accessible through religious television, began openly challenging the secularists by exposing their atheism, their lack of moral standards, and their social liberalism. Christian social critics such as the expatriate philosopher-theologian Francis Schaeffer, a Presbyterian; the psychologist James Dobson, an evangelical; the Republican presidential candidate and CBN founder M.G. "Pat" Robertson, a charismatic Baptist; and the former presidential counsel Chuck Colson, an Episcopalian, made compelling arguments against humanism and secularism. By no means the only contemporary apologists to do so, they utilized their vast formats and immensely popular styles of apologetic to effectively reach masses of American Christians. The unexpected emergence of the articulate, intellectually respectable Christian thinkers proved a formidable challenge to secularism. Since the debate forum was the unparalleled power of television and radio broadcasting, a Christian vs. secularist turf war was inevitable.

The audiences that primetime, network TV affords are huge compared to religious television. The producers and screenwriters of primetime's plethora of dramas, sitcoms, and news magazine shows know this. One swipe, jab, derogatory remark, or gratuitous depiction of a practicing Christian as a hypocrite, charlatan, or bigot can effectively "neutralize" an evangelist, preacher, or archbishop in the minds of millions of American viewers. By focusing on the foibles and moral failings of a particular clergyman, and playing up the scandal so that it exceeds all reasonable proportion, anti-Christian secularists know that they can cast Christianity as an unattractive, hypocritical, and self-righteous moralism that is ultimately repugnant to Americans who cherish their liberty and privacy rights.

So rather than taking on Christianity in the arena of fair, intelligent, and intellectually respectable debate, television and films, as well as a large segment of "talk radio," have turned to mud-slinging, libel, scandal, and defamation of Christian people. This denigration of believers is in large part deliberately designed to discredit and therefore expedite the defeat of Christianity before the public.

Lenin espoused a pragmatic approach to the expansion of communism. He believed that Communists had to be flexible and clever with strategies and tactics, adapting party programs in order to serve the goal of extending Communist domination in the world. The secularist-New Left forces have also adopted a pragmatism that allows them to cunningly appeal to the concerns of the middle class and to economically disadvantaged minority Americans. The overwhelming number of minorities in America espouse moral standards based on religious teaching, predominantly Christian, which is diametrically opposed to the agenda of the sexual revolution. However, the sexual revolutionary forces

ignore this reality and approach their goals in nearly indis-
cernible increments until the time is right. Average Americans find it difficult to wage a spirited fight about moral and
family issues when the New Left is making glowing promises
about economic, educational, and social improvements. The
result is that the average citizen abandons concern for the
underlying moral agenda, and its potential effects on them
and their families, and votes for the candidate that offers
economic improvement, regardless of the social policies he
or she represents.

The New Left and its allies have formed political coali-
tions in numerous county and state legislatures, courts, and
especially educational systems (an example would be in the
state of New York, where the overwhelming majority in each
case is secularist, liberal, and New Left). Once the party line
is established, any dissent is either ridiculed, ostracized, or
punished by threatened or real civil litigation. Opposition is
either silenced, ignored, lampooned, or otherwise defamed.
With these vital public institutions together with the media
(which in a later chapter, as I have pointed out, will be
proven to be biased toward secularist, left-wing ideology),
the platform is already created for the promotion of the anti-
religious consensus. Although this consensus may be far
afield from the core beliefs and values of the average religious American, the appearance of majority support is created by dominating these key public and quasi-public institutions.

On one occasion I was invited to speak on the subject of
abortion to the combined sociology and anthropology departments at a local state college. The policy of the school
was to provide visiting lecturers with a $100 honorarium in
appreciation for their efforts. Before I was to speak, however, the inviting professor—an African who had studied in
the Soviet Union—was appalled to find out that the university bursar declined to issue the check in my name "because
he was a Reverend."

"What difference is it?" he had asked.

"We can't write a check to a Reverend," was the reply.
"Separation of church and state."

This did not come as a surprise to me. I grew up in the

1970s going to public schools during the time when secularism's assault on Christian faith was on the ascent. It was during this period that I became a Christian. One day, after school had been dismissed, I was walking through the halls on my way to a Bible study clandestinely held by the honors humanities teacher. I encountered the superintendent of secondary education, and he asked me, "Where are you supposed to be?"

"I'm on my way to Bible study." I distinctly remember regretting letting that slip past my lips, realizing that the Bible study was considered "illegal." He raised his hands in a reflexive motion and covered his ears.

"I don't want to hear that. I don't want to know anything about that. Just get where you're supposed to be going."

Such anti-religious bias was expected from governmental institutions in those days. In fact, for many fundamentalist and evangelical Christians, it was the fulfillment of biblical prophecy. Christians could expect to be persecuted in the world; Jesus had predicted this. "If the world hates you, keep in mind that it hated me first." In John 15:18, Jesus said, "If you belonged to the world, it would love you as its own. As it is, you do not belong to the world, but I have chosen you out of the world. That is why the world hates you."

These scriptural teachings, together with the reality of the small numbers of conscientious Christians in our community, convinced many of us that there was little or nothing that could be done to stem the tide of anti-Christian discrimination at school or from other public institutions. In a host of eschatologically focused publications, we were led to believe that the conditions for the followers of Christ would only worsen, so there was no sense getting upset about it, nor trying to change it.

It was as if we reveled in this baptism of fire. Suffering persecution for the name of Jesus was most certainly a source of blessing. But we ignored the larger implications of anti-religious bias that would ultimately affect the nation. If Jesus was to return in power and glory soon, then persecution really didn't matter. But what if we had still another generation or more on the face of the earth? As American citizens? If we ignore the disintegration of religious liberties upon which the United States of America was founded, and those now secured by the Constitution, what kind of society are we leaving to our children? Are we de facto denying them a sacred freedom—one almost uniquely embraced by the founders of our country?

The struggle against religious prejudice and defamation is not a denial of the teachings of Jesus regarding the inevitable persecutions of Christians. The Apostle John wrote in his first epistle, "Dear children, this is the last hour; and as you have heard that the antichrist is coming, even now many antichrists have come. This is how we know it is the last hour."[11]

Antichrists there are, and antichrists there will be. But this does not absolve us of our responsibility to vigorously defend religious freedom for all people and for our children. It could be said that true martyrdom is that which culminates at the end of the struggle against evil. If we do not struggle against injustice, wickedness, and sin, then we must really be in complicity with it. Our complacency only facilitates the wickedness and infidelity. Therefore, in the end, the only way to determine whether a persecution is truly the one allowed by God to fall on the church for purification and on the world for judgment is if the saints have done everything they know and everything in their power to thwart it.

The most vigorous dissent and challenge to the false consensus must come invariably and inevitably from Christians. Although the number of conscientious Christian dissidents is almost always just a fraction, a tithe of the vast number of professing Christians, it is their conviction, spurred by their reliance on the Holy Spirit and their knowledge of the Word of God, that drives and compels them to confront and to contradict falsehood. They must be the ones to expose the elitist minority perpetrating the false consensus. The anti-religious, secularist-New Left coalition, however, has carefully prepared its defense: through court decisions and legislation, it has succeeded in all but banning religion, religious personalities, and moral issues based in part on religious conviction from the public sector. This includes banning from libraries, schools, colleges, universities, public buildings, public broadcasting and publishing, sports arenas, and courthouses, any and all references to God, Scripture, the gospel, prayer, and hymn-singing. What is not accomplished legally is accomplished illegally. A public librarian recently informed me that it has become impossible for the public libraries to keep pro-life volumes on the shelves. They are regularly stolen, mutilated, or checked out and never returned. She said that some libraries have just given up trying to keep pro-life books in stock!

When our church inquired about renting an auditorium at the University of Buffalo, we were denied the use of its facilities. A representative in the administrative office explained that the university could not do business with evangelical Christian groups because of "the separation of church and state." This in spite of the fact that they were available to all other groups, including Satanists!

One time I was driving downtown in my home city of Buffalo, New York, and I passed by an abortion clinic that was the site of regular, peaceful, and legal prayer presence. Frequently, I would see a small gathering of precious Catholic Christians huddled together, even in frigid Buffalo winter weather, praying the rosary. That day I noticed a group hastily making for their vehicles, which had been parked on the street. I just felt as if I should stop and inquire. I pulled over to the curb and rolled down the window. One of the participants in the "Rosary Witness for Life" came over to my car and told me that the police had just been there and told them that the abortionist, who was Jewish, had threatened to file charges of harassment against them because their "Christian prayers" were offensive to his religion! If they did not disperse, the officer told them, he would arrest them.

I left them and immediately went to my office where I called a number of Jewish pro-lifers, including my father, and they agreed to join me about two hours later to pray "Jewish prayers" on the same sidewalk at which those saying Catholic prayers were threatened with arrest. We gathered wearing yarmulkes and tallithot (prayer shawls) and began to recite Hebrew prayers from the Siddur, the Jewish prayer book. Just as I thought, a police officer arrived about ten minutes later and left his patrol car and went into the clinic. He emerged a few minutes later and approached us. I stepped forward as the spokesman.

"I'm going to have to ask you to cease from your praying and disperse. If you don't, I'm going to have to make arrests," he said sheepishly, as if he was duty bound to do what he didn't want to do.

"For what?" I asked indignantly.

"The doctor says your prayers are harassing him."

"You're going to arrest me on a public sidewalk in the United States of America for praying in Hebrew? Be my guest." And I raised both my wrists, palms up, as if to offer them for handcuffing. The young officer was nonplused. Red-faced, he looked at me as if to say, "Don't make me do this." I stared into his eyes. He knew this was wrong. He knew I had every right to the free exercise of my religion. Finally, he backed down. "I'm not going to do it," he muttered as he walked to his patrol car.

The tragedy is that many believers have suffered arrest, incarceration, stiff fines, and brutality at the hands of police and courts for doing nothing more than praying in public.

According to Keith Fournier, executive director of the famed American Center for Law and Justice, "Under the banner of . . . liberty . . . as redefined in our secularized state, unpopular speech and, in a particular way, Christian speech, is being censored from the public arena. Rather than free speech we now have a growing effort to enforce 'speech-free' zones throughout the country. The 'political correctness' movement is but one example of a growing intolerance toward religious speech." An example cited by Fournier in his pamphlet, "In Defense of Liberty," is a case in Stone Mountain, Georgia, where "a Jewish Christian evangelist was denied the right to hand out evangelistic literature. That park is owned and operated by the State of Georgia. Such public parks have traditionally been held to be one of the most appropriate places for free speech activities. However, the officials at Stone Mountain Park refused to allow protections of the First Amendment into its gates . . . park officials are seeking to suppress speech. Why? Because of its content. Because it is Christian."

In Buffalo, New York, when members of Project Rescue attempted to distribute religious tracts and pro-life literature on a public sidewalk to students leaving high school, they were told by school officials not to offer the literature and were threatened with arrest if they persisted. Students were told over the public address system not to take the literature, and according to a report published in the *Buffalo News*, students told them "that they were threatened with discipline if they accepted [the literature]." According to the newspaper, "About ten dour looking school officials stood among the activists on the sidewalk outside . . . and watched the students as they walked to their buses."[12]

A point should be made here about the freedoms accorded to religious broadcasting, publishing, and education in America. It is true that most states continue to offer almost unrestricted freedom to Christian radio and television, publishing, and Christian schools. This liberty, however, is already fragile. These religious institutions are totally dependent on charitable donations from constituents who support their message. As such, their future and their ability to promote their message is precarious, subject to the vicissitudes of voluntary giving. Public institutions, including public broadcasting, are funded by tax monies that are compulsory and not at all attached to the content of the message. An anti-Christian professor can manipulate a curriculum to serve his or her prejudices, funded by taxes paid by conscientious Christians who are not only the object of the message but often the victims of it!

Since secularism is far from the mainstream of American thinking and beliefs, the contrivance of the false consensus is only possible by controlling, as far as possible, the ideas and speech of the opposition. The Marxists in the old Soviet Union realized that this was their only hope in reconstructing the thoughts and perceptions of the general population, and the New Left is learning the same thing. The secularist-New Left coalition relies on a great deal of unsubstantiated claims and propaganda that distorts and convolutes the truth to serve their ideological and political ends. When their propaganda is challenged by the presentation of facts and of the truth, their theories cannot hold up. Therefore, they must "neutralize" dissidents by discrediting them, defaming them, or accusing them of the contemporary guilt-by-allegation crimes of "sexism," "racism," "homophobia," "sexual harassment," or just plain "harassment." (This writer was compelled by a U.S. District Court to pay to the court and the plaintiffs $30,000 in fines for "harassing" an abortionist by calling him "a pig" in public during an abortion protest.)[13]

In his syndicated column, Cal Thomas wrote about a *Washington Post*

> front page story on the impact of evangelical Christians, who have been flooding the White House and Congress with phone calls and mail [in response to President Clinton's call for lifting the ban on homosexuality in the military] in the exercise of their constitutional rights; *Washington Post* reporter Michel Weisskopf invoked the most bigoted of generalizations when he wrote that evangelicals were "largely poor, uneducated and easy to command."

> The *Post* ran a correction the next day, saying the conclusion had no "factual basis," but the damage had already been done. The *Post* was flooded with calls. People who said they were evangelical Christians offered their bona fides, incomes, and assertions of independent thinking . . .

> The caricature of evangelical Christians as inherently stupid because they believe in an authority higher than journalism, the government, or the culture (the unholy trinity of rampant secularism) would be repugnant to all if it had been applied to blacks or women or homosexuals. But it seems Christian-bashing is always in season.

On 27 February 1993, public television aired a cinematically beautiful nature program entitled "The Land of the Eagle." It was a gorgeous photographic depiction of the natural beauty of the unspoiled American wilderness. The photography itself would have served well the apparent ideological purpose, which was to stress the urgent need for environmental protections. During the commentary, however, was this very disturbing anti-Christian slander:

"The pilgrims who first came to this country came to establish their new Jerusalem. They believed that the natives were savages, their religion 'devil worship,' and their relationship to the land ungodly. They believed they were superior to the land. . . . The diseases they brought from Europe killed off nation after nation."

During a fund-raising break, the local TV announcer proclaimed, "Our message [in the program] is very important."

What does the young child or the nondiscriminating adult think about a message that depicts sincere, self-sacrificing persecuted Christians as pie-in-the-sky religious bigots who spread diseases to unwary natives "killing off nation after nation"? We will see later how these messages have become cumulative in contemporary culture and are constantly bombarding the public, pummeling them into submission to the secularist, anti-Christian consensus. This one came partly at taxpayer expense.

In the January 1993 edition of the *Christian New Yorker*, correspondent Dana Oakes reported on an 17 October 1992 incident at Cornell University. According to Oakes:

> The Cornell Coalition for Life sponsored a day-long Ivy League Conference for Life featuring psychologist and author Susan Stanford-Rue and National Right to Life attorney James Bopp. Before the event could begin, conferees had to endure nearly two hours of whistling, screaming, chanting and name-calling by approximately 150 pro-choice protesters. Attempts were made [by the pro-choicers] to pull conference organizer Mary Beth McCall away from the podium while others attempted to pull the microphone from her hand. . . . The wire leading to the microphone was later severed. A guest speaker was spat on as were other pro-life attenders. Eyewitnesses said that the same individuals attended the Rally for Choice, sponsored by Cornell Democrats the day before. The Rally

for Choice featured New York Attorney General Robert Abrams, local politicians, and an Ithaca College professor. Numerous announcements were made during the rally encouraging attenders to protest against the Conference for Life.[14]

This kind of intolerance for "politically incorrect" speech has become widespread among liberals on college and university campuses. So much is this the case that it has spurred the quintessentially liberal *Village Voice* founding editor and columnist Nat Hentoff to write a book on the subject, *Free Speech for Me, but Not for Thee*. It is, tragically, now spreading beyond the campuses and into the public. Typically, such intolerance and harassment has been ignored by authorities as it was in this case. Just the next week, according to the paper, homosexuals on the campus demanded that University president Frank Rhodes respond to anti-homosexual chalkings that began to appear on campus sidewalks. Rhodes issued a statement saying, "Members of the gay, lesbian, and bisexual communities should feel as free of personal intimidation as any other member of the University community. Violence and the threat of violence have no place at Cornell." No similar statement, however, was issued in response to the disruptions and assaults during the pro-life conference.

A case in which Christianity was officially discriminated against in the public square is the City of New York's denial of a parade permit to the Ancient Order of Hibernians, who, for 150 years, has sponsored the oldest, most celebrated parade in America. The St. Patrick's Day Parade is indisputably a Catholic event. But Mayor David Dinkins, in an attempt to impose the secularist consensus on New York City's Catholics, "declared" the parade a "secular" event and told the Hibernians that they would have to obey city law barring "discrimination" against homosexuals. The Hibernians refused, citing their religious beliefs that homosexuality is sinful and aberrant behavior. The mayor then denied them the permit and handed the parade over to another group claiming a similar name that would include homosexuals in the march. According to one member of the Ancient Order of Hibernians who was present at a meeting with the mayor,

Dinkins offered that if the Catholic church "would change its teachings on homosexuality," he would reconsider. In the end a federal judge decided that Dinkins was wrong and that the Catholic paraders were free to exclude homosexuals on religious grounds. In this case, at least, the Ancient Order of Hibernians had the resolve and the money to defend themselves in court. But what about smaller, poorer groups that cannot afford to do likewise? They are forced to relinquish their rights and submit to intolerance.

According to an article that appeared in *Christianity Today*, the science writer Forrest Mims III was fired as the "Amateur Scientist" columnist for *Scientific American* magazine because he was a Christian. The forty-six-year-old scientist has written more than seventy books and authored hundreds of articles for magazines such as *National Geographic*, *Science Digest*, *Popular Mechanics*, and *Modern Electronics*. According to *Christianity Today*, when Mims indicated he had written some articles for Christian publications, he was asked directly by the magazine's editor, Jonathan Piel, if he "believed" in Darwin's theory of evolution. Mims replied, "No."

> Mims says he left a 1988 meeting in New York thinking he had the job as the Amateur Scientist writer. But he was also given a stern warning from [the editor] that if he ever wrote anything on creationism, his pay could be cut or he could be dismissed.

> Mims, who teaches a Bible study in his local church, insists he has never used his science writing to promote his Christian beliefs, and that "he would never use that column to espouse my personal religious views." After he returned home, he wrote and submitted three columns.

> Several months later, however, Mims says he was questioned further by [editor] Piel and another editor about his views on abortion and his faith. Though describing Mims' work as "first rate," Peil expressed concern that the "good name of the magazine" might be "embarrassed" by Mims. . . . According to the writer, Piel asked, "Are you a fundamentalist Chris-

tian?" Mims objected to the question and said, "I will
not be discriminated against." [15]

After that, according to the magazine, Mims was fired.
This is an undeniable example of the intolerance of the
consensus at work. Dr. Mims was willing to stand up against
discrimination and bigotry, not to mention his willingness to
sacrifice the $2,000 per column pay he would have received.
But what about others less inclined to "make waves," endure
slander, or lose their employment? What about those who
cannot afford to lose their only source of income? Those
Christians are forced to submit, once again, to the intolerance and tyranny of the secularist, false consensus.

It is a travesty that such anti-Christian bias and prejudice
prevails and is even promoted in the last few years of the
twentieth century, a century that has seen such progress in
the area of civil and human rights. Twentieth century America
has recognized women's rights, the expansion of rights for
minority Americans, and huge strides in civil rights for all
American citizens. In an age of such liberal accomplishment,
a serious turn toward discrimination against people of sincere religious convictions and practices is a terrible contra-
diction to the meaning of the twentieth century. That this
discrimination and defamation is often perpetrated by people
who embrace liberal values is even more scandalous. It is the
epitome of hypocrisy for those who advocate equality for
homosexuals, women, and minorities to deny equal justice
and equal treatment for Christians. The reality is that advocacy for the "underclass" is much of the time a careful and
effective disguise for an underlying, anti-Christian, anti-religious political and social agenda.

Jesus taught that "you shall know the truth, and the truth
shall make you free."[16] Freedom is dependent upon the
truth. Freedom cannot thrive in an environment of lies,
deception, intrigue, or distortion. Neither can true freedom
survive when those who proclaim truth are stifled or punished for it. Religious beliefs are a pristine form of truth.
The framers of the Constitution knew this, and that is why
religious freedom was guaranteed in the First Amendment

and why it led off the Bill of Rights. Where people are not free in their souls to believe in the spiritual and to freely proclaim those beliefs and to make converts, they cannot be said to enjoy true freedom, in spite of any other liberties that they may be accorded.

THREE

A *Christian Kristallnacht*

————— | —————

On 7 November 1938, in Paris, France, a desperate, seventeen-year-old Jewish refugee named Herschel Grynszpan entered the German Embassy in Paris and shot to death a minor diplomat named Ernst von Rath. The youth's actual intention was to assassinate the ambassador, Count Johannes von Welczeck, in retribution for the deportation of his parents to a Nazi concentration camp. When the boy arrived however, the embassy staff determined that the rag-tag displaced person's inquiry did not deserve the chief diplomat's time, and instead dispatched von Rath, an undersecretary, to find out what the boy wanted. It was then that the distraught and confused prodigal discharged his pistol, mortally wounding the young officer. Von Rath was at the time under investigation by the Gestapo for his suspected opposition to the anti-Semitic policies of the Nazi party, which made his murder particularly ironic.

What would follow would be the most egregious, sinister political contrivance of the Nazis to that time. On the evening of 9-10 November, Dr. Paul Joseph Goebbels, the Nazi minister of propaganda, issued orders that demonstrations against the murder of the German diplomat in Paris be implemented throughout the night. Although the newspapers, which were under Goebbel's editorial control, represented the riots as "spontaneous," the truth was that they were perpetrated by the party that controlled the government. The resulting pogrom, or Kristallnacht (the night of the broken glass), was to become the first act of what would metastasize into the diabolical "Final Solution" to the Jewish problem.

In his memoirs, Rudolf Hoss described it as the night when "throughout all of Germany Jewish businesses were destroyed, or at least all the windows were smashed in retaliation for the killing of von Rath. . . . Fires broke out in the synagogues and the firemen were deliberately prohibited from fighting the fires." "To protect them from the wrath of the German people," all Jews who still played a role in commerce, industry, and business were arrested and brought to the concentration camps as "Jews in protective custody."[1]

The Nazis used what they knew to be an isolated and unquestionably non-representative incident—the murder of a minor diplomat by a frantic refugee—as an excuse to initiate a policy of persecution against the Jews of Europe. Before the killing of von Roth, Nazi propaganda had accused the German Jews of waging a "hate campaign" against the concentration camps, which the Nazis believed were admirable institutions. As a result, party leaders were just waiting for an occasion that could be exploited for the purpose of meting out retribution against the Jewish population.

Paul Johnson, in *Modern Times–the World from the Twenties to the Nineties*, observes that "the 'Jewish Problem' was central to [Hitler's] whole view of history, political philosophy, and program of action."[2]

Propaganda minister Goebbel's directives, which included instructions that synagogues could be burned down, Jewish businesses and apartments could be destroyed, and prominent Jews arrested and sent to concentration camps—which left the distinct impression that Jews could even be murdered with tacit impunity—were all in line with the viciously anti-Semitic policies of Hitler and his Nazi party.

In obedience to Goebbel's orders, party operatives hastily organized and deployed rank and file followers, whipping up anti-Semitic mobs to carry out the objectives of party leaders with an excessive fury. William Shirer, in his monumental, authoritative volume on the history of Nazism, *The Rise and Fall of the Third Reich*, documents: "It was a night of horror throughout Germany. Synagogues, Jewish homes and shops went up in flames, and several Jews, men, women and children, were shot or otherwise slain while trying to escape burning to death."

According to Shirer's account, a preliminary report made to Hermann Goering, the economic dictator of the Third Reich, showed that besides the hundreds of shops destroyed, houses and synagogues were torched, and tens of thousands of Jews arrested. "Thirty-six deaths were reported, and those seriously injured were also numbered at thirty-six."

In actuality, Shirer points out, the number of slain victims was "believed to have been several times the preliminary figure."[3]

All this devastation was wrought in supposed response to the murder of the third secretary of the embassy in Paris. What should have been responsibly treated as an isolated incident was used by the unscrupulous and opportunistic Nazis as an example of the danger of the Jews to the German state. The Nazi party bosses held the entire German Jewish population accountable for the killing. They knew very well that no conspiracy among any Jews existed, much less the whole of the Jewish population, but it served their twisted belief, in line with the Fuhrer's, that the Jews had to be expunged from the emerging Aryan empire if the Reich was to rise to its glorious apex.

Not only did the German Jews face the initial brunt of the anti-Semitic backlash in the form of murdering and pillaging mobs, but additional penalties beyond the "night of broken glass" further pressed the retribution:

"They were subjected, collectively, to a fine of one billion marks as punishment," as Goering put it, "for their abominable crimes, etc."[4] And Goebbels insisted "that the Jews be excluded from everything: schools, theaters, movies, resorts, public beaches, parks, and even from the German forests."[5]

"Count Shwerin von Krosigk, the minister of finance, and former Rhodes scholar who prided himself on representing the 'traditional and decent Germany' in the Nazi government, agreed 'that we will have to do everything to shove the Jews into foreign countries.'"[6]

At the meeting of cabinet officers at which the penalties were decided upon, Field Marshall Goering adjourned with this conclusion: "I shall close the meeting with these words:

German Jewry, shall, as punishment for their crimes, et cetera, have to make a contribution for one billion marks. That will work. The swine won't commit another murder. Incidentally, I would like to say that I would not like to be a Jew in Germany."[7]

The anti-Jewish riots of 9 November show how a single, unfortunate incident, in this case, the tragic murder of an innocent man, could be used as an excuse to initiate a violent crackdown on a "politically incorrect" segment of the population. The killing of von Rath was the perfect opportunity for the Nazis to put their anti-Semitic ideology into practice. It is my prediction that a recent, similarly tragic incident just possibly could lead to a Kristallnacht for Christians in America.

On Wednesday, 10 March 1993, Michael Griffin, an erstwhile anti-abortion protester, shot and killed Dr. David Gunn, an abortionist, at his clinic in Pensacola, Florida. The killing was committed, judging from Griffin's words to Gunn moments before he shot him, to stop Gunn from killing "any more pre-born babies."

The thirty-one-year-old Griffin had surfaced in several of the pro-life activist churches in the Pensacola area after his wife had contacted Linda Burt, co-direc or with her husband John Burt, of My Father's House, a shelter for women in crisis pregnancy. Mrs. Griffin volunteered her services, but when it was determined that she did not have the necessary skills to be of immediate help, she offered the services of her husband, whom she said was a "handyman."

According to Linda Burt, "Michael Griffin came around and helped fix some things around the house." The crisis pregnancy center had burned down suspiciously in January of 1992. The cause was officially listed as "undetermined," but the fire marshall said off the record that the fire was definitely of "suspicious origin." The Burts were convinced it was the work of opponents of the home's mission to provide a positive, constructive alternative to abortions. They eventually located another house and reopened in May of the same year.

Linda Burt describes Michael Griffin as a quiet, almost

withdrawn man. The Reverend James Kilpatrick, pastor of the Brownsville Assembly of God church, which Griffin left in 1989 after a dispute, said, "He had an eerie calm to him."[8] To the Burts, he appeared to be a sincere Christian. Eventually they became aware that there was tension in Griffin's family life. He had at least once and maybe twice filed for divorce, and there was some indication of violence in his home. His wife once obtained a judicial order of protection against him, which she eventually abandoned. At the time of the murder, Michael Griffin was not a member of any church, but sporadically attended various churches in the vicinity.

The Sunday before he killed David Gunn, Griffin had visited the Burts' church, Whitfield Assembly of God, located outside of Pensacola. In the service that morning he had requested prayers for abortionist Gunn, asking that the congregation "would agree with him that Dr. Gunn would give his life to Jesus Christ." That weekend he had accompanied the Reverend Joe Nettleton from Charity Chapel Church and seventeen other men on a retreat during which he asked the men to lay hands upon him and pray for him because he carried "such a burden for these aborted children." According to Pastor Nettleton, Griffin "prayed that Dr. Gunn would stop doing what the Bible said he shouldn't do."

The Tuesday night before the shooting, Michael Griffin called Linda Burt, and asked where the next day's pro-life demonstration would take place. Linda Burt was cautious; she sensed in Griffin's voice that something was wrong. Perhaps her knowledge of his previously contentious past contributed to her trepidation. In a subtle attempt to dissuade him from participating, she withheld information on the location of the demonstration from him. Somewhat bewildered, he told her that he had a doctor bill to pay in the area of the clinic, and that when he found the demonstrators, he would join them.

Michael Griffin did locate the picket at about 10:00 the next morning. According to a deputy sheriff at the scene, he appeared, "dressed in a gray suit like he was going to church," in the rear parking lot of the Pensacola Women's Medical Services Clinic, which the abortionist Gunn operated. Gunn had just gotten out of his car when someone spotted Griffin running up to him. While Gunn was turned away from him, Griffin shot him at least three times in the upper back with a .38-caliber, snubbed-nose revolver.

Raised in the theologically conservative Church of Christ, the forty-seven-year-old Gunn, a former obstetrician, had long since stopped delivering babies and was exclusively committing abortions and related procedures. His abortion work was something he never disclosed to his family, other than to his twenty-two-year-old son. His brother was shocked to find out he was even involved in abortions. His only allusion to it was a cryptic statement he had once made, that he was doing his part to "help with the population explosion."[9]

Michael Griffin's murder of David Gunn was a single act of a deeply troubled misfit. It was not at all connected to the strategies or goals of the pro-life movement, and much less to the practice of Christianity. Nonetheless, the media, reflecting the prejudice of the false consensus, attempted to connect the two in the popular mind. *Newsweek* took the opportunity to cast the rescue movement's civil disobedience, which racked up over seventy thousand arrests in five years with no convictions for violent acts, with "arson [and] fire bombings." Ralph Reed, executive director of the Christian Coalition, wrote in the *Wall Street Journal* (Tuesday, 16 March 1993), "A dark thread runs through the conventional explanation for Michael Griffin's behavior: He was a devout Christian. His pathology has been cast in largely religious terms."

As soon as news of the killing was out, a great hue and cry went up from the pro-abortion groups such as the National Abortion Rights Action League, the National Abortion Federation, and the National Organization for Women, calling for retribution against pro-life Christians through state and federal law enforcement agencies. United States Attorney General Janet Reno, who was being sworn in on the day of the shooting, said that "on the top list" of her priorities was using "the full force" of her office to guarantee unfettered abortion. Lobbying efforts were immediately catalyzed in Washington for a federal act guaranteeing access to clinics and asking for the federal protection of abortionists, and imposing stiff penalties on anyone convicted of preventing, impeding, or frustrating access to the abortion clinics. The murder of David Gunn became front-page headlines in newspapers all across the country. The *Virginian Pilot* and *Ledger-Star* ran an Associated Press story headlined "New tactic in pro-life circles: Death." It was the lead story on virtually all of the network news programs and commentary shows, and it instantly became the subject of several major talk shows. There was even a moment of silence decreed in several cities in memory of the slain abortionist. President Clinton, himself accused by a former mistress of complicity in the abortion of their child, in a somewhat tortured statement made at a White House photo-op, equated the pro-life movement's usage of civil disobedience with this one, aberrant act of murder. He said, "We must create an atmosphere in the country where women can exercise their constitutional rights." Furthermore, he insisted that "this must stop and we will use every available means to stop it." In a face to face confrontation with national pro-life spokesman Bob Jewett at the televised Michigan town meeting, Clinton reportedly told him, "I'm gonna make sure you Operation Rescue types spend the rest of your lives in jail."

Before any government officials, or for that matter even any pro-abortion spokespersons, were heard decrying the act, pro-life leaders across the nation were being quoted as deploring and denouncing the use of violence and homicide by Michael Griffin. Randall Terry, the founder of Operation Rescue, said that the murder was "inappropriate and abhorrent." Rev. Robert Schenck, speaking on behalf of the National Clergy Council, denounced the use of violence and said that the Bible clearly states, "He who lives by the sword shall also die by the sword." Dr. Wanda Franz of the National Right to Life Committee said, "Of course we deplore the use of violence and murder. Killing is never the answer—whether of abortionists or unborn babies." The United States Catholic Bishops' Conference issued a statement declaring, "The violence of killing in the name of pro-life makes a mockery of the pro-life cause. Violence is not a part of the pro-life message."

David Gunn's murder came shortly after the conviction of Dr. Abu Hayat, a New York City abortionist, who was known locally as the "Butcher of Avenue A." Hayat was charged with severing the arm of baby Ana Rosa Rodriguez in a late term abortion performed on her mother, Rosa Rodriguez. Hayat was convicted of three first degree assault counts, the first for the failed abortion of Rodriguez's daughter in the eighth month of her pregnancy. The baby was born several days later in a hospital emergency room, missing her right arm. He was also convicted of a charge of ejecting a woman from his office in March of 1991 in the middle of an abortion because her husband was unable to pay the $500 fee. Hospital doctors later treated the woman and found pieces of her unborn child left behind, including a foot. In addition to these charges, Hayat was also convicted of falsifying business records.

Although Abu Hayat, a licensed abortionist in the state of New York, was convicted of assaulting an unborn child (He was convicted of an "illegal" abortion only because the court determined the late term abortion should have been performed in a hospital, rather than a clinic—an abortion in the eighth month of pregnancy is legal in New York State), his conviction warranted only a small article buried in the second section of most newspapers. Meanwhile, abortionist Gunn's death became front-page headlines and the leading radio and television story for three full days after the shooting.

Furthermore, Hayat's conviction created virtually no cry for, nor any efforts to enact, better regulation on abortionists and their clinics. No women's organizations or advocacy groups called for tougher legislation to deal with unscrupulous abortionists. There was not a congressional call for more accountability on the part of the abortion industry and absolutely no call for the rescinding of *Roe v. Wade*, under which Hayat operated. For all we know the president did not even notice Hayat's conviction or the circumstances leading up to it.

There is only one reasonable explanation for this imbalance in the reporting of these two related incidents. The fact that abortion-on-demand and the advocates of it are *au courant* with politicians and with the news media, the current administration ran on a platform that offered more abortions and the Democratic party in charge of both houses of Congress as well as the White House is on record as the "pro-choice party." This puts the abortion industry and its proponents on the politically correct side of the issue while abortion opponents (99 percent most of whom are practicing Christians) are on the politically incorrect side.

In an unusually bold and telling series (published in the *Los Angeles Times*), staff writer David Shaw exposed the bias in the news media against the pro-life movement and in favor of the abortion industry:

"Most major newspapers support abortion rights on their editorial pages, and two major media studies have shown that 80% to 90% of U.S. journalists personally favor abortion. . . . The American Newspaper Guild, the union that represents news and editorial employees at many major newspapers, has officially endorsed 'freedom of choice in abortion decisions'."[10]

Furthermore, Shaw states, "A comprehensive *Times* study of major newspaper, television and newsmagazine coverage over the last eighteen months, including more than 100 interviews with journalists and with activists on both sides of the abortion debate, confirms that this bias (in favor of abortion rights) often exists."[11]

While we will examine the ramifications of this media bias in favor of the abortion industry in a later chapter, at this point it is essential that we consider its implications for fueling retribution against conscientious, pro-life Christians for the murder of Dr. David Gunn.

A biased media cannot be trusted to present the truth about the Pensacola murder. Broadcasts and printed reports about the killing linked it to the strategies of the pro-life movement. The press, partly following sensationalistic instinct, and partly reflecting its pro-abortion bias, depicted the pro-life movement as condoning, indeed applauding the murder. The media largely accepted the spin put on it by the abortion industry, that murder is a natural progression from picketing and protesting. Once again, in depicting pro-life

Christians as potentially murderous fanatics, the bearers of the false consensus attempt to discredit and neutralize the right-to-life cause, while confirming in the public's mind the image of the sincere Christian as a dangerous, crazed, homicidal maniac.

Pro-abortion forces in the United States have continuously expressed frustration with the pro-life movement. Apparently irrepressible and devoted beyond secularist comprehension, the predominantly Christian pro-lifers have been willing to endure ever increasing levels of suffering meted out to them by the plaintiff abortionists and their regiments, irritated law enforcement personnel, and biased courts. These penalties have included huge fines for the violation of dubious restraining orders and court injunctions, most of which were determined in the end to be unconstitutional when in January of 1993 the Supreme Court limited federal jurisdiction over abortion protests in *Bray v. Alexandria Women's Health Clinic*. However, before that ruling was handed down, pro-life Christians had been fined millions of dollars. They allegedly "interfered with women's constitutional rights" by offering last minute counseling outside clinics to those seeking abortions, distributing Christian and pro-life literature, and picketing the abortion clinics. In Houston, they were fined for merely praying at the clinic sites.

Advocates for Life, a Portland-based pro-life organization, was fined eight million dollars in a suit charging them with interfering in the "constitutional" business of abortion when they exercised their own constitutional right by picketing the abortion businesses in their city.

Convicted of violating an injunction which prohibited "hindering" a woman from gaining access to an abortion clinic, my brother, Rev. Robert Schenck, and I were fined $10,000 each and ordered to pay attorney's fees for the clinic operators. On Saturday, 27 December 1990, Robert and I, in our capacities as ordained ministers, went to a clinic site in Buffalo, New York, to proclaim the gospel and distribute copies of the Bible and Christian literature. We stood all morning on the sidewalk outside a building that housed, in addition to the clinic, a United States Post Office and a drug rehab counseling center, along with several businesses. There we distributed New Testaments and Christian tracts to passersby, including several women whom we thought may have been headed for the clinic (We were never certain since we could not tell whether in fact they went into the clinic). Eventually we were charged with five counts of contempt for allegedly "hindering," "trespassing," and "impeding" access by walking "in front of" a car pulling into the office complex driveway; by "offering" a piece of literature, a New Testament, to a couple not entering but exiting the complex driveway; by "impeding" when I offered a New Testament to a woman who happily received it; and by "trespassing" when I continued to speak to a woman after she had passed by me and "pirouetted" on an entrance tile supposedly belonging to the clinic! In a bench trial which lasted all of five months, we were both convicted. Not a shred of evidence that we presented in our defense was ever considered, nor were any of the supposedly aggrieved women brought to court or asked to testify against us. The judge, whose wife is connected to a professional health service which purportedly represents abortionists, found us guilty on every count!

In addition to these injustices, pro-life Christians who have dared to challenge the pro-abortion consensus have suffered lengthy imprisonment: sentences of up to six years for trespass. In other cases they have received six months in jail for praying on a public sidewalk and a year for "resisting arrest" by assuming a posture of kneeling in prayer. I myself witnessed two incidents in which people simply "praying" on public property, in the first case on a public street corner and in the other on the mall in front of a subway station, were subjected to physical abuse by law enforcement personnel. In the first case, a pastor participating in a lawful protest of abortion in Atlanta, Georgia, rose from his knees on the curb of a public street to read the Bible aloud. He was pounced on by two young police officers, who ground his face into the asphalt, handcuffed him, and whisked him away on a charge of "disorderly conduct." In the second case, again in Atlanta, as abortion protesters were being blocked by police from lawfully entering a subway station, a man kneeling in prayer before the barricades was kicked in the chest and knocked over backward by a police captain. None of this was trumpeted in the news, but it would have been had the protesters been some "politically correct" group.

These incidents demonstrate the extreme to which authorities sympathetic to the abortion industry are willing to go in their efforts to discourage and dismantle Christian opposition to freewheeling, unrestricted, and unregulated abortion-on-demand in America.

What potential abuses, what travesties of justice might eventually occur if, as the Clinton administration has promised, they or any future administrations use "every available means" to stop conscientious, pro-life dissent? According to broadcaster M. G. "Pat" Robertson:

> Acts of Congress, signed by the president of the United States, carry with them the full enforcement power of the F.B.I. and the Justice Department. The time may come in America when the federal government will hunt down and prosecute any Christian who dares protest the slaughter of unborn children or the flagrant practice of homosexuality. Instead of those who break God's laws being criminals, those who uphold God's laws will be considered criminals and enemies of the state![12]

This is exactly what is happening, and sooner than the Reverend Mr. Robertson predicted. During the 1992 Republican National Convention in Houston, Texas, State District Judge Eileen O'Neill issued a temporary restraining order restricting pro-life demonstrators from being within one hundred feet of abortion clinic entrances. The order, however, was written so broadly as to prohibit "preaching, praying, (and) hymn singing," among other traditional and First Amendment religious Christian practices. When local clergy became aware of the denial of religious rights inherent in the order, they deliberately penetrated the hundred-foot, "Gospel-free zone" and engaged in non-confrontational prayer, much of it alone, sometimes in a kneeling posture on the sidewalk, and they preached. Under normal circumstances, such activity would have been considered religious expression protected by the First Amendment, but not in the wake of the false consensus. In the wake of the false consensus, those clergymen who exercised their First Amendment rights to free exercise of religion were arrested, jailed, tried, and found guilty of contempt, most of them being sentenced by Judge O'Neill to six months in prison!

Eventually, Judge O'Neill's sentences were overturned by the Texas Supreme Court. But the fact that the judge could even issue such an order, that law enforcement agencies would have to take it seriously, and that innocent citizens who were merely exercising their constitutional rights would be imprisoned for days, and in at least one case for more than two weeks because his views and his actions were considered intolerable by the secularist, anti-Christian elite (Planned Parenthood made at least one financial contribution to Judge O'Neill's campaign chest), demonstrates how far the anti-religious coalition has gone to intimidate dissidents. As the hatred and frustration of the sexual revolution crowd mounts toward the non-violent yet persistently conscientious Christians, the prospect of a "night of broken glass" for the latter becomes very real.

Numerous Christians, including myself, have been harassed, arrested, maligned in the press, physically attacked, denied their constitutional rights, and otherwise abused simply because their beliefs, their practices, and their actions are not in lock step with the false consensus. They therefore cannot be tolerated by the secular propagandists.

On Holy Saturday of 1992, I went alone to an abortion clinic to pray and to lay flowers as a memorial to the nascent children who were slain there. Wearing a clerical collar and stole, I approached the yellow police line that demarcated the boundaries of a federal court order protecting the premises from pro-life demonstrators. It was of course the Easter season, and on Good Friday a group of one hundred pro-abortion protesters had assembled along the sidewalks leading to our church. Chanting obscenities, they spat on worshipers going into the church and swung coat hangers at them. In one case a demonstrator cut a man across the forehead. Now, this same cadre of pro-abortion extremists mobbed in front of the clinic. Two men had accompanied me in my car that morning, but I asked them to remain at a distance. I evaluated the situation. It was a surly mob, already agitated and obviously looking for trouble. I was aware of the fact that if I knelt to pray at the boundary line, I would likely be assaulted. Nonetheless, praying for courage and strength, I crossed the street and approached the mob.

As I drew closer, the gaggle began jeering and mocking, some people physically contorting their bodies and spasmodically ejaculating epithets and insults. Others gyrated, intermittently shoving their backsides into my face as I knelt to pray. I began to read Scripture as I laid the flowers down just an inch beyond the yellow line. The flowers were immediately ground to shreds by the demonstrators who then surrounded me and began pummeling me on the head and back and kicking me between my legs. At the same time others spat on my head and in my face and drooled onto the pages of my Bible. One man kept screaming through a megaphone into my ear while another person dropped cigarette ashes on my head. After that, someone stole my eyeglasses and ripped off my clerical stole. Then they picked me up under my armpits and dragged me into the main street without my eyeglasses and left me in the middle of the traffic. The banner under which I had been abused read "Buffalo United for Choice."

An editorial that appeared following the incident read, "Schenck incident unacceptably crossed barrier." *The Buffalo News*, in an unusual advocacy, deplored the attack on me, stating, "When pro-choice militants jostled, mocked, and spat upon the Rev. Paul H. Schenck while he read a Bible outside a downtown abortion clinic, they crossed a line of behavior that should not have been crossed at all."

"The shoving of Schenck, a local anti-abortion leader, contributes to a climate of extremism that threatens violence."

In March of 1993, I was cited in contempt of a federal injunction for speaking at a Washington, D.C., rally at which I called for a "holy rebellion" among Christian youth against the secular agenda. I urged the crowd to emulate others, including the war protesters of the previous generation who had contributed effectively to the demise of Richard Nixon's presidency. While I was careful to explain that my words were not a commentary on the rightness or the wrongness of that protest movement, I pointed out that those protesters were able to topple the president, or at least contribute to his fall. In a similar way, conscientious Christian young people who vociferously and relentlessly oppose the immoral policies of the current administration could have an effect on the tenure of Bill Clinton in the White House. For these remarks I was cited in contempt of the federal order that prohibited "aiding and abetting" actions designed to prohibit abortion! In one sense the motion to hold me in contempt was accurate, for opposing the policies of the Clinton administration would ultimately have an effect on abortions in America, since this is the most pro-abortion administration ever. On the other hand, to hold any American, much less a member of the clergy, in contempt with a possible $5,000 penalty, for merely speaking out is a blatant violation of the fundamental rights to freedom of speech and religion.

It is not just at the juncture of the abortion debate that Christians get identified with antisocial behavior, bigotry, and violence. Homosexuality, another sacred subject of the secularist-sexual revolution, is often the door to stereotyping people of faith:

Newsweek magazine seems to specialize in Christian-bashing by employing stereotype, innuendo, exaggeration, and outright anti-Christian bigotry in numerous articles reporting on so-called "Gay rights." For instance, in the 14 September 1992 cover story "Gays Under Fire," the "religious right" (the epithetical designation so frequently invoked by the secularist press to show that orthodox, biblical Christians are off center and probably dangerous) was blamed for "a powerful backlash" against "Gay America's struggle for acceptance." *Newsweek* traced this invidious animus toward homosexuals to the Christians' belief in the Bible. Referring to St. Paul's Epistle to the Corinthians 6:9-11, the writers state that the Bible "promises that homosexuals shall never inherit the Kingdom of God."

These statements, made in contrast to the "struggle for equal treatment" by the downtrodden homosexuals, leave the distinct impression that conscientious Christians are mean, hard-hearted, and most likely a danger to a fair society. In addition, the article's consistent equating of orthodox Christianity's moral rejection of homosexuality to "gay-bashing" (an ambiguous term that seems to connote violence but that really designates any opposition to homosexuality) conveys the erroneous idea that Christians support, if not clandestinely engage in, acts of violence perpetrated against homosexuals.

In another article on the subject, which appeared in the 1 March 1993 edition, *Newsweek* again promoted the idea of a dangerous Christian population in America. The headline in the "Society" column, under the heading "Religion," read "Onward Muscular Christians!"—once again connoting a potentially violent group. The writers portray Colorado Springs as "the capital city of muscular Christianity" and say that evangelical organizations have moved their national headquarters there "like Muslims to Mecca," a veiled allusion to the terrorist violence associated in the popular mind with fundamentalist Muslims. According to the article, "Not surprisingly, most of the fundamentalists focus on gay rights." The writers alarmingly refer to the "hate campaign" being waged by the Christians against homosexuals in Colorado. The inference is undeniable: Wherever conscientious Christians gather, you can be sure that hatred, bigotry, and possibly violence will be there.

Note that during the six months separating these two articles the target of this stereotyping widened. In "Gays Under Fire," only so-called "fundamentalists" were impugned, but in "Muscular Christians," the category of dangerous types has been expanded to include evangelicals and even Presbyterians. "The volume of hate seems to be rising," prophesy the authors. "Moral crusades, however heartfelt, too often take no prisoners" (still another allusion to the potentially lethal nature of committed Christians).

The volume of hate that is rising is not hatred by Christians, whose "God is love," but rather it is the animosity directed toward these people of faith by the media. That is where the hatred is to be found. The accrual of mockery, suspicion, prejudice, stereotype, animus, and hostility toward serious Protestant and Catholic Christians in America is escalating the potential for anti-religious violence, preparing the way for vigilantism and violence.

A recent popular opinion poll asked the question, "What kinds of people would you least like having as a next door neighbor?" The designation described as "fundamentalist Christian" was ranked fourth on the list of least desirable. This demonstrates the extent to which the negative portrayal of traditional, biblical Christians has affected the public's acceptance and toleration of their beliefs and practices. A prerequisite for persecution is making it onto the "undesirable" list. Thanks to the bias and prejudice of the American news media, the entertainment industry, the education establishment, and the liberal law establishment, Christians are fast rising to the top of the list.

Another arena that displays unmistakable antipathy toward biblical Christians is the arena of science and education. The creation/evolution debate has staked out the safety zones for Christians. Today, if anyone denies the veracity of the theory of evolution, and instead embraces a creationist cosmogony, he or she can be expected to be ostracized and banished by the scientific and academic communities. According to Dr. Henry Morris, president of the Institute for Creation Research:

> Every discipline of modern thought is now contaminated and controlled by evolutionism. The schools and colleges are everywhere dominated not only by evolutionary thought but also by evolutionary methodology. Furthermore, all the devastating politico-economic movements of the past century, including the great wars, have been motivated by evolutionary philosophy.[13]

Conscientious, orthodox Christians largely reject the theories of evolution in deference to the biblical depiction of a single act of creation of the universe and the populations of the earth. Furthermore, they believe there is substantial scientific evidence for creationism and have produced a tremendous amount of credible research on this subject. However, as pointed out by Dr. Morris, "evolutionism," as he calls it, is now the control ideology of scientific and educational institutions, and any rejection of the various evolutionary theories all but automatically disqualifies one from being taken seriously and often results in ostracism and defamation in those circles.

Harold Lindsell, in his book, *The New Paganism*, wrote about a group of prominent scientists who banded together to oppose a law in the state of Louisiana that would have mandated the giving of equal time in public schools to creationism alongside evolutionism as an alternative viable theory of cosmology. According to Lindsell, "The brief said that teaching religious ideas mislabeled as science is detrimental."[14] The inference is that holding religious beliefs about the world is deleterious and damaging to intellectual development.

The same acrimony is often heard from the educational establishment. The former Secretary of Education William Bennett, writing in his book, *The Devaluing of America*, said, "It is ironic that anyone who appeals to religious values today runs the risk of being called 'divisive' or attacked as an enemy of pluralism."[15]

Add to this the depiction of Christians in contemporary films and television as hypocrites, charlatans, rapists, murderers, and cannibals, and the defamation is complete.

So far, we have reviewed the prejudicial and defamatory characterizations of Christian convictions and practices as they conflict with the secularist agenda in the arenas of sexuality, science, and education. Customarily applied to Christians who do not consent to the secularist agenda in these areas are loaded terms such as "muscular," "hateful," "violent," "detrimental," "bigoted," and "gay-bashing." These are often used in the same contexts as "fundamentalist," "evangelical," "conservative Catholics," and "religious right." This leaves the undeniable impression that conscientious Christians, Protestant or Catholic, are an imminent danger to a secular, so-called pluralistic society. At best these inexplicable hold-overs from the dark ages must be tolerated in a country that still pays lip service to the Bill of Rights. But a movement is growing among secularists, who now have serious sponsorship in the administration, to marginalize and muzzle the religious opposition by using every means at their disposal. This arsenal of discrimination already includes intimidation, ostracism, and firings, exaggerated and false accusations of criminal or quasi-criminal activities, false arrests, and imprisonment. What weapons remain but the fomenting of popular hatred and prejudice toward Christians, which ultimately might erupt into pogroms? And who would blame a society that persecuted such a cadre of miscreants?

FOUR

Prime Time Prejudice

———————— | ————————

If you are a Christian, you may be rather surprised to discover that numerous popular musical groups, television shows, and major motion pictures are consistently and incessantly depicting you as a stooge, a hypocrite, a charlatan, a racist, an anti-Semite, mentally ill, a thief, a con artist, a child molester, a rapist, a murderer, and a cannibal!

In its unabashed contumacy of the Judeo-Christian tradition, the entertainment industry has heaped on the public an endless supply of malignant specimens it pawns off as Christians. Basically, these stereotypes come in two versions—Catholic and fundamentalist, although more recently a third type has begun to appear in the Hollywood line-up of defamatory depicture: the rabid, lunatic Pentecostal.

The Catholic Christian is often portrayed as a neurotic, timid paranoid who is obsessed with superstitious practices that more accurately resemble witchcraft than Christian devotion. This Catholic is often a middle-aged woman or a young female misfit. More often than not, she is portrayed wearing drab, slightly outdated clothing and bearing the wear and tear of unfounded fear and worry on her face. She is sexually inhibited and cannot enjoy life because of her tedious observance of religious ritual.

The male version of the Catholic Christian stereotype is equally paranoid, but where the female is timid and nervous, he is aggressive and belligerent. Many versions of this stereotype demonstrate a mental and emotional instability that prohibits the stereotype from relating to the opposite sex

normally and that often works itself out in anti-social and/
or violent behaviors. In another edition, he is a sort of
warlock that perpetrates terrible crimes that are accompanied by pseudo-Catholic rites.

The fundamentalist is by far the most sinister of all the
Christian villains in the media. The fundamentalist is invariably white, more often male than female, and exhibits unparalleled bigotry, chauvinism, racial prejudice, ignorance, hypocrisy, and malevolence. In music, television, and movies,
the fundamentalist Christian has thought every horrible
thought and committed every heinous act in his acting out
of excessive self-righteousness and in the guise of piety. The
Pentecostal is invariably portrayed as a crazed, homicidal
maniac that is given to spasms of tongue-speaking and religious delusions that lead to unspeakable atrocities.

Twisted, distorted, and demented images of Christians
are plenteous and unrelenting in contemporary entertainment, and the use of cruel and exaggerated stereotypes knows
no boundaries. Today, they are just as likely to show up in
a serious dramatic series such as "L.A. Law" or "In the Heat
of the Night"—or in respectable sitcoms like "The Carol
Burnett Show," as they are in irreverent comedy shows like
"Saturday Night Live," perhaps even more so!

As we have already seen, stereotypes of traditional Christians are being promoted in America today in an attempt to
nullify their influence on the contemporary culture. Conscientious Christians stand in dramatic contrast and, I might
add, protest to the prevailing hedonism that is so widespread among entertainment's elite. For this reason, the
media moguls have taken sharp exception to the presence of
conscientious Christian faith and have targeted
its practitioners for ridicule, sarcasm, derision, and scorn.

Rock and rap musicians, stand-up comics, Hollywood
screenwriters, TV talk show hosts and news commentators,
journalists, and novelists have all employed stereotypes when
depicting Christians.

As in just about every other category, contemporary
music has been the least discreet when it comes to Christian
bashing. In popular tunes irresponsibly discharged over the
airwaves and into the ears, minds, and hearts of unsupervised

(and many supervised) children—social sponges soaking up whatever the latest label has to dish up—bigoted bards have sung about Christians who abuse their children, commit incest with their daughters, seduce otherwise celibate songwriters (is anything unbelievable anymore?), and even kill with Bible verses on their lips and Jesus in their hearts.

Television has enlarged on these misrepresentations by carefully placing negative stereotypes in juxtaposition to clever, poised, and admirable skeptics who inevitably expose the pretender's hypocrisy and put the lie to his reverence for religion. As we will see, these images include the most gross exaggerations of Christian beliefs and practices. Inaccuracies, embellishments, and sheer fiction abound in the denigration of characters who represent religious life.

When the aural power of music and the visual power of television and film are combined, the defamation of Christian people and symbols escalates. I hesitate to mention the pop icon Madonna, whose use of Christian imagery is purposeful and obviously designed to raise the ire of the religious community, twice molesting them by using them as free promotion. Yet there is no discounting the "model" role she has played, especially with teens and pre-teens. Setting aside for now Madonna's pornographic and pedophilic adventures, her theft of sacred images, such as the statue of a saint with which she copulates in one of her music videos, denigrates the great heritage and the high moral, ethical, and spiritual traditions which that statue represents.

Malignant and vicious characterization inevitably affects young people's attitudes and preconceptions, not only about religion in general but also about their own family members who cherish and practice religious faith as well. It creates in the minds of a generation of youth images of religious people as hypocritical, sanctimonious, and loathsome. Furthermore, it animates their rebellion against their parents and grandparents, who most often represent the family's religious heritage.

The frequent depiction of Christians as superficial, dangerous charlatans also seriously diminishes the eventual impact of religion on the formation of a child's personality. While there are religious hypocrites that young people should be warned about, the stereotypes that show up in popular music, television, and movies paint all Christians with the same broad brush. Kids need faith, and they need the ethical and moral foundation that religious belief and instruction bring to them and nurture in their souls. The history of civilization has proven beyond any doubt that religious beliefs are essential to a moral and ethical society. I believe that the most significant reason for the moral and ethical crisis in America today is the diminishing of religion in young people's eyes. The role of religious faith in helping young people to define themselves, to comprehend the illusive and potentially confusing and disappointing world into which they have been thrust, and to help them understand their roles, responsibilities, and relationships to God, to themselves, and to others has been amply demonstrated.

Recent studies have shown that kids who pray, study the Bible, and attend church or synagogue (or for that matter, other houses of religious worship) are far less likely to smoke or drink, use illicit drugs, engage in premarital sex, or become involved in criminal activity. Children raised in religious homes are also shown to be more comfortable and secure and more able to face the crises of life with confidence.

Yet those who ought to be encouraging and supporting young people in exploring the treasures of religious faith are precisely those who are often joining in on the put-downs. A middle school offers an elective course as a substitute for literature and history called "Myth, Magic and Religion," in which prayer is reduced to the level of magical incantations and the Bible is made the equivalent of the Egyptian Book of the Dead. The United States Supreme Court calls it unconstitutional for a rabbi to deliver a non-sectarian, general "prayer" at a high-school graduation. A U.S. district court judge declares a prayer before a school football game "illegal." A federal judge in Michigan ordered that a portrait of Jesus that hung in a high school next to one of Dr. Martin Luther King, Jr., in the foyer for over twenty-five years violated the "separation of church and state" and directed the school's administration to remove it.

What is particularly onerous about these anti-religious

measures is that the institutions that are typically counterbalancing the negative and destructive cultural influences on young people are seen by youth as siding with them against the Church. While the courts and the "druggies," the schools and the rappers, and the community groups and pornographers are invariably juxtaposed to one another on just about every topic relevant to a modern teen-ager, they seem to be united on one thing: the idea that religion can be downright dangerous!

How can Christians be expected to continue to exercise a positive influence in their communities—strengthening families fighting drug abuse, racial prejudice, discrimination, and unfair housing policies; helping the hungry and the homeless, the abused and abandoned; working to keep kids in school and chaste; endeavoring to develop good character in young people—if the schools and other governmental authorities keep sending out the signal that robust Christian faith is, in the words of the political scientist Christopher Atterton, "a contagion from the right"?[1]

"The religious right can provide an important counterweight to the trend toward a materialistic society that sees all values as relative, views truth as a matter of interpretation and rejects the lessons of 3,500 years of Judeo-Christian experience," wrote David Awbery, an editor of the Wichita, Kansas, *Eagle*. Yet the majority of media voices continue to disparage earnest Christian faith.

I believe that much of the opposition to the practice of religion is based on the numerous stereotypes appearing in the American media. I have already quoted the *Washington Post* reporter Michael Weisskopf describing evangelicals as "largely poor, uneducated and easy to command." When Christians are portrayed like this in such a prestigious and prominent publication as the *Post*, why would educators present them as desirable models to put before their students? Of course, they're going to steer their charges away from such decadence!

The stereotypes of believers in the entertainment/news media are so abundant that this entire work could encompass an exposé of the way the conscientious practice of religion is treated by Hollywood. A huge debt of gratitude must be paid to the PBS film critic Michael Medved for exposing this scandalous reality in his telling volume, *Hollywood vs. America—Popular Culture and the War on Traditional Values* (New York: Harper Collins Publishers/Zondervan, 1992). In a rare and remarkably honest evaluation of the contemporary entertainment industry, the forty-three-year-old critic and erstwhile speech writer for the Democratic presidential candidate George McGovern clearly demonstrates that the liberal Hollywood elite, with very little exception, has literally nothing good to say about faith.

The February 1992 edition of the *American Family Association Journal* reported on the results of research on the status of religion in prime time television. The study, commissioned by the AFA, was conducted by Dr. Thomas Skill of the Department of Communications, University of Dayton; Dr. John Lyons of the Department of Psychiatry, Psychology and Medicine at Northwestern University; and Dr. David Larson of the Duke University Medical Center. The researchers analyzed one hundred prime time network programs that appeared on ABC, NBC, CBS, and Fox during the month of November 1990. The research looked at the religious and spiritual behaviors of the characters portrayed in the shows and also analyzed the appearance of religious images, artifacts, and rituals such as crosses, churches, and prayer services.

Of the 1,462 characters studied, only eighty-one had any identifiable religious affiliation. There were fifty-one Catholics, twenty-one Protestants, five cult members and three "New Agers." According to the research, 94.5 percent of all speaking characters on television have no religious affiliations.

In the sixty-eight hours of programming that was the subject of the analysis, researchers witnessed only 115 behaviors by ninety-one characters that were considered even remotely religious or spiritual in nature. Most of these behaviors consisted of statements or actions as insignificant as someone exclaiming "Thank God!" or words to that effect, after a close call.

What was most revealing, though, was the media's pervasive contempt for religion; in over 50 percent of the rare instances when religion was displayed, it was presented, in the words of the report, in a "clearly negative" way.

Here are some examples of prime time television shows that have depicted practicing Christians in disparaging ways:

1. Christians as fools:

In the 12 March 1992 episode of the NBC sitcom "Wings," the show's main character, Joe, accidentally destroys Lowell's model blimp, which Lowell has worked on for six years. Lowell is a "simple-minded, slow-witted dunce." At first Lowell won't speak to Joe, but eventually he attempts a reconciliation. He tells Joe he can't forgive him, but turns to "prayer," insisting that Joe pray along with him. He thrusts Joe to his knees, calling on his "Heavenly Father above." When the prayer appears ineffectual, Joe tries to squirm out of it. Lowell tells Joe they must stay on their knees until they have a "sign." Joe's foot falls asleep, and Lowell declares that it is the requisite omen, and off they go for beers. In this episode, prayer is clearly displayed as a silly, stupid, ineffectual thing to do.

In the 16 December 1992 episode of NBC's hit comedy series "Seinfeld," the show's character Elaine is mocked by the star, Jerry Seinfeld, for dating a "religious guy."

"What are you doing Saturday night?" asks Seinfeld.

"Date with Fred."

"The religious guy?" Jerry exclaims.

"He's not that religious," Elaine responds defensively.

Standing up, Jerry intones derisively, "LET US PRAY . . ."

On the 2 January 1993 episode of NBC's political farce, "The Powers That Be," Caitlyn, the adult daughter of Senator Powers, is converted to Christianity. She turns to Christ after having her hair done—she hates the new "do." She locks herself in her bedroom for four days, after which her mother and husband break the door down and discover the newly "born-again" Caitlyn, who was led to Jesus through the movie *The Greatest Story Ever Told*, which she watched during her depression.

Later in the segment, Sen. Powers tells his mistress that, as a result of his daughter's testimony, he might "even give church a chance." When the woman asks if that means an end to their Sunday morning liaisons, he replies, "Well, you don't have to get fanatical about it." At the end of the episode, Mrs. Powers storms into her husband's office, protesting, "Christian values are destroying this family!"

2. *Christians as bigots:*

At first such mockery may appear harmless, a given in a society that is generally recalcitrant when it comes to the Ten Commandments. After all, the scripture itself says, "All have swerved, one and all have gone wrong, no one does good, not a single one. Their throat is an open grave, they are treacherous with their tongues" (Rom. 3:12-13). Such spiritual impudence is to be expected; indeed, it is a condition that we all share as sinners. But it is the cumulative effect of such stereotypes on the American populace—a nation founded upon the profound respect for the practice of religion—that is detrimental. It is the mockery of religion and especially of religious persons that threatens to seriously injure the status of religious freedom and persons of faith in American society, not to mention the damage that is done to society itself when it relentlessly scorns what is best within it. Consider these further traducements of believers:

In the 11 December 1992 segment of CBS's "Picket Fences," Sheriff Brock interrupts a school Christmas pageant rehearsal, declaring that the court had deemed the pageant a violation of "church and state." The teacher, Miss Talbot, defies the order, proceeds with the program and is arrested. The school board backs her until it is discovered that she is a transsexual, whereupon they dismiss her. The sheriff's wife encourages the teacher to go to court. The judge overturns the school board's decision and gives her back her job. Parents withdraw their children from the pageant, forcing Miss Talbot to withdraw. The Christmas pageant proceeds, not in school but in a church.

As the wise men enter, however, young Zack Brock stops them, declaring, "The children of Rome hereby reject the prejudice of its parents—we reject your fear and narrow-mindedness!"

"We are afraid," adds Zack's brother, "that the wise men might condemn the children because of what they are. We're afraid that the wise men will judge us by our race, our religion, our sexual identity and not our character." The children invite Miss Talbot onto the stage with them, and encourage their parents to join them. One by one the parents and other townsfolk renounce their Judeo-Christian prejudices. The audience breaks into applause in acceptance of the transsexual Talbot. Once again, the show depicts traditional Christian morality as bigoted, hypocritical, and cruel.

In an episode of NBC's "Reasonable Doubts" that aired 17 March 1992, a professed "Christian" member of a white supremacist group is convicted of the murder of a Jewish man. A scene in the show depicts Christians as anti-Semites when a prospective juror is questioned. The show's prosecuting attorney, Tess Kaufmann, asks the woman, "What does it mean to be a born-again Christian?"

"It means accepting Jesus Christ as your personal savior."

"Then how do you view people of the Jewish faith?" Ms. Kaufmann continues.

"Personally, I believe the Jews crucified Christ."

"Should I conclude that you could not be a fair and impartial juror in a case where the victim is Jewish?"

"The Jews bring a lot of problems on themselves" is the Christian's response.

This segment invokes the worst and most malicious stereotype of earnest Christians, deliberately mixing images and drawing on old prejudices that have long since become unacceptable to conscientious people of faith. The kind of prejudice evinced by the fictitious juror is exceptionally rare. Rather, born-again Christians have been the most ardent supporters and defenders of the Jewish people and of the state of Israel outside the Jewish community. A veritable "Christian Zionism" prevails among the vast majority of born-again Christians who are overwhelmingly dispensationalists and recognize the state of Israel as a fulfillment of biblical prophecies. The preservation of the Jewish people is seen by most evangelical Christians as a sign of God's covenantal promises to them and as a precursor to the second coming of Jesus Christ. To paint Christians with the broad brush of anti-Semitism is itself an act of bigotry.

3. Christians as Hypocrites:

In the 1 November 1992 episode of "In Flesh n Blood" on NBC, Arlo, a self-proclaimed Christian, is sought out by Starr, a high-school girl friend he'd jilted seventeen years before. When she finally tracks him down, she invites him to her motel room, where the "born-again" and the "bimbo" go to bed.

The 30 October 1992 segment of ABC's "Good and Evil" presented a hypocritical Catholic priest who uses profanity, laughs at adultery, and makes a mockery of a wedding ceremony in which the groom is a known adulterer.

In an 18 March edition of ABC's post–World War II drama series, "Homefront," the focus is on the pregnancy of an unmarried Catholic matriarch, Ann, who has been the paragon of morality and decency in the series. A devout Catholic widow, Ann is impregnated by a divorced Jewish man named Al. Al talks her into marriage, and they begin premarital counseling with the parish priest.

In the latter episode, Ann and Al have an argument over whether they will raise their child Catholic, which results in Ann's breaking off the engagement. She says she'll go stay with a friend until her baby is born and return later with the "adopted" child.

4. Christians as dangerous:

In the 17 March 1992 episode of "Reasonable Doubts," the accused murderer, a white supremacist, was a professed "born-again" Christian.

A 16 February movie, *In The Best Interest of the Children*, depicts Cally, a mother of five, some illegitimate, as a praying Christian and an irrational, manic-depressive who has mood swings, violent outbursts, and mental illness. She has had numerous live-in lovers.

She goes into a rage one Christmas Day and makes her children return the gifts her brother has given to them. That night she leaves her children alone to go out and pick up a man whom she brings back to her home. When she gets home, nine-year-old Jessie (the oldest child who plays mother to her siblings) confronts her mother about forgetting to take birth control pills. The child tells Cally she'd better take the pills because she doesn't want any more children to take care of and she doesn't want "another ugly man hanging around."

Eventually, Cally is persuaded to seek help in a mental hospital. In a counseling session she apologizes to one daughter for hitting her with a dog chain, saying that she hit her because "it was as if the Bible was speaking to me . . . because it says 'Spare the rod and spoil the child.'"

These are just some examples of the scores of prime time programs that have depicted Christians in a negative light. These defamatory portrayals promote an image of conscientious people of faith as fools, bigots, and hypocrites, implying that people of earnest religious observance might be secretly sexual psychopaths and murderers. The result of this can only be further religious prejudice and division sown into communities where people of different faiths wish to live side by side in harmony and understanding. This is a flagrant violation of liberal sympathies that stress multicultural tolerance, pluralistic understanding, and mutual acceptance of different ideas and beliefs. Franky Schaeffer, in his 1982 book, *A Time for Anger*, sarcastically defined "liberal" as meaning "an indefinite tolerance of everyone and anything, except those who disagree about issues on the basis of moral principle."

The characterizations of religious people on television evince a deeply rooted antipathy toward the morality that is inherent in religious tradition. They are rarely portrayed in a positive light, and when they are, their apparent goodness is usually surpassed by their naivete. The most prevalent condition of religion in television, though, is nonexistence.

According to an article that appeared in the *Cable Guide*, "The conventional wisdom is, beyond Sunday morning programming and televangelists, TV and God are mutually exclusive."[2]

In her article, the writer Sharon Boone quotes several television producers and executives who blame the potential for offending members of various sects who hold "narrow-minded religious views." But virtually all the examples of opposition to religion in television programming raised by the same representatives are ascribed to secularists who are offended by the mere invocation of the name of God. For instance, Donald Bellisario, the creator of the hit TV program "Quantum Leap," describes the opposition he received when he originally suggested that "God or fate or time is leaping Sam."

"I was told by a lot of people, 'You can't say it's God leaping him around because it will turn a lot of people off.' When we did the research, 40 percent of the people said it would turn them off because it implies that the show would be preachy."

This is not the response of religious viewers with "narrow-minded views." It is instead the response of secularist, anti-religious sentiment, which sees the mere mention of God or religious belief as intolerable.

This attitude toward religion is pervasive in television programming. According to Michael Medved, "a 1983 public opinion survey of 104 of the most influential leaders of TV's creative community showed that a full 45 percent claim no religious affiliation whatsoever and an astounding 93 percent say they seldom or never attend religious services."

The result of this negligence of the spirit on the part of the makers and shakers of prime time is an appalling ignorance of religious practices and an easy willingness to use stereotypes when depicting persons of faith.

Made-for-television movies have again depicted Christian leaders, ministers, and evangelists as hypocrites and charlatans and Catholic priests as fornicators and child molesters. One TV movie, *Flight of the Black Angel,* was "centered on an Air Force officer and born-again Christian whose apocalyptic visions lead him on a mad mission to 'nuke' Las Vegas."

Milder incidents recorded by Medved include:

(1) An episode of "T. J. Hooker" in which the star, William Shatner, "finally manages to track down a ruthless, scripture-spouting crook who leaves Bibles as calling cards at the scene of his crimes."

(2) A 1989 broadcast of "The Women of Brewster Place" shows a preacher propositioning a woman after his sermon and eventually luring her to his bed."

In NBC's UNSUB, Bishop Grace murders two teen-age girls in his congregation.

(3) In "In the Heat of the Night," another production of NBC, a "Reverend Haskell" dies after enjoying an adulterous affair with one of his parishioners.

(4) An episode of "Knot's Landing" features a crazed, born-again character who attempts to murder his ex-wife's fiancee.

(5) "Shannon's Deal" shows two more fundamentalist kidnappers (denounced in the script as "Bible-thumpin' hayseeds"), together with a devout Christian who murders his wife and justifies the killing as "an act of God . . ."[3]

(6) Two recent episodes of "Law and Order" have taken aim at religious fanatics who happen to be active in the pro-life movement: one of them is exposed as a vicious wife-beater while another attempts to kill one of her Christian colleagues who has hypocritically visited a clinic to seek her own abortion.[4]

In another segment of the article that appeared in the *Cable Guide*, Father Andrew Greeley, a Roman Catholic priest and best-selling author, is quoted as saying, "Normal programming and TV news ignore religion—[they're] embarrassed by it. Journalists are not religious, it makes them uneasy."[5]

Ignorance of religion and religious practices increases the employment of stereotype in television. For instance, it is typical for television to depict a clergyman dressed in black clerical garb, wearing a Roman collar, and carrying a large, leather-bound black book with the words "Holy Bible" emblazoned on the cover. This ignores tradition and mixes images to create a potent stereotype that is not reflective of the truth. Catholic priests do not typically carry Bibles, much less standard King James editions. These Bibles are used by evangelical and fundamentalist ministers, since their tenets of faith embrace the Bible as the "final authority in matters of faith and practice." Roman Catholic, Greek Orthodox, and Anglican priests, on the other hand, rely on Apostolic tradition to define their faith and turn rather to the lectionary, breviary, and the Book of Common Prayer, which appear altogether different from the Protestant preacher's Bible. But this kind of accuracy doesn't interest the anti-religious bigots in TV land; the mixing of the symbols creates a conglomerate target of prejudice, Catholic and Protestant Christians, all in one!

In television news the accuracy is no better, and derogatory terms, stereotypical images, and defamation are often utilized when reporting on religious subjects, especially when religious convictions or actions dissent from the secularist ideology that permeates the newsroom. According to the best-selling author Charles Colson, "Studies of the leading journalists and news anchors consistently show that their opinions bend sharply towards the left."

In a revealing series on news bias in the abortion debate, the *Los Angeles Times* reporter David Shaw quotes the media spokesman John Buckley, who explains that "the culture in the newsrooms just assumes that abortion is right."[6]

Abortion is a topic very often associated with religion. In fact, the majority of pro-life abortion protesters can be fairly described as religious. Although many of those associated with the pro-life movement are Roman Catholic, evangelical, or fundamentalist, the movement is not exclusively associated with these branches of Christianity. Several conservative denominations, including Presbyterian bodies, the Episcopal Church, the United Methodist Church, the United Church of Christ, among major so-called mainline liberal denominations, have officially recognized pro-life organizations within themselves, representing a significant number of their members who support the right to life in almost all circumstances. The same is true among Jews. While relatively small in number, there are Jewish pro-life organizations and representatives, including Rabbi Yehudah Levin of Brooklyn, an outspoken critic of liberal abortion policies in the United States.

In January 1993, four national Jewish organizations, representing two thousand rabbis, issued a joint statement declaring the twentieth anniversary of *Roe v. Wade* a "time of mourning." Rabbi Abraham Hecht, president of the Rabbinical Alliance of America, speaking for the coalition, which included the Alliance, the Union of Orthodox Rabbis of the United States and Canada, the Rabbinical Council of America, and the Central Rabbinical Council, said that the twenty-year period was a "generation of unspeakable immorality and disrespect for human life." The statement went unreported in virtually every national major news outlet. The same treatment was given to the "Atheists Against Abortion" that joined in the "March for Life" in Washington in 1993.

According to news reporter Shaw, "Abortion opponents are often described as 'conservatives,' while abortion-rights supporters are rarely labeled as 'liberals.' Abortion opponents are sometimes identified as Catholics (or fundamentalist Christians), even when their religion is not demonstrably relevant to a given story; abortion rights advocates are rarely identified by religion."[7]

Even when representatives do not wish to be identified by their religious affiliations—or do not accept the stereotypical labels placed on them by news reporters—they're often identified as "fundamentalists."

I have never identified myself as a "fundamentalist," though I have profound respect, admiration, and affection for my fellow Christians of that designation. My first church of membership was the United Methodist Church, which I joined after my baptism. I was raised in a nominally Jewish family and converted to Christianity when I was fifteen years old. I attended a Pentecostal Bible college and was ordained a Pentecostal minister in 1982. Pentecostals, who derive from a revivalist and holiness background, are not properly called "fundamentalists." Although many Pentecostals would consider themselves "fundamental" when it comes to a literal interpretation of the Bible, historically and sociologically they belong to an altogether "third" branch of Christianity.

One time when I was being interviewed on a television talk show, the host kept referring to me as "fundamentalist minister" Reverend Paul Schenck. As soon as I had an opportunity off the air, I corrected her. "I'm not a fundamentalist," I insisted politely. "What are you then?" was her surprised response.

"I'm a Jewish-Christian, ordained a Pentecostal minister," was my admittedly complex answer. It may have been cumbersome, but it was the truth.

"We're back," said my host as we reentered the airwaves, "with fundamentalist minister, Reverend Paul Schenck . . ."

Some stereotypes just die hard.

Why is this the case? Why, for instance, are pro-life protesters consistently identified by their real or supposed religious denominations while pro-abortion protesters are not? Why are Pentecostal, charismatic, evangelical, and conservative ministers all lumped together under the one, inaccurate category of "fundamentalist"? Why are Catholics so often identified as such when liberal spokespersons are almost never identified as "Catholic" unless their position opposes the official teachings of the magisterium?

The answer is plain: because the terms "fundamentalist" and "Catholic" invoke stereotypical images which have been adopted widely by the print and broadcast media.

I have deliberately connected the news and entertainment industries because I believe that they are essentially one and the same thing. As news networks proliferate and the network news no longer has the monopoly over news reporting—and as national newspapers and magazines compete more effectively with local newspapers in cities and towns all across the nation—news sources are becoming more concerned over ratings and are sensationalizing and dramatizing the news more and more. Re-creations and reenactments, once almost taboo in the newsroom, are now fairly commonplace.

Two examples of this breaching of traditional newsroom ethics are the GM truck incident at "Dateline NBC" and the Clearwater National Forest story on "NBC Nightly News." The "Dateline" program did a supposed exposé of General Motors pickups that allegedly exploded when they were broadsided. A clip of a car's ramming the truck and the truck's exploding into flames was shown. General Motors uncharacteristically went on the offensive and turned up evidence that the truck had been fitted with an incendiary device that was detonated at the time of impact. NBC was forced to confess and issued an apology. The Clearwater segment showed dead fish floating in a stream where forest clear-cutting was going on. The images were designed to show how clear-cutting pollutes streams and kills fish. But they weren't dead fish; they had been stunned by forest officials to count them and check their conditions.

National news looks more today like an entertainment media then ever before. There is also more interaction between the news media and the entertainment shows, with anchormen and women of the major news programs making cameo appearances on sitcoms like "Murphy Brown."

The news shows borrow stereotypes originally intended for the prime time line-up of sitcoms and action shows and replay them in their news coverage as if they were unquestionably factual, when they are demonstrably not. But these stereotypes "work" for newscasts. They play on preconceived images of people, thus allowing reporters to cut out time-consuming backgrounds to stories. The only problem is, these stereotypes misrepresent, exaggerate, and erroneously depict individuals, their beliefs, and ideas.

According to David Shaw, "Abortion opponents are often described as 'militant' or 'strident.'"[8] Operation Rescue participants in Wichita, Kansas, in the summer of 1991 were described in most press releases as "storming abortion clinics" when in fact they were crawling on their hands and knees under police billy clubs. But the word "storming" coincides with the media's stereotype of "militant" and "violent" pro-lifers. A segment of "CBS Evening News" showed a cadre of angry, screaming protesters struggling with police and assaulting other protesters. The voice-over was describing pro-life protests. The only problem was that the footage was of pro-abortion protesters. A minor detail!

The same can be said about the coverage of other conscientious Christians. Shaw points out that "the more money and education a person has and the less religious a person is, the more likely the person is to favor abortion rights. Since most big city journalists tend to be better paid, better-educated, and less religious than the general public, it's not surprising that they also tend to favor abortion rights."

The object here is not to point to the news media's bias on abortion, although it is relevant, but to point out the irreligiosity of the journalistic crowd. This condition exacerbates the stereotype of Christians in news reporting.

In the summer of 1989, Christians gathered outside CNN headquarters in Atlanta, Georgia, to protest the showing of the film *Roe vs Wade* on the Turner Broadcasting System. The TBS founder and chairman, Ted Turner, called the demonstrators "bozos" and "idiots."

At a pro-life protest in which I participated in Buffalo, a reporter with the local CBS affiliate station, WIVB TV channel 4, took me aside, off camera, and, using his right hand to carefully position me square in front of him so that we were staring into each other's eyes, said, "Look—off the record—I think what you do stinks."

Another time I was interviewed on "Canada AM," the Canadian national morning news program like "Good Morning America," in which the interviewer, inquiring about my Christian position against abortion, asked, "Doesn't that make you basically the same as the Ayatollah Khomeini?" My announced, unequivocal commitment to non-violence notwithstanding, the association between my uncompromising position on biblical morality and Islamic fundamentalism was too tempting, and invoking the megalomaniacal visage of the Iranian ayatollah was an easy draw on another, convenient stereotype. To my host, any degree of religious commitment beyond the basics of high holy days, marriages, births, and burials was scary.

In a segment of "CBS Morning News," the correspondent Morley Safer reported on the Wycliffe Bible translators' work in Central America. Safer said that the aim of the literacy specialists, whose work includes teaching children and adults how to read and write, was "to resettle people into areas where they can be controlled and thus converted." According to Safer's view, the professional linguists, teachers, medical doctors, engineers, and artists who serve sacrificially, raising their own personal support and often living in the same impoverished conditions as the people they so earnestly serve, created "instant slums" and "instant disillusion." Safer portrayed the missionaries as inflicting great harm on the indigenous populations.

What the viewers were not told in the ostensibly "objective" report, was that Safer's wife, Jane, was at the time head of the U.S. division of Survival International, a London-based organization opposed to Christian missionary activities.

At the same time the report was aired, Jane Safer and her U.S. chapter of Survival International were holding a symposium in New York City to focus public attention on their objections to the work of Christian missionaries.

This kind of bias undermines the integrity of news reporting and seriously damages the credibility of the networks in their ability to present facts without insidious interpretations that scandalize religious groups and persons. The potential backlash that this deliberately distorted coverage could provoke makes the irresponsibility of the media even more acute.

It should be emphasized that no Christian organization, not the American Family Association, or the Christian Action Council, or the Family Research Council, or the Christian Coalition, has called for the further censorship of television programming. What is called for is objective, responsible, truthful, and temperate reporting of news, responsible and edifying entertainment, and programming that reflects the true nature of religious faith and practice in America today.

As it is, the usage of stereotype in television is encouraging bigotry and taking the culture down the slippery slope toward greater intolerance, especially of religious beliefs. The resulting isolation of the practicing Christian sets him or her up to be a target of prejudice and makes the believer a candidate for the scapegoat who will be blamed for all of society's ills. This is an unconscionable development in a liberal society.

FIVE

Big Screen Bigotry

———————— | ————————

The American motion picture industry has provided a vast venue for two components of the secular assault on Christianity: the promulgation of the false consensus and the defamation of Christians.

There is no medium in the world today that surpasses the magnitude of power to convey ideas and to persuade people as movies do. The ambiance of the theater, that final moment of darkness enveloping the moviegoer, the height and breadth of the screen unveiling the panorama before the viewer, and the sweep of the images that march across it are enough in themselves to move the viewer. Add to that the ethereal characteristics of great cinematography, grand musical scores, and superb acting, and the movie takes on an almost transcendental quality. Hollywood knows this power, and to its shame it has blatantly exploited it for its own, secularist biases.

The Hollywood agenda undeniably includes the defamation of Christianity and of Christians in particular. Just a cursory review of the motion pictures made in the ten-year period between 1982 and 1992 demonstrates the high degree of antipathy, bigotry, and prejudice that many of Hollywood's producers, directors, and screenwriters have toward people of earnest Christian faith.

The Christian stereotype is pervasive in contemporary entertainment. But the motion picture industry has gone far beyond television's depiction of believers as bungling hypocrites. Hollywood's producers and screenwriters have embraced a vicious form of anti-Christian propaganda that typically portrays practicing Christians as malevolent devils who prey upon earnest, sincere humanists who only want to live and let live.

Filmmakers admit taking advantage of the powerful medium of communication at their control to advocate for their causes. In an article that appeared in *USA Today* (22 May 1992), the director Richard Donner (*Lethal Weapon, Lethal Weapon 2,* and *Lethal Weapon 3*) stated that "under the guise of entertainment you can sneak a lot of messages in. . . . If one person gets interested, then you've served [the cause]."

Indeed, many anti-religious messages have been cleverly sneaked in "under the guise of entertainment." This has served the cause of militant secularism well.

Michael Medved has documented much of the anti-religious stereotype and prejudice in his book, *Hollywood vs. America.* His list includes many of the most influential contemporary movies that have employed all kinds of skewed, exaggerated, and erroneous images of people of faith:

Medved describes the 1979 film, *The Runner Stumbles,* which had veteran performer "Dick Van Dyke . . . in his deadly serious role as a small town priest who falls in love with a sensitive young nun . . . and then stands trial for her murder." This "clergy kills illicit lover" is a recurrent theme in modern films. It portrays Christian clergymen in particular as dangerous murderers disguised as peaceful clerics. There appears to be an underlying desire to discredit clergy by creating in the mind of the general public a dark image of the priest or minister as a hypocritical hunter preying on innocents.

In a 1982 film called *Monsignor,* another priest, this time a cardinal, "engages in every imaginable sin," seduces a glamorous nun—and is complicit in her death. "His shady dealings with the Mafia to control the Vatican bank eventually bring him to the peak of power under the approving eye of a shriveled, anorexic Pope." Once again, the priest is the malefactor, the devil in disguise as an angel of light.

In *Agnes of God* (1985), "the movie opens with the uplifting spectacle of a disturbed, young nun, Meg Tilly, giving birth in a convent, murdering her baby, and then flushing the tiny, bloody corpse down the toilet." The allusion here with abortion is unmistakable. The nun, symbolic of all women captured and imprisoned by Catholicism (or all Christianity for that matter) is forced to endure the anguish of the bloody birth of her child, conceived in opposition to her church's moral teaching, and then to sacrifice the baby because she could not abort it. Medved points out that the film was advertised as examining the conflict between religion and science. But the favoritism shown toward science—Jane Fonda is a cool-headed, enlightened psychologist that helps to guide the benighted nun out of her dungeon—exposes the overtones of the false consensus.

Medved describes the 1985 comedy film *Heaven Help Us* as "raunchy." Originally produced under the title *Catholic Boys*, it supposedly "exposes the horrors of a parochial school education." The false consensus often draws on resentments that are held against religious education. A similar theme is incipient in the otherwise skillfully crafted Woody Allen picture *Radio Days*, when the young Allen is dragged to the rabbi's study by his parents to be disciplined for collecting, then keeping, National Jewish Fund contributions. The boy's parents argue with each other and the rabbi over who will beat him as each takes turns whacking him on the head and bottom. Although the incident is comical and even reminiscent of similar scenarios from every Jewish boy's past, the only depiction of the rabbi in the film is the negative one.

In *The Penitent* (1988), Raul Julia "plays a farmer in New Mexico who joins a primitive and brutal Catholic cult. . . Every year, the scowling, sadistic sect reenacts the Crucifixion, selecting a lucky nominee . . . performing the service on screen with a maximum of blood, gore, cockeyed camera angles, and whacked-out, quasi-religious visions." The desecration of the Crucifixion, the Mass, worship, preaching, and baptism is also thematic in much of Hollywood's antireligious fare. It is not insignificant that baptism and communion are rites of admission in Christianity and that worship and preaching are expressions of evangelization and propagation. By lampooning these, filmmakers are making the message of the Church as well as the Church itself less inviting. At times it appears that achieving this effect is a deliberate goal on the part of some film producers and directors.

In another film described by Medved, *We're No Angels* (1989), "Robert DeNiro and Sean Penn play two lunk-headed petty crooks who escape from prison and pretend to be priests. The two sleazy fugitives are instantly honored as distinguished Church scholars by the stunningly stupid and superstitious members of a religious order who run the monastery where they seek refuge."

The mockery of religious communities and churches seems to agree with the mockery of religious people. It is simply too tempting for Hollywood to imagine all kinds of perverted, preposterous, and pornographic behavior going on behind those Gothic walls. Although there is little evidence that anything like this mayhem occurs with regularity, Hollywood would like the moviegoing public to believe that it does. By misrepresenting religious communities as concentrations of demented misfits or foolish scoundrels, it cooperates with the false consensus and makes religious life very unappealing.

Still another Catholic-bashing flick, *Nuns on the Run* (1990), "features a long monologue in which [lead character] Robbie Coltrane attempts to offer a garbled and offensive explanation of the concept of the Trinity before concluding, 'It's not supposed to make sense! It's religion!'" This line aptly summarizes the film industry's inability to treat the subject of religion with anything close to understanding. They simply don't get it. The Hollywood elite is so overwhelmingly irreligious that few can be found that truly comprehend the meaning, significance, and importance of religious faith. In contrast to the tens of millions of Americans who are religiously affiliated, who attend church or synagogue, and who read the Bible and pray, Hollywood finds religious faith incomprehensible. Therefore, Hollywood can only ridicule such beliefs.

Medved asserts that "while the Catholic church provides one prime focus for Hollywood's anti-religious animus, it is by no means the only faith to feel the wrath of the entertainment industry."[1] Here is a brief description he offers of some of the movies that have stereotyped Protestant Christians in a similarly brutal fashion:

The 1984 film, *Crimes of Passion*, portrays "a sweaty, Bible-toting skid row evangelist." According to the author, "Anthony Perkins generates the same warmth and charm he brought to his famous role . . . in *Psycho*. He grits his teeth and twitches constantly, and in some scenes even drools, quoting biblical verses at the same time he amuses (and abuses) himself at sleazy peep shows. Obsessed with a part-time hooker, this preacher pervert plans to 'save her soul' by murdering her through the sexual insertion of a huge stainless steel cylinder with a lethally sharpened tip."

The Handmaid's Tale (1990) is a "pointedly political polemic about what life would be like if Christian fundamentalists came to power in America. . . . These religious zealots are considerably less lovable than Nazis. . . . The vicious, theocratic government enslaves and degrades all women, pursues genocidal policies against ethnic minorities, burns books with 'non-scriptural' messages, oppresses working people, assembles huge crowds to watch public hanging and torture, and uses brute force to enforce the most arcane regulations from the Bible. . . . The evil evangelists who run the country aren't even sincere in their fanaticism: they emphasize modesty and purity and sobriety in all their rules and pronouncements but secretly operate . . . bordellos for their private pleasure."

Again, the evil religious community is depicted as torturing the happy hedonists and hanging the harmless humanists.

In the 1991 film *The Rapture*, "Mimi Rogers plays a buxom swinger, addicted to group sex with strangers, who sacrifices these satisfactions when she makes a sudden commitment to Christ. At first, her religious transformation appears to have positive consequences, but before the end of the film, her 'faith' causes her to take her six-year-old daughter out to the desert where they wait for days in the burning sun for the Rapture that is supposed to precede Christ's second coming. When nothing happens, the heroine takes a revolver and holds it to her daughter's head and, while mumbling invocations of the Almighty, blows the child's brains out."

This film clearly manifests the contention of the false consensus that religion is dangerous to children. Hollywood's image of children is not unlike the Lost Boys in *Peter Pan*. Parental authority oppresses children who would otherwise be free and unrestrained. Religion is seen as a component of restrictive adult authority, like Captain Hook. The boomers who make many of these films, as well as the veteran producers and directors who think like them, depict the danger they sense in religion's ordered life by portraying it as kidnapping and killing the children. This is why secret child sacrifice is often the theme in anti-religious films.

In *At Play in the Fields of the Lord* (1991), Medved shows that "no faith is spared: In addition to the psychotic, repressed, relentlessly obnoxious and mean-spirited Protestant missionaries, the cast of characters also includes a foul-smelling, cynical Catholic priest and an alcoholic, whore-mongering, heavily tattooed Jewish mercenary who offers contemptuous recollections of his own Bar Mitzvah. The script could hardly be more straightforward in laying out its anti-religious agenda in one incident after another."

And neither could Hollywood.

In *Guilty as Charged* (1992), "Rod Steiger is a murderous maniac who just happens to be a Christian fanatic. He . . . imprisons . . . poor souls in a homemade dungeon . . . and one by one . . . executes them in a huge electric chair, decorated with religious motifs. . . . As the victims fry, howling in fear and pain, Steiger exults at the top of his lungs: 'We praise the Lord for the Department of Water and Power! The Holy Spirit is electricity, and the chair is God's instrument of Justice and Salvation!'"

One that didn't make it into Medved's list was the 1992 B-film *Breaking the Rules*, which starred C. Thomas Howell and Jonathan Silverman. The movie depicts a "gratuitous bedroom scene where Silverman's 'wisecracking Jewish character' picks up a blonde at a skating rink and goes back to her apartment. As she takes off her clothes, she says, 'Did you know evil Jews killed our Lord?' She then sets up a baptismal font in her bathroom and tells Silverman she won't go to bed with him until he gets baptized and becomes a 'born-again' Christian, which he agrees to do to get the sexual reward. According to Dr. Michael Rubinoff, writing in the *Christian News*, 'It is the most insulting imaginable portrayal of born-again Christians.'"[2]

These films, and many more like them, promote derogatory, dirty, and defamatory stereotypes of conscientious Christians. The cumulative effect of a diet of these depictions is a community of practicing Christians viewed by the moviegoing public as disturbed, demented, and dangerous people who are more than likely a threat to your safety and that of your family and your neighborhood. After viewing any number of these bigoted, anti-religious films, who in his right mind would voluntarily choose to room with, move next door to, or hire a practicing Catholic or Bible-believing, born again Christian? Furthermore, who would deny the necessity of government keeping a watchful eye on the practices, actions, or movements of such rascals?

If the above films distort the true record of Christian practice and character—and exaggerate it so far as to go beyond the credibility level for many, if not most, common sense Americans—consider the subliminal messages of two of the most powerful motion pictures of 1991-92, *Cape Fear* and *Alien 3*.

In *Cape Fear*, the Hollywood superstar Robert DeNiro plays a Pentecostal Christian homicidal misanthrope who sports a body-sized cross tattooed on his back (which unmistakably identifies him as a Christian fanatic in one of the film's opening scenes), a subtle, almost undetectable fish on his left wrist (the fish was the ancient, secret symbol of Christians under persecution), a well-worn Bible, and a tendency to speak in tongues. The vengeful ex-con is hunting down his former attorney, played by Nick Nolte, who, realizing DeNiro was guilty of violent rape, sold him down the river by withholding evidence in the defense. Now it is fourteen years later, and upon his release from prison, DeNiro is intent on punishing Nolte and his family for the traitorous act.

When DeNiro's ominous visage and threatening manners provoke the film's leading lady, Nolte's wife, to inquire about his religiosity, Nolte's character replies, "Oh, some kind of Pentecostal crackers—from the mountains."

Something should be said here about the emergence of Pentecostalism as a favorite for Hollywood stereotyping. As a relatively young religious community, very little is actually known or understood about America's Pentecostals. Pentecostalism takes its name from the biblical Day of Pentecost (the Jewish holiday of "Shavuot," or "First Fruits," celebrated fifty days after Passover). It was on this Old Testament feast day that the New Testament book of Acts, records that the Holy Spirit came upon the members of the gathered church in a Jerusalem upper room, and "tongues of fire" appeared above their heads, and each one "spoke in other tongues as the Spirit gave them utterance."

This phenomenon was repeated at least three more times in the Bible when the Spirit fell on believers. Pentecostals, who trace their roots to the religious revivals of the turn of the century, share with the historic churches the orthodox Christian doctrines expressed in the ancient creeds, a literal belief in the Bible and an expectation of Christ's second coming, but also believe in a baptism of the Holy Spirit that is accompanied by "speaking with other tongues" unknown, or rather unlearned, languages with which they praise God.

Because Pentecostalism has historically and sociologically been the religion of the poor and of minorities in America (the largest Pentecostal denomination in the world, the Church of God in Christ, is African-American, and Pentecostalism is growing faster in Latin America than in any other continent), it is typically the target of prejudice and anti-religious discrimination. Few Pentecostals are aware of the intense antipathy toward them in the entertainment business, mostly because their stress on personal holiness leads them to avoid the carnal excesses of films and TV. As such, they are frequently the victims of anti-religious propaganda and stereotype.

The *Cape Fear* film, a remake of a 1962 classic starring Robert Mitchum and Gregory Peck, injected horrendous religious stereotypes that played no part in the original. DeNiro's "Pentecostal-Christian" character smokes pot, at-

tempts the seduction of a teen-age girl, brutally rapes and
partly cannibalizes a woman, and eventually commits serial
murder before sinking to his own watery grave, "speaking in
tongues."

I saw this film. It was a riveting horror film that kept me
on the edge of my seat. As drama goes, this was an excellent
cinema, exquisitely acted and photographically impressive.
But that's just it. The young minds that watch this compelling, and in many respects, overwhelming film, unmistakably
identify a Bible-believing Christian with a horrible, homicidal maniac.

Add to this the similar depiction of Christians in *Alien 3*.
This third installment in the *Aliens* trilogy once again casts
Sigourney Weaver as the intergalactic heroine whose unfortunate lot in life is to engage the hideous, spindly exoskel-
eton alien, dripping with mucous and slime, and devouring
the weakling frontiersmen and women of the universe.

In this episode, Weaver crash lands on a penal planet
that has been abandoned by the department of corrections,
except for a handful of ex-cons who voluntarily remain behind. The prison's doctor revives the haphazard crash victim
and nurses her back to health. He warns her that the planet's
inhabitants are a strange cabal who wear sackcloth and in-
tone nightmarish prayers and that "none of them have seen
a woman in years."

When Weaver's character, Lieutenant Ripley, ignores
the doctor's orders and sits down in the mess hall with the
prison's religious leader, he says to her, "I don't know why
you're talking to me. You don't wanna know me, Lieutenant.
I am a murderer and a rapist. Of women."

And which denomination, according to the screenwriters,
does this chaplain from hell represent?

"I don't know," says the prison's doctor. "Hard to say.
Some sort of millenarian apocalyptic Christian fundamentalist brew."[3]

Here again is Hollywood's not-so-subtle equivalence:
Christian fundamentalist equals murderer equals rapist.

In its attempt to negate the influence of religious faith
on America, the secularist, sexual revolutionary agenda of

Hollywood's elite has seized upon a stereotype that could not be further from the truth. Inspired by the foibles of fallen televangelists, confident that the viewing audience knows little or nothing about the beliefs and practices of Pentecostals, has no interest nor sympathy for fundamentalists, and that they reject the repressive morality of the Catholic Church, the movie screenwriters, directors, and producers unabashedly pour on erroneous, exaggerated, and libelous misrepresentations of the truly sincere, respectable, and self-sacrificing Christians of America.

The result of this bigotry is a pervasive suspicion of religious persons among many Americans, leading to the potential for anti-Christian bias, discrimination, vandalism, and even violence. Already, several American cities are reporting a marked increase in vandalism against churches and religious cemeteries, as well as violence against and even murder of religious leaders—something exceptionally rare, if almost nonexistent, in the past, when even criminals respected the sanctity of the sanctuary.

But today religion is no longer sacred, thanks in part to the sick stereotypes and defamation of Christians by Hollywood. The Christian villain has become a favorite of film writers and directors. These images go a long way in vilifying people of strong moral conviction, blaming them for every conceivable crime against humanity. The baleful, pernicious Camorra so grotesquely represented in contemporary films should have no part in a "great society."

Hollywood's malignant depiction of Christians could well pave the way for the ultimate extermination of Christianity from popular American culture.

SIX

Injustice in the Courtroom

———————— | ————————

I leaned forward toward the antique wood and wrought-iron railing that separated the gallery from the courtroom. In the front of the courtroom, above the judge's head, emblazoned in gold leaf letters were the words "IN GOD WE TRUST." I bowed my head and quietly prayed, asking the Holy Spirit to guide the proceedings. This was a special session of the supreme court of the state of New York. My brother Robert and I had been sentenced to thirty days in the county jail for violating Judge Bestry's ban on prayer. We had begun our sentence by spending two days in jail but were released on an emergency stay obtained by our attorney, William J. Ostrowski, a retired supreme court justice. Now the court would decide whether or not we could remain free, pending our appeal of the conviction.

As I opened my eyes after my brief prayer, I noticed a slim, white, middle-aged attorney whisk into the courtroom and whisper to a neatly dressed, black, female attorney seated just ahead of me beyond the railing: "Can you believe this? Have you ever seen anything like this? Can you believe they expect us to prosecute this?" He was waving a photocopied form in front of her. That was the first time I saw the information detailing the reasons for my arrest and incarceration:

At a trial term of the Amherst Town Court,
held at the Court House, 400 John James
Audubon Parkway, in the Town of Amherst,
New York, on the 7th day of August, 1992.

Present: Hon. Sherwood L. Bestry
Amherst Town Justice
State of New York, County of Erie
Town of Amherst

People of the State of New York
vs.
Paul Schenck d.o.b. 10-1-58

The above named defendant, having appeared in court this date as an observer of a multi-defendant jury trial, did participate in a religious demonstration by leading others in prayer in the courtroom in the presence of the jury pool and was brought into chambers and advised by the court to cease and desist but . . . did open a large Bible and held it up to the judge and started praying after having been advised that any religious demonstration . . . would result in a finding of summary contempt and a jail sentence . . . . Ordered that the defendant, Paul Schenck, be and hereby is sentenced to imprisonment in the Erie County Correctional Facility for a period of thirty days, to commence forthwith.

Dated: 8/7/92   Sherwood L. Bestry
                                 Amherst Town Justice

Now it became obvious to me why the deputy sheriffs at the county jail were so surprised when my brother and I were brought in for processing. They had passed the instrument of arrest around and expressed various degrees of dismay and of disbelief. I had assumed the judge would have been more discreet, perhaps charging me with contempt of court or some other charge of disorderliness without any detailed explanation. But the judge saw nothing wrong with jailing a clergyman for praying in public.

I had read about Judge Bestry's ban on prayer in the newspaper. During the course of the trial of pro-life demonstrators who had been arrested in the "Spring of Life" rescue campaign in Buffalo, the judge had ordered that any prayers anywhere in or near the courthouse would be punishable by thirty days in the county prison. Judge Bestry considered public prayers "disgusting" and would not tolerate "any religious ceremonies" that include clergy vestments in or around the courthouse.

After reading the article, I felt that I should attend the proceedings and test out the ban, whether or not it could hold up in a higher court.

When I arrived at the courthouse, a small group of spectators were gathered on the steps outside. It was Judge Bestry's habit to convene the court sometimes hours later than scheduled, so it wasn't unusual for defendants, spectators, and attorneys to be forced to wait outside, even in inclement weather, until the judge ordered the doors opened. About the only people who didn't have to wait outside were the prosecutors, with whom the judge cooperated.

While we waited, I invited the group of people to join me in prayer. Some took me up on the offer; others withdrew against the large glass doors of the courthouse, obviously discomforted. We first knelt on the concrete patio and recited the Lord's Prayer together in unison, then I read the litany of the Great Thanksgiving from the Episcopal Book of Common Prayer. As we sang "Alleluia," I could hear the shuffle of shoes, and I could feel the breeze created by the swinging of the doors. I was conscious of the opening of the courthouse and suspected that the deputies had rushed to unlock and open up the doors so that the non-praying spectators and prospective jurors could escape the "praying mob."

As we gathered in the courthouse foyer, the courtroom was still locked, as it customarily was, and I could sense a stiff tension in the air. The deputies stood, taut, at the courtroom doors. One glowered at me across the room, and I got the feeling I was being monitored. Once again, I assembled the group for quiet prayer. I had chosen a Psalm and invited those present to join me in the recitation of it. I draped a stole bearing the indusia of the cross and crown around my neck, and in a hushed tone, I began reading:

Lord, remember David and all the hardships he endured. He swore an oath to the Lord and made a vow
to the Mighty One of Jacob: I will not enter my house
or go to my bed—I will allow no sleep to my eyes, nor
slumber to my eyelids, till I find a place for the Lord,
a dwelling for the Mighty One of Jacob.

As I read, I sensed someone draw up just behind my
right shoulder, and he was peering over it. When I finished
the sentence, I turned my face toward him.

"You'll have to stop doing that," the deputy said tersely.

"Doing what?" I tested.

"You know what the judge said."

"What did the judge say?"

"You know."

"What? Can you tell me?"

"If you don't stop, you're gonna be arrested," he shot
back with an inflection that was half-warning, half-taunting.

"Then arrest me for praying," I said politely, but he
withdrew.

When court was called into session some time later, I
was barred from the courtroom because I had failed to
conform to another of Judge Bestry's peculiar procedures,
signing in and identifying myself to the court. I had no
practical objection to it, though it did seem to me that it
could be intimidating to the average spectator; I simply wasn't
aware of the sign-up sheet. I was forced to remain outside in
the foyer during the proceedings, while my brother, a defendant, was admitted.

Some time later, the courtroom doors flew open and
there was a bustle of movement. A cacophony filled the
foyer as spectators, defendants, jurors, and deputies spilled
out. Someone rushed up to me and blurted out, "They've
just arrested your brother and another guy—"

"For praying!" somebody else added.

During a recess, while the judge and the attorneys were
in chambers, several of the defendants and onlookers, including my brother, either knelt or bowed their heads in
prayer. The prayers were reported by a deputy to the judge
via a note that said, "Rev. Rob Schenck is leading people in
prayer," which he was not.

Upon reading the note, the judge jumped up from his chair and burst into the courtroom. His index finger raised above his head, he lowered it accusatorially and thundered, "All-right—go ahead—defy me—thirty days in the county holding center!" And off went the malefactor. But wait! The deputy misjudged the trajectory of the judge's finger—he took the wrong man into custody. Never mind! The poor young man went to jail anyway, for thirty days!

Then came the clarification. The man he really wanted was the Reverend Robert Schenck. My brother stood up and considerately identified himself. "I think you want me," he offered to the irate judge. "Thirty days in the Erie County Correctional Facility!" went the redundant sentence. And off he went to join the other.

I asked an officer for an account of my brother's arrest, which I had not witnessed. "Why was he arrested?" I inquired.

"You know," came the stock reply.

"No, I don't know. Can you tell me?"

At that, another young officer took me gently by the forearm and escorted me to the front of the courtroom. It was a strange assist, almost indicating where the arrest had taken place. I donned my stole, opened my Bible, and began to pray. Another officer approached. "You'll have to come with me."

"I cannot. I'm reading the Word of God," I replied. "When I am finished reading the Psalm, I will come." Amazingly, he waited. I finished and notified him I was ready to answer to the judge.

I was escorted into the judge's chambers. The room was cluttered and disheveled. The judge was slouched behind his desk, his robe hanging open and stacks of papers and books scattered atop the desk.

He condescendingly reported the arrests and the summary sentencing of my brother and the other poor fellow, and then he warned me not to emulate their illegal behavior, which had landed them in prison. I began an explanation of my actions when he interrupted me shouting, "Don't talk or I'll have you gagged!" At that I opened my Bible and dropped to my knees, muttering a quick prayer before I was whisked away with the edict: "That's it—thirty days in the Erie County Correctional Facility!"

The deputy that arrested me shoved me in the back as he forced me to walk a fast pace down the hallway into the jail. While he strutted and I tried to keep up, he tore my stole away from my neck, and grabbed my Bible from my hands. He repeated the judge's condemnation, calling my prayers "disgusting." My shoes, belt, eyeglasses, and Bible were taken from me, and I was put into a cell. I walked the length and breadth of it, two-thirds blind, singing and worshipping the Lord.

I soon became aware of the presence of my brother and the other man in adjacent cells, and we carried on a good conversation about spiritual matters until we were shipped out to the holding center downtown at about 2 A.M. When we arrived, the deputy sheriffs were astounded to learn the circumstances of our arrests. "You're free to pray all you like here!" one particularly jovial deputy quipped. "I'm not sure I'm going to be doing all that much praying," I rejoined, as I surrendered my clerical collar. "That's what got me in trouble in the first place!"

At the first stage of the appeal, the county court judge who had originally released us had determined his court did not have jurisdiction over the matter. The state supreme court didn't want it either, but the chief judge ultimately assigned the case to special term. The court clerk's office then announced that the case would be heard by a supreme court judge with whom I had served on a committee for the Billy Graham crusade. We had prayed together in his chambers many times. I opened my mouth and was about to exclaim, "Praise God!" when an attorney counseled, "Don't say anything." Eventually that judge recused himself, and the case bounced like a hot potato until a lower court judge was appointed by the supreme court as an acting justice to hear it. That appeals court determined that Judge Bestry had acted improperly and that our jailing was illegal. In addition, the higher court dismissed charges against the third man and my brother altogether. Some of my friends and colleagues asked me why I deliberately violated the ban, an action I knew would likely result in a jail sentence. I answered that the judge's ban on prayer was just another example of the frightful move of government toward restricting "offensive" religious speech. In his book, *Free Speech for Me, but Not for Thee*, Nat Hentoff, an atheist, wrote, "The urge—indeed, lust—to interfere with the 'wrong' thoughts and speech of others is often manifested in anti-religious zealotry."[1] Judge Bestry was exhibiting just such anti-religious zeal. This is precisely what we're witnessing on college campuses all over the country, and the chief offenders are the law schools. Speech and conduct codes in some liberal institutions are looking as if they belong in Beijing or Havana.

An example is a resolution adopted by the law school faculty at the University of Buffalo. According to Dinesh D'Souza, it "warned students not to make 'remarks directed at another's race, sex, religion, national origin, age, or sexual preference, including ethnically derogatory statements as well as other remarks based on prejudice or group stereotype.'" D'Souza goes on to observe that

> students who violate this rule should not expect protection under the First Amendment, the faculty rule says, because our intellectual community shares values that go beyond a mere standardized commitment to open and unrestrained debate. The faculty agrees to take strong and immediate steps to prosecute offending students through the use of ordinary university procedures. The faculty also resolves to write to any bar to which such a student applies, offering where appropriate, our conclusion that the student should not be admitted to practice law.[2]

This resolution has been used to intimidate and silence conscientious Christian students despite the inclusion of religion in its list of protected classes. Actually, the resolution has had the opposite effect. One female student, who happened to be a Christian and pro-life, was warned by two of her professors that if she were to "get involved" in assisting pro-lifers in legal defense, she would be "blackballed in the legal community" and that the professors would "personally see to it" that she "never practiced law anywhere."

This kind of discrimination and intimidation has been repeated many times at other law schools, including Georgetown and Harvard.

Judge Bestry's ban on prayer is an example of the same kind of bias that shows up in scores of judicial decrees in the forms of restraining orders, injunctions, and decisions that have intruded upon that form of speech once considered sacrosanct (religious exercise). In fact, utilizing their enormously broad powers, "politically correct" judges have seriously curtailed the First Amendment rights of Christians and other religionists, under the spell of the false consensus.

There is a growing trend throughout the country for secularistic organizations, groups, and individuals to petition the courts to restrict religious expression in public.

For instance, a state court judge in Houston, Texas, granted relief to abortion groups by issuing an injunction barring preaching, hymn singing, witnessing, and Bible and tract distribution on public sidewalks around abortion clinics. Similar injunctions were issued in Atlanta, Georgia; Wichita, Kansas; and Buffalo, New York. Someone reading about this may feel that these restrictions have more to do with abortion than with religious liberty. But think for a moment of the opposite case: a particular church goes to court and requests an injunction barring atheists from making speeches, singing atheistic songs, talking to people about atheism, or distributing atheistic literature on sidewalks or in parks situated in the vicinity of churches. What chance would such an injunction ever have of being granted, or in the unlikely event that it was, of being upheld? None. It is preposterous to imagine such an injunction ever being written. It would be a terribly dangerous precedent if it was. In a nation that stands for freedom of speech, it is unthinkable that atheists would be barred from the public sidewalks outside of churches, but this is exactly what is happening to conscientious Christians in city after city, throughout the United States. Federal and state court injunctions have enjoined the proclamation of the gospel as a component of restrictions on protest activities.

Similarly spooked by the "separationist" doctrine, a federal appeals court in Zion, Illinois, ruled that the one hundred-year-old city seal, which incorporated a cross and the motto "God reigns," was unconstitutional. There is a significant historical reason for the presence of the cross and the motto. Zion was founded by John Alexander Dowie, an American healing evangelist who was raised in Australia. Returning to the U.S. in 1888, he founded Zion Tabernacle outside Chicago and announced his plans to establish a "holy society" there. His vision materialized as "Zion City" (later only Zion), Illinois. The mother church of the denomination that he founded, the Christian Catholic Church, is still active there, and Evangelist Dowie's home is now the Historical Society building. But because of the court's ruling, the seal, which was supported by over 90 percent of the townspeople, was removed from sight. In a similar denial of religious heritage, a county court in San Diego, California, handed down a decision in December 1991 ordering that a monument that was designated a historic landmark must be removed because it contained a cross. The marker, situated at Mt. Soledad, was originally on private property. When the property was bequeathed to the state of California, it was agreed that the cross marker would remain. The court, however, broke the contract and gave the county ninety days to remove the cross.

Here is a list of anti-religious cases from around the country compiled by the American Center for Law and Justice:

An elderly man was arrested and held handcuffed for distributing religious literature outside of an office complex. The charges were later dropped, and the man has filed a suit against the city for abridgment of his civil rights. Two New York street preachers were arrested for preaching without a permit and charged with disorderly conduct. The preachers had been ministering in virtually the same manner for over ten years. Once again, the charges were eventually dropped. A midwestern school district was sued for allowing the Gideons to distribute Bibles to students requesting them. The practice had been going on uninterrupted for forty-one years. A North Carolina pastor was denied the use of a public building because he intended to put on a Christmas play there. A group of Christian students were denied access to the school newspaper by their local school board after they requested to announce their after-school meetings.

Law enforcement personnel are bombarded by anti-religious stereotypes in the media, an increasing amount of legislation that is unfavorable toward religious practices, and a proliferation of court decisions biased against religious defendants and litigants. As a result they have developed an intolerant attitude toward religious expression. Just as academia has concluded that the mere presence of religious expression is enough to violate the "separation of church and state," law enforcement officials have begun to draw the same erroneous conclusion. Actions that once were clearly protected by the Constitution are presently being prohibited, and law enforcement agencies are enforcing stringent measures against religious public practices.

Right now the punishment of religious expression is, in the majority of cases, related to either protests or public education. In the cases where there is an appearance of state approval of religious symbols, belief, or practice, the courts tend to rule against public displays or demonstrations. At first this may seem to be reasonable in light of the establishment clause of the First Amendment. It is admittedly difficult to determine just when it is appropriate for the government to accommodate religion and yet not promote doctrines. It does appear that neutrality would be called for and is really the only viable way to protect all religious faiths from government control, intrusion, or sponsorship.

The problem is not with neutrality, which any conscientious Christian would and should accept. The problem is with the way that neutrality plays out. Human beings are not good at neutrality. We are human beings of passionate beliefs. Those beliefs define us and our thinking and in many ways affect our relationships with others. Even a cursory reading of American history shows that the nation itself is a product, not of dispassionate indifference, but of ardent devotion to the ideals of liberty, and, chief among them, religious liberty.

Today, however, the ardent devotion once reserved to

religious liberty is energizing the push behind secularism.
Secularism no longer plays out as "indifference" or neutrality toward religion but rather a determined rejection and
exclusion of religion from the public domain.

Perhaps the most important case affecting religious ex-
pression in the United States today would be the *Lee v.
Weisman* decision handed down by the Supreme Court on 24
June 1992.

Deborah Weisman was a fourteen-year-old eighth grader
when she graduated from Nathan Bishop Middle School in
Providence, Rhode Island, in 1989. As part of the graduation
ceremony, Rabbi Leslie Gutterman, from Temple Beth El in
Providence, prayed:

> God of the free, hope of the brave:
>
> For the legacy of America, where diversity is celebrated
> and the rights of minorities protected, we thank you.
> May these young men and women grow up to enrich
> it.
>
> For the liberty of America, we thank you. May these
> new graduates grow up to guard it.
>
> For the political process of America in which all its
> citizens may participate, for its court system where all
> may seek justice, we thank you. May those we honor
> this morning always turn to it in trust.
>
> For the destiny of America, we thank you. May the
> graduates of Nathan Bishop Middle School so live
> that they may live to share it.
>
> May our aspirations for our country and for these
> young people, who are our hope for the future, be
> richly fulfilled.
>
> Amen.

At the conclusion of the ceremony, the Rabbi prayed:

> O God, we are grateful to you for having endowed us
> with the capacity for learning which we have celebrated
> on this joyous commencement.

Happy families give thanks for seeing their children achieve an important milestone. Send your blessing upon the teachers and administrators who helped prepare them.

The graduates now need strength and guidance for the future; help them to understand that we are not complete with academic knowledge alone. We must each strive to fulfill what you require of us all: To do justly, to love mercy, and to walk humbly.

We give thanks to you, Lord, for keeping us alive, sustaining us, and allowing us to reach this special, happy occasion.

Amen.

It was the custom of the Providence public schools to allow individual principals to invite local clergy to participate in the graduation exercises. The Middle School principal, Robert E. Lee, had invited Rabbi Gutterman and had given him a booklet entitled "Guidelines for Civic Occasions" published by the National Conference for Christians and Jews. The rabbi's prayers conformed to the ecumenical and non-sectarian prayers presented in the book.

But that was not good enough for Deborah Weisman's father, Daniel. A self-styled "non-believer," Mr. Weisman objected to any prayers being said at his daughter's graduation. He went to the federal court for Rhode Island and asked the judge for a temporary restraining order that would ban the rabbi and the prayers. The judge denied his motion, stating that there wasn't enough time to research his request. The ceremony went ahead as planned, and the prayers were said as part of the commencement.

But Mr. Weisman did not give up. Deborah enrolled at Classical High School in Providence for the 1989-1990 term. In July of 1989, Mr. Weisman asked the federal court for a permanent injunction that would prohibit any clergy or prayers at any future graduations.

The court ruled in Mr. Weisman's favor and banned any prayers at all the schools in the state of Rhode Island. The judge held that the school principal's invitation to the rabbi created "an identification of the state with a religion, or religion in general" and that the effect of the invitation was to "endorse religion." This was determined to violate the three-part test of the *Lemon* decision.

The school district and the United States government appealed the judge's ruling, and the United States Supreme Court heard the case on 6 November 1991. The following spring, on 24 June, the high court held that "[i]ncluding clergy who offer prayers as part of an official public school graduation ceremony is forbidden." Thus, the Court made any official prayers at school functions in the United States illegal.

Keith Fournier, ACLJ Executive Director, writing in the *Regent University Law Review*, said that in light of *Weisman*, "any state action that can be perceived as creating even indirect social or peer pressure can be declared unconstitutional." According to Fournier,

> Now . . . there are three categories of speech which are significantly restricted inAmerica today. The first, obscenity, is not given the status of "speech" under the First Amendment, and thus is not constitutionally protected at all. The second, comprised of seditious or libelous expression, is restricted because of its inherent threat to individual and government rights. The third category, almost unbelievably, is religious speech. Despite the First Amendment's clear promise of freedom to exercise religion, religious speech has been restricted by means of the criteria set forth in Lemon v. Kurtzman and now by Weisman. . . . The "wall of separation" has become a wall of hostility to religious speech.

That hostility is a logical extension of the "rejection" of religion that is inherent in secularism.

In a series of cases in the 1980s and into the 1990s, the courts have begun to force "secularism" on religious Americans via the 1971 "*Lemon* test." In that decision, the high court ruled that a three-fold "test" must be applied to any government action (the decision actually involved a state statute) to determine whether or not it is permissible.

First, it must have a "secular" purpose. Second, its principle or primary effect must be one that neither advances nor inhibits religion. Finally, it must not foster an "excessive government entanglement with religion."

At first glance the *Lemon* test appears to guarantee government neutrality when it comes to religion, probably the safer side for government to be on. But what the *Lemon* and the more recent *Weisman* decisions ignore is the fact that secularism, as it is currently expressed in popular American culture, is not synonymous with neutrality. Secularism has become ideologically antagonistic to religious speech and practice. Consequently, the decisions of the lower courts that have been derived from *Lemon* in particular have contributed to the steady erosion of religion's high standing in American society.

The most pernicious aspect of the legal treatment of religion in the public sphere is what the law professor Gerard V. Bradley has identified as the "privatization" theory espoused by the U.S. Supreme Court: "Privatization is the Court's final solution to the problem of religious faction." According to Professor Bradley, the Supreme Court, since World War II, has conducted a "war of attrition upon religious consciousness."[3]

The war began in 1947 when the court decided on *Emerson v. Board of Education*. In that case, the Court ruled that "[n]either (state nor federal government) can pass laws which aid one religion, aid all religions, or prefer one religion over another." The Emerson case served as the inauguration of the Court's subsequent doctrine of the complete "separation of church and state." The justices concluded, without any reference to American history, that the establishment clause of the First Amendment (which reads "Congress shall make no law respecting the establishment of religion") prohibited the government from providing any material assistance to a religious effort. This was a novel interpretation, with virtually no previous precedent in law. That idea was reaffirmed the following year in *McCollum v. Board of Education*.

In that case, the school district in Champaign, Illinois, had joined in voluntary cooperation with the Champaign Council on Religious Education in a program designed to reduce the incidents of juvenile delinquency in the county. The program consisted of religious instruction provided at school during a release time approved and requested by the students' parents. Every religious body and denomination in the community was invited to participate, and students were given the choice of which religious instruction they would receive. Everyone was treated equally, and nobody was left out.

However, one student, James Terry, was the son of an avowed atheist and humanist, Mrs. Vashti McCollum. She filed a lawsuit claiming that her son was being discriminated against because he was the only child in his class who opted for no religious instruction at all. In her suit, she claimed that the Illinois law was unconstitutional. Furthermore, it was her intent to "ban every form of teaching which suggests or recognizes that there is a God."[4] The supreme court of the state of Illinois found that there was nothing wrong with the plan, since it was wholly voluntary and treated every religion equally.

The nation's highest court disagreed. They held that the arrangement violated the Constitution by involving "the use of taxpayer-supported property for religious instruction" and that it involved "the close cooperation between school authorities and the religious council in promoting religious education." Thus began the Court's war on the public role of religion in society. The case also introduced the notion that religious belief is nothing more or less than a completely private affair.

Professor Bradley demonstrates that the Supreme Court has conjured up a doctrine that religious convictions prohibit "state legislators from distinguishing worship from bowling." In other words, religion holds no more a significant place in American society than recreation or amusement does. In fact, later in the *Lemon* case, the Court insisted that:

> To have states or communities divide on the issues presented by state aid to parochial schools would tend to confuse and obscure other issues of great urgency. We have an expanding array of vexing issues, local and national, domestic and international,

to debate and divide on. It conflicts with our whole history and tradition to permit questions of religion clauses to assume such importance in our legislatures and in our elections that they could divert attention from the myriad issues and problems that confront every level of government.[5]

In this historic decision compromising religious liberty in America, the Court dismissed the importance of religious issues, sweeping them aside in favor of more "vexing issues . . . and problems" that face Americans.

The *Lemon* decision dealt with another Rhode Island law that allocated state funds to subsidize the salaries of teachers in private schools. The vast majority of those schools were affiliated with the Catholic diocese. The law carefully prescribed that the subsidies would only go to teachers of so-called secular subjects, such as math, science, and history. Furthermore, it required that teachers not teach any religious doctrine in their classes. At least one teacher indicated that he no longer "prayed with his classes" in respect to the law. Leaving aside the wisdom of such a statute, it was drafted to carefully send every signal of fairness to all religions, treating them alike. In the end the justices ruled that the Rhode Island law violated the separation of church and state. That decision, more than any other, reveals the growing hostility of the secular ideology of the court toward religious believers. Here are some excerpts from that now notoriously anti-religious opinion, delivered by Justice William Brennan:

> The entanglement [between the state and religion] arises . . . because of the religious activity and purpose of the church affiliated schools, especially with respect to children of impressionable age in the primary grades, and the dangers that a teacher under religious control and discipline poses. . . .
>
> Political division along religious lines was one of the evils at which the First Amendment aimed . . .

Referring to the Catholic Schools of Rhode Island:

The church schools involved . . . are located close to
parish churches. The school buildings contain identifying religious symbols such as crosses on the exterior
and crucifixes, and religious paintings and statues
either in the classrooms or hallways.

We cannot ignore the danger that a teacher under
religious control and discipline poses . . .

In our view, the record shows these dangers are
present to a substantial degree.

[T]he potential for impermissible fostering of religion is present.

The history of many countries attests to the hazards
of religion's intruding into the political arena. . . .

From Justice Douglas' concurring opinion:

We deal [here] not with evil teachers, but zealous
ones who may use any opportunity to indoctrinate a
class.

One can imagine what a religious zealot, as contrasted
with a civil libertarian, can do with the Reformation
or the Inquisition.

I can think of no more disrupting influence apt to
promote rancor and ill will between church and state
than this kind of surveillance and control.

This is the language of juxtaposition and of contradic-
tion. In *Lemon*, the Supreme Court drew the line in the sand.
On the one side are "civil libertarians," good citizens who do
not hold "rancorous" and "divisive" religious convictions,
and on the other are "evil zealots" who would take advantage
of government accommodation and impose their perverse
religious beliefs on "children of impressionable age."

In fairness, the language of the various decisions of the
Court does try to mitigate the hostility that they have fostered between the public trust and believers. They are quick
to point out that their decisions are not to be construed in
any manner to "denigrate" religious beliefs, but they fail to

realize, or willfully deny, that is exactly the outcome of their language. The justices wittingly or unwittingly have adopted the terminology of militant secularism—the purposeful and ideological rejection and exclusion of religious considerations.

The net result of these decisions, and especially the language employed by them, is an image of religious faith and practice in America that is in stark contrast to reality. In reality, religious faith has contributed illustriously to American society and culture. In any city or town across the continent, religious bodies have founded and administrate schools, hospitals and health clinics, counseling agencies and youth programs, public shelters, drug and alcohol rehabilitation, food pantries, and legal services. Christian clergy can be found to be involved in efforts to eliminate drug abuse and crime, promote fair housing, conduct preschool and after-school educational programs, and a myriad of other positive enhancements to community life. Yet the language of the Supreme Court and lower court rulings that follow its dicta make it sound as if religion is a dormant evil in America, a combustible material that could explode in an incendiary conflagration at any time, inflicting pain and suffering on our tender democracy. Just a brief reading of some of the religious clause decisions exposes an imagery of religion that is inherently "anti-democratic," "divisive," "exclusive," and "dominant."

The descriptive terminology of these decisions follows the lead of the false consensus. According to Professor Bradley, the message of the Court has been "[I]f religion possesses any objective truth claims at all, they are not public truths. Religious individuals instead are propelled into politics by the pursuit of money or unwarranted preferences in the hierarchy of public symbols."[6]

The Supreme Court was determined to drive religious beliefs out of the public domain and into the secret, relatively harmless world of the private conscience of citizens. As such, it holds no prospect of ever "intruding" into public policy. This situation is a fundamental denial of what the framers of the Constitution really meant when they adopted the First Amendment's protection of religious liberty.

In his scathing dissent in *Weisman*, Justice Antonin Scalia, joined by Chief Justice Rehnquist and Justices White and Thomas, contends that "[t]he Court—with nary a mention that it is doing so—lays waste a tradition that is as old as public school graduation ceremonies themselves, and that is a component of an even more long-standing American tradition of non-sectarian prayer to God at public celebrations generally." He goes on to refer to the decision as an "instrument of destruction," and a "bulldozer of . . . social engineering." He accuses the majority on the Court of presenting religion as a

> purely personal avocation that can be indulged in entirely in secret, like pornography, in the privacy of one's room. For most believers it is not that, and has never been. Religious men and women of almost all denominations have felt it necessary to acknowledge and beseech the blessing of God as a people, and not just as individuals, because they believe God to be, as Washington's first Thanksgiving Proclamation put it, the "Great Lord and Ruler of the Nations." One can believe in the effectiveness of such public worship, or one can deprecate and deride it. But the long-standing American tradition of prayer at official ceremonies displays with unmistakable clarity that the Establishment Clause does not forbid the government to accommodate it.

By inferring that that is just what the *Weisman* decision does, deprecates and derides religious faith, Justice Scalia explained why Judge Bestry could announce, on the record, his opinion that public praying is a "disgusting" act. That designation agrees with the denigratory but much more sophisticated language used to express the highest court's disdain for the public expression of religious belief and practice.

A change, though, is in the wind. Provoked, we are confident, by Justice Scalia, the Court is now demonstrating some contrition and a tentative willingness to reconsider its antipathy toward religion.

The Supreme Court heard the *Lamb's Chapel v. Center Moriches School District* case on the same day as the *Zobrest* case. We describe the case in detail in the next chapter.

In the course of the colloquy before the Court, the attorney of the school district argued that school facilities are neutral, and the district therefore opposed the use of its buildings by religious groups.

"Is that neutral—permitting no one with a religious perspective?" asked Justice O'Connor.

Justice Stevens inquired, "Are left-wingers neutral? What if Communists and Socialists want to speak?"

Justice Scalia scorned the position taken by the New York state attorney general, that religion "serves the community only in the eyes of its adherents and yields a benefit only to those who already believe."

"It used to be thought that if there was a lack of religious institutions, there would be more people to mug me and rape my sister. How is this new regime working? Has it worked very well?" he chided. Furthermore, he pointed out that many school districts in Virginia allow churches to hold services in school buildings, inferring that no social harm had resulted from the arrangement.

Chief Justice Rehnquist, and Justices Scalia, Thomas, and White [7] appear ready to stem the tide of anti-religious discrimination inherent within the establishment clause cases of the last half-century. Justice Scalia made it clear in his dissent in *Weisman* that he recognizes the critically important role that religious faith plays in society.

> The history and tradition of our nation are replete with public ceremonies featuring prayers of thanksgiving and petition. Illustrations of this point have been amply provided in our opinions, but since the Court is so oblivious to our history as to suggest that the Constitution restricts "preservation and transmission of religious beliefs . . . to the private sphere," it appears necessary to provide another brief account.

> From our nation's origin, prayer has been a prominent part of governmental ceremonies and proclamations. The Declaration of Independence, the document marking our birth as a separate people, "appeal[ed] to the Supreme Judge of the world for the rectitude of our intentions" and avowed "a firm

reliance on the protection of divine Providence." In his first inaugural address, after swearing his oath of office on a Bible, George Washington deliberately made prayer a part of his first official act as President. . . . Thomas Jefferson . . . prayed in his first inaugural address . . . James Madison . . . Most recently, George Bush . . ."

In outlining the usage of prayer by the presidents, Scalia emphasized the key role religion has played in American history and politics.

> The founders of our Republic knew the fearsome potential of sectarian religious belief to generate dissension and civil strife. And they also knew that nothing, absolutely nothing, is so inclined to foster among religious believers of various faiths a toleration—no, an affection—for one another than voluntarily joining in prayer together to the God whom they all worship and seek. Needless to say, no one should be compelled to do that, but it is a shame to deprive our public culture the opportunity, and indeed the encouragement, for people to do it voluntarily. The Baptist or Catholic who heard and joined in the simple and inspiring prayers of Rabbi Gutterman on this official and patriotic occasion was inoculated from religious bigotry and prejudice in a manner that cannot be replicated. To deprive our society of that important unifying mechanism, in order to spare the non-believer what seems to me the minimal inconvenience of standing or even sitting in respectful non-participation, is as senseless in policy as it is unsupported in law.

The addition, however, of a secularist justice to the court by Clinton or a subsequent administration would continue to deprive the culture of just such a blessing and would hasten the demise of religion in American life. Christians and other religious believers are already on the defensive in many American courts; some are in jail, and others have been deprived of their possessions, their dignity, and their civil and constitutional rights.

SEVEN

Ignorance in Academia

The brief reign of the New York City Public Schools chancellor Joseph Fernandez is a dramatic example of the conflict between the educational establishment and ordinary American citizens, whose children are compelled by law to attend school.

The story reads like a chronicle of just how insidious the false consensus is and how it operates in a community. The demise of Chancellor Fernandez, and the more important triumph of Queens District School Board president Mary Cummins, reveals all the intrigue, power-politicking, deception, and propaganda that are the basic components of the secularist-sexual revolution agenda.

Joseph Fernandez came to New York from Miami where he had gained the reputation of an educational reformer. He assumed the helm of the nation's worst school system. The dropout rate was at 17 percent, and SAT scores were more than one hundred points lower than the national average. Violence in the schools had reached an epidemic proportion that required the school system to employ an internal police force larger than some metropolitan areas of the country.

Fernandez had been hand-picked by Mayor David Dinkins, and his nomination was rubber-stamped by the "nominating committee" that had been assembled to choose the best candidate. It didn't take long for Fernandez to become a part of the political landscape of New York that was designed by City Hall. Mayor Dinkins had depended on the homosexual lobby to inch out former Mayor Ed Koch in the

Democratic primary. His victory in the general election was
by only one percentage point, and the homosexuals claimed
that they put him over the top. They insisted that it was
"payback" time. Dinkins responded to the pressure by pushing homosexual issues to the top of his list. He extended
spousal benefits to homosexual partners and took the St.
Patrick's Day Parade permit away from the Ancient Order of
Hibernians, a Catholic organization, and gave it to an ad hoc
group that promised to allow homosexuals to march openly
in the parade, then suggested that if the Catholic church
would change its position on homosexuality as sin he might
give the permit back to Catholics.

Depriving Catholics of the First Amendment right to
free exercise of religion was not enough for Mayor Dinkins.
He further acquiesced to the revolutionaries' demand that
homosexuality be taught as a normal, valid lifestyle throughout the schools. This is where Joseph Fernandez appeared
on the scene.

Fernadez's mandate to turn around New York's deterio-
rating academic condition was early on subordinated to the
false consensus. True to the precepts of the sexual revolution, the chancellor's first major initiative—in the face of an
unparalleled academic crisis that threatened the students'
futures, rampant violence that jeopardized the safety and the
lives of students and faculty, and a crumbling infrastructure
of dilapidated school buildings, in some cases literally posing
the threat of collapse—was to announce that condoms would
be made available in unlimited quantities, and that homosexuality would be taught from preschool to graduation!

In spite of the fact that New York requires that parents
submit a consent form for sex education instruction, the
chancellor rescinded consent requirements for the condoms,
explaining that if parents had to give their permission, students would be less likely to use them. This is a major
feature of the false consensus, that parental involvement in
their children's private lives, and especially in their sexual
decisions, frustrates educational professionals' efforts to in-
struct children in risk-free sexual behaviors.

The chancellor's prophylactic plan was overwhelmingly
supported by the New York media. The *New York Times*

editorialized in favor of Fernandez's initiative. Across the nation, newspapers backed the chancellor. Opponents of the plan, including the archbishop of New York, John Cardinal O'Connor, were portrayed as head-in-the-sand conservatives and religious fanatics who denied reality and insisted on imposing their morality on the school system, endangering the sexual welfare of the students.

When the New York State Board of Regents, the highest governing body in state education policy, reversed its initial decision to delay the plan for further study, and instead, under pressure from Governor Mario Cuomo, approved it, it appeared that Chancellor Fernandez had won the day. Actually, the war that would ultimately lead to his ouster had just begun.

Mary Cummins, a seventy-three-year-old grandmother from Queens, was serving as president of the school board there when Fernandez's homosexual curriculum, "Children of the Rainbow," was introduced.

"I was horrified," she later said of her first reaction to the reading list for the first grade. *Daddy's Roommate* and *Heather Has Two Mommies* portrayed inviting images of homosexual couples raising children. "It was to be taught every day, in every subject, all day long, including playtime," she explains. "If a little boy concentrated on playing with trucks, and made no move to play with a doll, the teacher was supposed to guide him over to the dolls and take a little girl and put her with the truck." Mrs. Cummins saw the curriculum as undermining the family. The material instructed students that "school is your family" and was designed as a complete behavior modification program, teaching students that homosexuality was a normal, even desirable lifestyle.

Mrs. Cummins launched a campaign against the curriculum and against Fernandez. She wrote a letter to each of the school boards in New York and exposed the nature of the material to them. Because the curriculum stressed multiculturalism, Fernandez expected support from African-Americans and Hispanics. But leaders in those communities, particularly the clergy, vehemently opposed it on moral grounds. Both religious and community leaders backed Mrs. Cummins and opposed Fernandez.

In an attempt to put down the insurrection, Fernandez suspended the Queens Board of Education and Mary Cummins. But she did not relent. A public outcry was heard, a meeting was convened at City Hall, and the Queens school board and Mrs. Cummins were reinstated. Fernandez was subsequently turned out of office.

In spite of the fact that the New York City administration, the Democratic party, and the media unanimously backed Fernandez and the curriculum, the people of New York, across the ethnic spectrum, overwhelmingly rejected them. Although the media and the educational and political establishments attempted to foist on New York families a false consensus, in this case, the truth prevailed and the false consensus lost out.

Prejudice, bigotry, discrimination, and defamation are dependent on an absence of truth. "You shall know the truth," Jesus said, "and the truth shall make you free." If there is any "secular" institution where the truth should be ardently sought, tenaciously guarded, and carefully transmitted, it ought to be public education. Tragically, this is not the case. The American campus today has become a social and intellectual gulag where wayward religious dissidents are forcibly reeducated in the finer points of the false consensus.

The new "outcomes-based education" programs, like the one adopted by the Northwest Suburban high-school district outside Chicago, show a frightening potential for not only ostracizing students who hold to traditional moral values but for punishing them academically.

In the case of the Northwest district, the school board adopted ten "general learner outcomes" that students must achieve by their senior year. They include the development of verbal, quantitative, and technological literacy; skill in communication and group interaction; skill in problem solving and decision making and in expressing themselves creatively and responding to the creative works of others; civic understanding through study of American culture and history; and understanding past and present cultures, and concern, tolerance, and respect for others. Students must also show skill in adapting to and creating personal and social change.

While appearing advantageous on its face, the system needs only a quick second glance to see the frightening potential for abuse. What OBE proposals threaten to do is, first, take away the primary right of parents to inculcate their children with moral values and religious beliefs; and second, they present the specter of children being ostracized, disciplined, perhaps even punished, for not falling in step with the classroom "new think."

It does not take an extraordinary imagination to create a scenario in which students are "publicly examined" on their attitudes toward abortion, suicide, euthanasia, and homosexuality. This would fit in with the development of skills in "communication and group interaction" as well as demonstrating a capacity for "adapting to, and creating, personal and social change." Given the average adolescent's need for peer approval, this stage may be enough to "do the trick." Should the student, however, continue to demonstrate that she is not "sufficiently tolerant" or "respecting" of such behavior or persons who engage in it, then she would be held back for what has elsewhere been called "reeducation." This kind of behavior and thought modification is being applied on every level of education in secular America.

In the scathing conclusion of his examination of the "politics of race and sex on campus," author Dinesh D'Souza stated:

> By the time . . . students graduate, very few colleges have met their need for all-round development. Instead, by precept and example, universities have taught them that "all rules are unjust" and "all preferences are principled"; that justice is simply the will of the stronger party; that standards and values are arbitrary, and the ideal of the educated person is largely a figment of bourgeois white male ideology, which should be cast aside; that individual rights are a red flag signaling social privilege, and should be subordinated to the claims of group interest; that all knowledge can be reduced to politics and should be pursued not for its own sake but for the political end of power; that convenient myths and benign lies can substitute for truth; that double standards are accept-

able as long as they are enforced to the benefit of
minority victims; that debates are best conducted not
by rational and civil exchange of ideas, but by accusation, intimidation, and official prosecution; that the
university stands for nothing in particular and has no
claim to be exempt from outside pressures; and that
the multiracial society cannot be based on fair rules
that apply to every person, but must rather be constructed through a forced rationing of power among
separatist racial groups. In short, instead of liberal
education, what American students are getting is its
diametrical opposite, an education in closed
mindedness and intolerance.[1]

While D'Souza's research demonstrated the negative effect
of "political correctness" on academics and the social life of
the American college campus, its impact upon the free exercise of religious faith has been just as destructive. Political
correctness is fast achieving the secularist goal of eliminating
the meaningful presence and participation of religion in the
process of education. Speech codes have sanctioned students for opposing homosexuality, denied them a degree for
adhering to a scripturally consistent cosmogony, and expelled them for their recalcitrance when they refuse to kow-
tow to the false consensus. To be sure, today, if you are a
practicing, believing Christian, the American campus can be
a very scary place.

What is more ominous, though, than the intimidation of
the religious community on the college campus is the intimidation and punishment of Christian students in the nation's
high schools. There, the subtleties of speech and conduct
codes are often turned into fiat decrees pronounced by
school boards and administrators that seriously limit students' First Amendment rights and their individual civil liberties. Students have been failed or denied a grade because
they chose to write an essay on a religious topic; they have
been disqualified from school assemblies or special programs
because they selected a piece of religious music to perform;
and they have been arrested and removed from the campus
by police, as if they were dope dealers, simply for gathering
in prayer around the flagpole!

The intrinsic discrimination against religious expression on the part of the educational establishment is nowhere more blatant than in the circumstances leading up to the Supreme Court case *Lamb's Chapel and John Steigerwald v. Center Moriches Union Free School District et al.,* which came before the Court in late February 1993:

The Long Island village of Center Moriches is a quiet residential community founded in 1700 and situated in the campestral, forested region on the Great South Bay. John Steigerwald and Allen Snapp moved there in 1988. The two young graduates of Christ for the Nations Bible College in nearby Stony Brook had teamed up to share the pastorate of the Lamb's Chapel, a fledgling evangelical congregation that had formed just five years before.

Numbering about sixty members in all, the fellowship of predominantly young, middle-class families rented another church's sanctuary on Sunday afternoons for worship. Emphasizing "personal relationships" over "church programs," the pastors sought to reach out to the community by showing a film series about family values that was produced by the Christian psychologist James Dobson. Being optimistic about their prospects of attracting families interested in improving their parenting skills and family lives, the pastors printed flyers and advertised the films in local papers.

Judging their rented sanctuary as too austere and even threatening to visitors that may have been unchurched, the pastors decided to seek out a more "neutral" setting that would also provide more seating for the events.

Aware that the high school was rented by a variety of community groups and organizations, including the Boy Scouts and the Salvation Army band, John Steigerwald wrote a letter to the Center Moriches School District asking to rent the school's auditorium for five successive Wednesday nights. At the time it seemed to be a practical solution to help facilitate the church's mission, but he had no idea that the incident would eventuate in a Supreme Court decision that would focus the nation's attention on the anti-religious discrimination practiced by much of the education establishment.

Pastor Steigerwald received an ambivalent reply from the district indicating that it was their "suspicion" that the films were "religious in content" and if that was the case, the district would not rent the auditorium to show them to the public. After several letters were sent back and forth, the district denied the request.

The church's attorney advised the pastors that the denial was a "clear case of unconstitutional discrimination against religious speech" and referred them to Mark Trubnick, then chief counsel for Concerned Women for America (CWA). Trubnick flew in and met with the church's leadership. He told them that there was a clear potential for winning this case, but that it could become a huge demand and a distraction to the small congregation that was just walking through a difficult time of healing after the tragic deaths of two small children.

Initially, the three elders and four deacons determined that the church was not up to the fight, but six months later they changed their minds and called Trubnick back. A suit was filed, and two lower courts that heard the case and the appeal ruled in favor of the school district policy. By the time the case reached the Supreme Court for review, the legal office of CWA had merged with the American Center for Law and Justice. ACLJ chief counsel Jay Sekulow took the case, and it was argued on 24 February 1993. In an unusual alliance, the American Civil Liberties Union, the People for the American Way and the Union of American Hebrew Congregations sided with the church in amicus briefs. The usually extremist "separationist" groups agreed that the film series, and the use of public properties generally by religious groups, posed no "threat" of government entanglement with religion.

Defending the state of New York's discriminatory policies, state Attorney General Robert Abrams argued in a brief that religion is no good to anyone but the people who believe in it.

The justices hearing the case in the Supreme Court seemed incredulous as the school district's attorney, John Hoefling, asserted repeatedly that the school's policy was to deny religious organizations, even religious persons, access to school facilities while allowing "secularist," "communist," "socialist," "anti-religious," and "atheist" speakers to utilize them. During the argument, Hoefling, to the dismay of Justices Sandra Day O'Connor and Clarence Thomas, insisted that ten atheists could present their views against religious faith, but if one Christian showed up to defend it—it would be disallowed!

Arguing before the Court, Hoefling asserted that the school district had been consistent with the New York state law and the U.S. Constitution in insisting that "the premises would not be used for religious purposes."[2] When Mr. Hoefling was questioned by the Court as to whether the district would "permit someone to come in and urge the adoption of a particular lifestyle that was not based on any religious precepts . . . proselytizing, so to speak, of a secular nature, secularly inspired but not religiously inspired," he responded, "Yes, Your Honor." Pressed further, he was asked if the school district then meant that "on a secular basis . . . subject matter is permissible. But a speaker who urges the adoption of a lifestyle based on a religious passage could not do it." Again, Mr. Hoefling responded, "That's correct, Your Honor."[3]

Later, asked by the Court if "you had a Communist group that wanted to address the subject of family values and they thought that there was a value in not having children waste their time going to Sunday school or church and therefore they had a point of view that was definitely antireligious, they would be permitted, under your policy, to discuss family values in that context?" Mr. Hoefling answered emphatically, "Yes. Yes, Your Honor, that's correct."[4]

The school district's attorney was just expressing what most of the educational establishment, under the spell of the false consensus, believe about education's relationship to religion. Allen Snapp, who was assistant pastor of Lamb's Chapel at the time of the incident, said that the district had repeatedly demonstrated a hostile attitude toward the church, even subsequent to the Supreme Court's hearing of the case. When a high-school sophomore, who happened to attend Lamb's Chapel, requested permission to begin an after-school Bible club, she was told she would have to wait for the outcome of the case. When she told the principal of the school that the Supreme Court had already approved the use of school facilities for Bible studies in the 1990 *Westside Community Schools v. Mergens* case, he demanded a list of the students' names who would be involved, and whether any of them attended Lamb's Chapel. When Pastor Allen Snapp contacted the principal to complain about the scrutiny, he was told the district would want to know who was "involved in a group they were having trouble with."

According to the former Secretary of Education, William Bennett, "In too many places in American public education, religion has been ignored, banned, or shunned in ways that serve neither knowledge, nor the Constitution, nor sound public policy."[5]

Indeed, the paranoia over the "separation of church and state" in the academy has provoked some educators and educational institutions to exhibit virtual hostility toward religion and religious persons. The prevalent false consensus has made education the opponent, rather than the compliment, of religion.

The New York University School of Law teaches in some courses that the First Amendment actually consists of two, opposite clauses. The so-called "establishment clause," which prohibits the federal government from establishing a particular national religion, is interpreted as encouraging "suspicion" and "hostility" on the part of government toward religious faith. The "free exercise" clause disallows the government from outlawing any religion. In this view, the perennial polarization between the two clauses is part of the framers' plan: Allegedly, the drafters of the Bill of Rights believed that religion was "dangerous" and that any government entanglement with it could lead to tyranny and despotism. On the other hand, government must make room for the irrational and illogical beliefs of the common man, and therefore should be prohibited from denying the people their superstitions!

The position taken by the law school is not unique nor novel, but it is recent, going back only to the mid-1920s. If the government is to be "suspicious" and even "hostile" toward the religion of its subjects, how is a balance to be maintained? The government has all the guns, the religionists, few. The government conducts the courts, and the churches conduct none. Submission to the government is mandatory, to the church, voluntary. The government maintains the prisons, and the church only fellowship halls. When the torque between the two clauses exceeds its careful balance and the force becomes favorable to one side, which is the more likely to prevail on earth?

Furthermore, when it is the student-teacher relationship into which this constitutional "hostility" is introduced, which one is the more likely to succumb? Is it the young student expected to be submissive, deferential, and respectful, or is the teacher expected to be the expert, in command, exerting the tutor's authority?

My experience with the "church-state" conflict goes back to my own days as a public school student in Grand Island, New York. The Grand Island school system was considered a model of modern education in the seventies. The system was a well-run, well-funded program consisting of three elementary schools (grades kindergarten through five), a thoroughly modern "middle school" (one of the first in the nation) with grades six, seven, and eight, and a central highschool.

The school's curriculum was as modern as the new construction: Students as early as the sixth grade were able to choose their course configurations, travelled from classroom to classroom (like their college complements), and got to opt out of some courses they didn't like and opt into electives that sounded more interesting (and the truth is, entertaining) to them. Furthermore, students were allocated to different levels of math, science, "social studies" instead of history, and "humanities" instead of "English" based on their grades, aptitude, and proclivities.

In the ninth-grade science class, I distinctly recall one day when, as a nominally Jewish student from a basically agnostic family, I was personally troubled by the announcement made by the respectable, if not severe, biology instructor concerning the unit on evolution.

"In the next unit we're going to be studying evolution." I remember to this day his beady eyes darting to and fro as he deliberately leaned over the long, high, brown-black demonstration counter that ran the full length of the front of the classroom.

"If there's anyone here whose parents won't allow them to study this subject, they can leave the room now and go to the library for the next eight weeks."

This amounted to a virtual expulsion from the classroom, a Leninesque consequence of Christian "fundamentalism's" unwillingness to concede the Scopes trial and acquiesce to the inevitable superiority of Darwinism over faith.

The classroom waited, like a frightened pack of political prisoners wondering if any one of their downtrodden number would have the *kishkas* to stand up to the great academy and actually walk out of the room and down to the library in modern, public educational exile.

After a few moments, two girls, one the daughter of the local Presbyterian pastor and the other a member of his congregation, silently rose and, while all eyes fixed upon the two contemporary Joans of Arc, silently gathered their books into their arms. With an air and posture of dignity, they left the room.

The deed done, the sentence handed down, the exiles now safely removed to the library-gulag, the class rid of the ignorant dissenters was free to embrace Darwin. I was horrified by their treatment, and I grew silently indignant.

It was that obscure event that in part inspired me to become a Christian.

Tragically, this scenario has been repeated innumerable times in any variety of ways in public schools all across America. A whole generation of students educated in America's public school system have graduated with the idea that religious faith—with all of its virtues and its higher calling—is incompatible with intelligence and the honest pursuit of knowledge. There is very little attempt, if any at all, to present a reasonable comparison, or accommodate the dialogue, between faith and science. Educators have fostered hostility toward the faith of their students, and instead of respecting religious expression and diversity, they have treated religious students with condescension and contempt. Unfortunately, the education establishment has accepted the false consensus which views science and religion as mutually exclusive.

"Public education is the training ground, the hot house, the farm team, for the next generation of liberals (a.k.a. secularists)," says syndicated columnist Cal Thomas.

> How else to inculcate multiculturalism, political correctness, and historical revisionism into children? How else to drum into them the view that they evolved from slime, that sex is an intramural sport, and that the liberal agenda is best? Children might not be expected to counter these "truths" on their own and are even less likely to learn them in private schools, especially private religious schools where a real education, a moral conscience, and wisdom can still be found.

> Public education is not about education. In too many instances it is about propagandizing and controlling the minds and hearts (and bodies) of the next generation.

The propaganda comes in huge doses when evolution and sexuality are the subjects. In fact, there are no two arenas where the conflict between faith and science rages more furiously. Of course, it need not be so. There is a great deal with which both faith and science share an interest: the origin and definition of life, the composition of the universe, man's place in it, and the destiny of man and the universe. Science has much to inform faith of, and faith has as much to teach science. But the secularist-New Left coalition has ruled out any cooperation between the two. The false consensus depends upon an uncompromised materialist definition of the origin and meaning of the universe and of life. This atheistic presupposition has no place for the supernatural, much less for a transcendent, personal Creator-God with an intelligent plan for the universe and its inhabitants.

The scientific aspects of the false consensus are reliant upon Darwinism, which has evolved itself into an immutable dogma of the educational establishment. Any other theory of cosmogony is held in contempt and is summarily dismissed by the postulators of the materialist-evolutionary paradigm. Indeed, recent court cases that have challenged the singular position that evolutionism holds in public education have consistently upheld its privileged status.

Conscientious Christians object to evolution's paramount post in the public school curriculum. They would like it reduced to a position of parity with other theories, specifically with scientific creationism. The reason for this is to expose students to other credible and viable ideas about the origins of the universe and of life. Furthermore, Christians have come to recognize that the theory of evolution has much greater implications for society than merely what students will be taught about the origination of the planets, stars, and species.

Inherent within the thesis that the universe began accidentally, the belief is that there is ultimately no meaning or purpose to life. Materialism denies the supernatural, and with it any supra-intelligence guiding the inhabitants of the universe to anything greater or better. Humanity is, in the words of Harvard University's Stephen Jay Gould, "a thing so small, in a vast universe, a wildly improbable evolutionary event well within the realm of contingency. Humanity is just a species of 'large, reasoning animals' without any 'intrinsic meaning' or 'transcendent purpose.'"[6]

Christians not only disagree with this definition and description of mankind, they also believe that teaching this theory as indisputable fact is destructive. It not only deprives their children, and other students for that matter, of the truth, but it also impugns the scriptural teaching that human beings were created with a special purpose and that it is incumbent upon every person to discover that purpose and strive toward its realization. This is the essence of Christianity and the essence of being Christian.

Christians object to the forcible teaching of their children that their lives mean nothing more than a rock, that their coming into being is as purposeless as a toad's, and that their futures are filled with only meaningless flux and uncertainty. Furthermore, they object to the use of taxpayer moneys and of governmental authority to force this theory on them and their families via their children. They take these impositions to be a violation of their civil and human rights.

Rather than having their constitutionally protected, inalienable rights of belief treated with respect, Christian students and their parents are treated with condescension, scorn, and contempt. Their creationist views are represented as medieval myths, unscientific and unintelligent, and are unwelcome in a serious classroom. When the Supreme Court struck down a Louisiana statute that would have mandated that evolution be balanced with a creationist theory, Albert Shanker, president of the American Federation of Teachers, said that the Court had "rescued the nation's public school system from narrow minded fanatics." Is this the way the nation's teachers should refer to students and parents who hold sincere religious faith?[7]

To understand Christian indignation over this situation, one must look hard at the implications of it. Parents who are compelled by law and who, for economic or any other reason, send their students to public schools (in many places there is no other choice), are forced to defend their religious beliefs and practices with their own children. Their children are being taught that what they and their families believe is unintelligent, irrational, and untrue.

This puts parents in an unfair and unacceptable position. The integrity of the family requires that the government not sow seeds of discord between parents and their children. To intrude on this most basic of human relationships is to violate the most sacred rights of the citizens that government is sworn to protect. To violate the family unit, without just cause, and as a matter of policy, is a most egregious dereliction of governmental responsibility. Throughout history, the attempts of governments to redefine and reconfigure families have ultimately resulted in rebellion and the overthrow of those regimes. Government loses its capacity to rule when it loses its respect among families.

Such is the case with the imposition of the false consensus on schoolchildren through the exclusive teaching of evolution in public education. To be presented as theory, a scientific hypothesis of origins, is one thing; to be imposed and enforced upon all the nation's students as national doctrine is another. To require adherence to such a doctrine, as the old oaths of despots imposed on their oppressed subjects, is a discriminatory act that relegates Christians and their non-Christian co-religionists to the status of intellectual slaves.

Cornell University professor Dr. Richard Baer states, "Public schools are no genuine market of ideas, but are instead a state monopoly with a captive student clientele."

Even beyond the violation of basic civil rights that the dogmatic teaching of Darwinism equates to is the defamation that is brought to bear upon the Christians because of their unwillingness to concede the battle over cosmogony. Science, like its culture-making counterparts, has succumbed to the temptation to deride its opponents, slandering their character and impugning their motives rather than just sticking with "the facts."

None of the materialist-science-evolutionists expresses the contempt of the false consensus for believers better than the guru of anti-supernaturalism himself, Carl Sagan.

Perpetuating the stereotype of God-worshippers as narrow-minded ignoramuses who disguise their secret agenda of hateful control under a cloak of sanctimonious pomposity, Sagan drones contemptuously, "Religions can be so shamelessly dishonest, so contemptuous of the intelligence of their adherents."[8]

In derogating teachers of religion, Dr. Sagan is giving expression to attitudes widely held by members of the educational establishment. This disdainful, condescending reproach of persons of faith is too common among college professors and, to a lesser but still significant degree, among the high-school teachers of America's public education system.

Despite Sagan's gratuitous reference to the "intelligence" of religion's adherents (one has to wonder just how intelligent someone can be to believe in falsity and nonsense), believers are generally considered ignorant by the paragons of materialistic science. The further down the totem of scientism you go, the cruder the condescension becomes, until, at the bottom, close to the common man, it is plainly expressed as scorn and mockery.

The Christian student, whether in high school, college, or graduate school, definitely gets the idea that he or she is empty-headed, naive, and has willingly traded away his or her hard-earned evolutionary status as a "large, reasoning animal" for divine dribble and pie-in-the-sky delusions. Some have fared worse. Because of their non-evolutionary views, students have been denied entrance into certain university degree programs, and others have been disqualified even after enrolling. It is a travesty that, during the "winner-takes-all" stakes of the battle over cosmogonies, science has become the locus of a fundamental denial of academic freedom.

I once had a conversation with a graduate student who had been severed from a Ph.D. program because she had asserted her objections to the Darwinian theory of evolution. Her committee explained that her views were incompatible with the division of biology in which she was seeking her degree. Already more than two years into her program, she was dropped. She appealed the decision but was told that unless she was able to embrace evolutionary theory, as a matter of fact, she would not be readmitted.

I spoke to a Christian law student who told me, "If I ever let my professor, who is a pro-choice lesbian, know that I was a Christian, I know I'd fail her course, and I need that course to get my law degree." Whether or not her fears were well-founded, they were there. Why? I would suggest that it is because of the atmosphere of hostility that exists in academia toward conscientious Christian faith. The educational establishment has taken on an adversarial role toward the practice of religion.

What is most insidious about the denigration of Christians by the educational establishment is that it is not based, as it is widely thought to be and purported to be by educators, on empirical evidence that clearly disproves the existence of Divinity and proves the divine record wrong but rather on an anti-supernaturalistic presupposition—in other words, on anti-religious prejudice!

This pervasive prejudice has been exposed by Professor Phillip E. Johnson of the University of California at Berkeley School of Law in his book, *Darwin on Trial* (Regnery Gateway-Intervarsity Press). Johnson, a lawyer, examines the evidence and the logic used to confirm the theory of evolution. After a careful analysis, Johnson concludes that the scientific evidence is not enough to verify evolution. His thesis is that Darwinism is an unempirical expression of dogmatic naturalism and not a true scientific hypothesis. So he then turns to exposing the philosophical underpinnings of the theory.

It is here that Johnson's challenge to evolution becomes so controversial. Johnson maintains that scientists have purposefully altered facts to fit their preconceived ideas about the random and accidental manner in which the universe and species came into being. In Johnson's view, the evolutionists are guilty of the very thing they accuse religionists of: unwillingness to subordinate their beliefs to empirical evidence. Johnson doesn't say that the evidence proves creationism, but he clearly demonstrates that it fails at every point to prove Darwinism.

Scientism was rocked in 1989 when evidence began to surface that one of the most significant fossil finds in history was a forgery. *Nature* magazine published the claims of an Australian paleontologist, John Talent, that fossils of invertebrates, which the Indian paleontologist Viswa Jit Gupta said he unearthed in the Himalayan mountains, were in fact from other regions and had been purchased in curio shops. According to a report in *U.S. News & World Report*, "Talent discovered that a site where Gupta claimed to have found a particularly fragmented fossil had undergone such tremendous geological deformation that Talent assert[ed] no fossil could have survived intact."[9]

The report goes on to state that "the new allegations are the latest in a series of troubling exposures of fraudulent scientific research to appear over the past few years, and many researchers are beginning to wonder whether the problem has less to do with a few unscrupulous scientists than with science itself."

Referring to scientific methods of research as "acts of faith," the article quotes Nicholas Wade, author of *Betrayers of the Truth*, a book about scientific fraud, who contends, "Scientists are trained to believe that research is an entirely objective process." Faith? Belief? The inference is that much of what has been promoted as sound, objective, scientific research has actually been the product of scientific predilections.

A basic staple of the evolution theory over the past century-and-a-third, since Darwin first articulated it for the world in *The Origin of Species*, has been the postulate that life forms move through a slow, gradual process from lesser to greater complexity. According to a report, however, published in the *New York Times* (30 March 1993), "researchers say they have been unable to detect any overall evolutionary drive toward greater complexity."

According to Dr. Dan McShea, a paleobiologist at the University of Michigan, "the perception of drives toward complexity may be more a reflection of scientists' desire to see some sort of progress in evolution rather than a reflection of any biological reality."

What makes the leading scientists' harsh rejections of religious faith most egregious is their unwillingness to admit their own, demonstrable presuppositions.

It is particularly onerous that the educational establishment has derided, ostracized, and expelled otherwise esteemed members of its own ranks because of the secularist, anti-religious bigotry of its hard-core Darwinist members.

When Forest Mims III was fired as the writer of the "Amateur Scientist" column for the *Scientific American*, he was asked by the editor of the magazine if he believed in Darwin's theory of evolution. "No," said Mims. Mims recalls his editor's giving him a stern warning not to write anything about creationism for the column. Afterwards, Mims was told by the editor that the "good name of the magazine" might be "embarrassed" by him. At the final inquisition that preceded his dismissal, Mims was asked "Are you a fundamentalist Christian?"

For the publishers of the magazine, the connection was obvious: Rejection of the materialist-evolutionary dogma could mean only one thing—fundamentalism! Christian fundamentalism alone was enough to stigmatize, not just the scholar, but the publication itself! Mim's firing was nothing less than a blatant form of scientific McCarthyism, guilt by allegation and association.

Mims was fired in spite of a growing body of research that has challenged the bias toward Darwinian evolution. Although the scientific world is not ready just yet to give up on the dogma that it has venerated for over a century, evolution, nonetheless, has been seriously injured by the new data. The truth is that evolution is not a settled matter, yet it has consistently been utilized in the ostracism of religionists in education.

In addition, we find that American education shares with the other two great contemporary culture makers, media and law, the bias against the conservative morality of religion in favor of the moral relativism of secularism.

In an essay appearing in the *Public Interest* (Summer, 1987), Charles L. Glenn refers to a report commissioned by the Connecticut Mutual Life Insurance Company entitled "The Impact of Belief." According to Glenn, the study "surveyed approximately 1,800 leaders in nine major occupations and found them—especially those in law, education and media—consistently more 'liberal' on moral issues than the general public. 'Because leaders are among the less religious Americans,' the authors conclude, 'the study observes that they may be out of touch with the current of faith which appears to be gathering strength among the public in this decade.'"

The report is in. While religion is reaching the heart of America, secularism is capturing its institutions. Since those whose hearts have been filled with faith eventually must respond to the institutions, preeminently education, an ideological conflict has become inevitable.

The conflict erupted in the eighties in a series of critical court cases that challenged public education's dogmatic allegiance to secularism. Key Supreme Court cases decided mid-decade clearly established secularism as the credo of public education.

The seven-to-two high court decision ruled in June 1987 that Louisiana State Senator Bill Keith's law requiring schoolteachers to teach both evolution and scientific creationism was a "sham," in the words of Justice Brennan, and that it was devised "clearly to advance the religious viewpoint that a supernatural being created humankind." This is in spite of the fact that the Court had found in a 1952 case, *Zorach v. Clauson*, that "we are a religious people whose institutions presuppose a Supreme Being." Apparently the justice, affected by the deep animus of the liberal legal establishment toward religious faith, was able to deduce from the strictly non-religious language of the Louisiana statute that, lurking ominously behind this ostensibly scientific, albeit minority, theory of origins was a higher power that had been permanently expelled from school twenty-five years before when the court decided against school prayer in *Engel v. Vitale.*

The cumulative effect of these and a handful of lower court decisions has been the strengthening of the bias against religion that has become pervasive in the American educational establishment.

Because of these decisions, publishing companies that provide the nation's school districts with their textbooks have carefully avoided most references to religion. As a result, the supreme importance of religious pilgrims and pioneers, religious thinkers and leaders, and religious reformers has been ignored and, in some cases, misrepresented. Even in the cases in which the religious nature of those predecessors is mentioned, there is almost no explanation of what their religious beliefs consisted of, and why they believed and did the things they did.

The diminishing of religion in education has only further exacerbated the hostility between education and the faith practices of students. Lack of knowledge and understanding contributes to prejudice and bigotry. With only the media stereotypes of believers to go on, children require a balanced, truthful, and respectful treatment of the variety of religions adhered to in our country.

The absence of information on religious beliefs and practices is so much the case that teachers, as well as students and their parents, feel that their First Amendment right to the free exercise of their religious faith is being inhibited. Writing on the "My Turn" page of *Newsweek* magazine, high-school teacher and baseball coach Peter Huidekoper, Jr., laments this oppressive environment in the classroom:

> I think I speak for many teachers when I confess that
> something, be it the state or society or our own fears—
> our own embarrassment about discussing religion in

front of our classes, and the embarrassment too, of our students—interferes with the freedom to reflect on and wonder about religious beliefs in the classroom. Something interferes with a general willingness to consider whether God might exist and whether his being might not have some correlation to the work we are studying. . . .

Haven't we retreated too far in the other direction when as teachers we feel required to curb our instincts—which are in fact intellectually and professionally sound—to encourage our students to explore beliefs, concerns, and meanings, from time to time, in the context of our religious traditions, and in light of faith in a caring and personal God?[10]

In a ruling upholding a U.S. district court's decision barring the teaching of creation science, a federal appeals court in Chicago equated "propagating a religious creed" with "impairing intellectual inquiry." This kind of disparagement of sincere religious beliefs, whether they are appropriate in the public classroom or not, reveals the underlying contempt that the elite of the liberal law establishment holds for religion. Such characterizations contribute to the further denigration of Judeo-Christian traditions in American public education.

In a federal court in Mobile, Alabama, in 1986, secular humanism was determined to be a non-theistic religious doctrine that permeated public education. The case, in which six hundred parents and teachers challenged four dozen textbooks that either ignored or distorted religion and in its place promoted varying degrees of secular humanistic philosophy, exposed the pervasiveness of secularism as a creed in America's classrooms. During the trial, witnesses, such as Catholic scholar James Hitchcock of St. Louis University and University of Virginia sociologist James Hunter, testified that secular humanism was a substitute for traditional theistic religious beliefs.

As to its pervasiveness in public education, expert testimony established that it shows up mostly in the aversion to any references to traditional religion, and in the substitution of subjective "value clarification" and the usage of jargon associated with pop humanistic psychology. One instance that was introduced into evidence was the alteration of a story by Isaac Bashevis Singer in which "Thank God" was changed to "Thank goodness" in a sixth-grade reader.

In the end, the judge hearing the case ruled in the favor of the plaintiffs, concluding that humanism was a secular religion and thus should not be taught in schools. His ruling was later reversed.

With this degree of mounting authority against the religious practices of students, parents, and teachers involved in the educational systems of this country, it is no wonder that practicing Christians feel discriminated against by the education establishment.

Sex education is another flash point in the conflagration over religious rights in schools. Over the last twenty-five years, public education has forged ahead with a huge variety of innovative, explicit, and controversial curricula having to do with human sexuality. Public school classrooms have been the locus of discussions about "deep kissing," petting, fondling, masturbation, "outer-course" (mutual masturbation), how to place a condom on an erect penis (in at least one case the information, complete with demonstration, was supplied to eighth-grade girls), contraceptives, and abortion.

A group of teachers that attended a conference on human sexuality for educators in San Francisco at taxpayer expense complained about spending "two whole days trying to get a condom on a cucumber"! In another case, a high-school health class was shown a film of a man and a woman, completely nude, having sexual intercourse. A high-school in northern California regularly invites homosexual men and women in to explain their lifestyles to students.

This bold affront to Christian beliefs about morality is bound to drive a wedge between religious families and the local school board, not to mention one between students and their teachers and the administrators. In one instance, a suburban elementary school administration held a school-wide assembly with representatives of the Red Cross and Planned Parenthood. This included a lecturer who told the students that, as they entered their teen years, they "were going to have sex," so they should learn what "safe sex" is. During a response time, when members of the audience were allowed to ask questions about safe sexual practices, a sixth-grade teacher rose and took issue with the speaker's assumption that his students were "going to have sex" as teens. "I don't know where you get your information," protested the youthful, Jewish instructor, "but you obviously don't know my students. We've discussed this thoroughly, and my students intend to exercise their self control, and wait until they're ready for marriage!" His students gave him a standing ovation. The next day, he was called into his principal's office and told, "You and I both know what you did was right, but you've also got to understand we're all under political pressure here, and so never do anything like that again!"

The kind of flagrant sexual revolutionary pressure that the school principal was referring to has become disturbingly more frequent in public education. The false consensus has led many otherwise sensible and professional educators to abandon common sense and traditional Judeo-Christian moral standards and embrace extremist positions on sexuality education that, in many instances, have been proven ineffective, even destructive.

A predominant manifestation of the sexual revolution in education is the push on the part of so-called family planning agencies for the availability of free condoms and Norplant contraceptive implants in public schools. Several school districts in the country are currently providing these contraceptive devices to students without parental knowledge or consent.

News media, talk show commentary, and the education establishment have, for the most part, backed these measures. The specter of the AIDS epidemic looms larger and larger on the horizon of the nation's schools. Sexually transmitted diseases such as syphilis, gonorrhea, herpes, chlamydia, as well as over fifty other strains, are infecting more than 33,000 a day, or twelve million new cases each year. At this rate, one out of every four Americans will become infected by a sexually transmitted disease.

Rates of teen-age pregnancy and abortions continue to

climb. According to the National Center for Health Statistics, the number of births to unmarried women hit a record high in 1990 of 1,165,384, a 7 percent increase over the previous year and an incredible 75 percent increase over the decade. These numbers translate into more than one child out of four being born to an unwed mother. A majority of these babies were born to teen-agers, most of whom are forced to drop out of school and go on welfare.

In response to these gloomy statistics, an alarm has been sounded throughout the American educational establishment. Frantic family planning agencies, school boards, administrators, and politicians rushed toward the statistics with expedient solutions. At last count, teen-agers could obtain contraceptives in more than seventy high schools nationwide. In most cases, this means condoms and Norplant implantations. Some school systems, like those found in Rochester, New York, provide prescription services for other birth control devices such as pills and diaphragms through the school health office. In Rochester, parents are not notified when a student is given such a prescription.

These extreme measures might be understandable, even to Christians who disagree with the moral message such programs send, if they were effective, but the available statistical data prove that they are not. In 1987 the National Research Council published a report called "Risking the Future: Adolescent Sexuality, Pregnancy, and Childbearing." The report advised that contraceptives and unrestricted abortions be provided to teens at low or no cost, without parental consent. It advocated condom distribution and school-based clinics to provide these services. These measures were advocated despite the report's finding a correlation between increased rates of sexual activity and provision of family planning to adolescents, along with an acknowledgment that the services themselves may be causing the increase in teen sexual activity!

With the tremendous growth and outlay of federal dollars in family planning for teens, policy-makers might expect to see a marked reduction in adolescent pregnancy and abortion. But from 1971 to 1981, where there was a 306 percent increase in federal funding for contraceptive services to teens, there was a corresponding 48.3 percent increase in teen pregnancies and a 133 percent increase in teen-age abortions.[11]

Adams City High School, near Denver, was one of the first schools in the nation to distribute condoms to students. The program proved to be a huge failure. In the three years between 1989 to 1992, the birth rate soared to 31 percent above the national average. That figure does not represent the students whose pregnancies ended by miscarriage or abortion.

Christians who raise a conscientious objection to contraceptive measures, birth control, and abortion in public education have been routinely ridiculed as being unrealistic, old-fashioned, and puritanical. When Christian parents speak up against these programs at school board meetings, they are often dismissed as religious fanatics who would endanger the safety of children in exchange for the imposition of their peculiar morality on the public schools. Branded "fundamentalists," "Moral Majority-types," and "anti-family planning" fanatics, their protestations are ignored, and the programs are adopted willy-nilly by school boards under political pressure from birth control and pro-abortion groups.

What are the implications of these programs for conscientious Christian families with students in the public schools? Imagine a religious family, whose teen-age son or daughter is enrolled in a public school. Posted on the health office door is information directing students to Planned Parenthood, which in turn will provide them with contraceptives or abortions. In a conversation with a fellow student, the Christian child is told, "You go there if you want to have sex." When the time comes, the child, who would otherwise turn to his or her parents, a teacher or counselor, to clergy or conscience, instead decides to "check out" Planned Parenthood even though he or she is conscience stricken over this.

What happens at Planned Parenthood? According to researcher Douglas Scott:

> Planned Parenthood distributes pamphlets and other materials designed for teens. It is not necessary for parents to approve of the literature before Planned Parenthood gives one to any teen.

Planned Parenthood tells teens the purpose of dating in "The Problem with Puberty." The pamphlet reads, "If you're not supposed to go after a girl for sex, what are you supposed to do?"*

The pamphlet "Choices" outlines various methods of birth control. It also states that "[y]ou can have mutual masturbation or interfemoral intercourse (penis between the legs) . . . You can have 'petting to climax' which is just fooling around until you come. Just keep the penis away from the pubis or vagina."

"The Great Orgasm Robbery" states, "Sex is fun and joyful, and courting is fun and joyful, and it comes in all types of styles, all of which are OK. Do what gives you pleasure and enjoy what gives you pleasure. Don't rob yourself of joy by focusing on old-fashioned ideas about what's 'normal' or 'nice.' Just communicate and enjoy."[12]

Endorsements of promiscuous sex like these from an agency that the child was referred to by his or her school may be too much to resist. Not only has the child been led to believe that the moral standards he has been raised with, taught in the Scriptures, and encouraged toward in church are "old-fashioned," but he has been offered the necessary equipment to embark on a sexual adventure that will, at least according to the advertisements, be fun-filled and enjoyable.

The child is encouraged in this without the parents' knowledge, permission, or counsel. In fact, the child has been deliberately steered away from parents and church because their ideals are to be considered "old-fashioned."

What is worse, some schools surreptitiously refer students for abortion. One young woman told me that when she was sixteen, she became pregnant. Her parents were, in her words, "devout Catholics," and she believed that if they

---

* The editors at Huntington House contemplated omitting this entire quote, but they decided that parents ought to have the luxury of reading what their children have already read at school (as graphic and offensive as it might be).

learned she was pregnant, "it would kill them." So she sought advice from her high-school guidance counselor. Her counselor told her that her parents needn't know about her pregnancy. "A volunteer can come to school and take you to see a doctor, who can perform an operation on you so that you won't be pregnant anymore." The news came as a great relief to the desperate girl. An arrangement was made, and a "counselor" came to school and took her, during school hours, to the abortionist.

After school, she returned home. She was feeling sick and went to bed. Her mother thought she might have the flu or a virus. Then the hemorrhaging began. Her mother and father rushed her to the emergency room at the hospital. After what seemed like an eternity, the doctor came out and told them they almost lost their daughter. "Why? What was it?" they asked in desperation. "A punctured uterus," was the doctor's reply. "You didn't know? Your daughter had an abortion!" They were horrified. Not because their daughter had committed the sin, but because their baby went through the horrid drama and nearly died without their knowledge. Her parents' response was not to throw her out of the house but to become more concerned about their daughter's well-being.

The courts and the educational establishment have given the schools license to exercise such liberties without accounting to parents. The Christian family feels threatened by these developments and rightfully so. Christian parents are traditionally family oriented and believe strongly in their exclusive right to determine what and how their children will learn. For any institution, especially the public school, to usurp that role, is a fundamental violation of the rights of families. It shatters the confidence of the American people in not only the educational establishment but also in the government that fosters it. Without this confidence both are prohibited from performing effectively and successfully for all people.

In addition to its assaults on academic freedom and family rights, public education has also violated the constitutional rights of students to freedom of speech and the free exercise of religion. These two rights, articulated in the First

Amendment, are inalienably the first rights of a free citizen in a free society. Yet the educational establishment has made them applicable only to "secular" expression.

The American Family Association Law Center filed a federal lawsuit in Jacksonville, Florida, against a school district that ordered an eleven-year-old fourth grader to remove his T-shirt because it contained a Christian message. The lawsuit alleges that the student at Green Cove Springs Elementary School near Jacksonville was denied his constitutional rights to free speech by the school district. The suit also alleges a violation of the First Amendment free exercise clause that prohibits the public school from acting in a hostile way against religion. The T-shirt contained a Christian message referring to the Gospel of John 3:14.

According to Nikolas T. Nikas, the AFA Law Center attorney who filed the suit on behalf of the student, "Students are allowed to wear the most outrageous, blasphemous, and offensive T-shirts imaginable and are not restricted in any way. However, wear a T-shirt with a Christian message to school and the full force of the state is aimed at crushing your free speech."[13]

Christian students at Massac County High School in Metropolis, Illinois, were arrested and detained by police when they gathered after school hours around the flag pole to pray for their nation, their families, and their school officials. Administrators pushed the "separationist" panic button, believing the false consensus that a prayer event on public property is felonious. The school board ultimately issued an apology to the students and their families, but the very fact that the incident occurred in the first place demonstrates the inherent hostility toward religious faith that the secularist agenda has inculcated in American education.

In Las Vegas, Nevada, school officials told an elementary school student she could not sing "The First Noel" at the school's winter concert because the song was "religious."

A Florida high school student was suspended for ten days for distributing Christian literature at school. A Kentucky high-school canceled its graduation ceremony rather than risk violating the "separation of church and state." Students in Reno, Nevada, were told they could not pray at their own graduation. An eighth-grade student in South Carolina was told by the principal she and other students could not hold a Bible club on school property. A student in Jefferson County, Kentucky, drew a cross as part of his depiction of "What Easter means to me." The school refused to display the rendering along with the other students' posters because of its "religious theme."

This kind of discrimination is unconscionable and deplorable in a nation that was founded on freedom and esteem for religious faith and practice. The secularist elite, aided and abetted by the educational establishment, have launched an all-out war on faith, and the ultimate loser will be all of the citizens of this great country, the vast majority of whom, whether black or white, male or female, whether of one ethnic heritage or another, are believers in, and worshipers of, God.

EIGHT

Five Steps to Disaster

While the Jews under Hitler and the Christians under communism suffered their persecutions for different, even opposite, ideological reasons, there were certain critical elements that paved the way for the two holocausts that were ominously similar. Hitler had heaped on the Jews the blame for German woes, accusing them of dominating the European economic world and dissipating Aryan ingenuity. Hitler believed that if the Jews were eradicated from the world, it would pave the way for the ascent of the Aryan race that would ultimately redeem the world. Of course, he would be the leader of that "superior" race, and thus the Jews stood in his way, becoming his personal nemesis. Therefore, the Fuhrer himself had to design the Jews' destruction and see to it that it was carried out.

The Communist persecution of the church was somewhat more complex. Rooted in a Marxist philosophical disdain for religion, which Marx viewed as a tool of bourgeois oppression, Communist persecution was implemented as a program to "liberate" humanity from ancient bondage. In the words of one Russian public school textbook, "Religion is a fantastic and perverse reflection of the world in man's consciousness. . . . Religion has become the medium for the spiritual enslavement of the masses."[1]

It soon became apparent that religion was not going to go away easily. Religious faith was deeply rooted in the hearts and souls of the people. Rather than being a source of sinister oppression, religion was a source of spiritual strength and comfort for those under Soviet domination. As a result, the Soviet government had to devise ways to forcibly eradicate religious faith in order to complete the revolution.

The Communists found their most tenacious opponents in the "sectarians" (Baptists, Evangelicals, Pentecostals, and Adventists) and Roman Catholics. The Orthodox Christians, and particularly the priests, also firmly resisted the purgation of religion from Soviet life. Millions of individual Christians and thousands of clergy suffered fines, internal exile, imprisonment, internment in labor camps, and even death for resisting Communist atheism in those years.

The Communist persecution of Christians took a more subtle and sophisticated turn after World War II. Before the war, Soviet anti-religious propaganda openly denounced the church, called for the eradication of Christianity and other religions, and threatened individual church leaders with arrest, imprisonment, deportations, and exile. But Christians had proved loyal soldiers and comrades during the war. Because of this, after the war the campaign against religious faith avoided attacking Christianity and Christian leaders directly. Instead, propagandists adopted a tactic of positively asserting atheism. The primary conduit of atheistic propaganda was science and public education, as well as popularly published anti-religious articles, pamphlets, cartoons, and films that continued to employ malicious pre-war stereotypes that defamed believers.

Khrushchev issued a report in 1958 on education reform that called for the development of a materialistic world view in youth. Although the document did not specifically attack religion, it was implied that the development of a materialistic world view among students meant that education would become the subtle tool of atheism and anti-religious propaganda.

Scientists and educators produced an endless supply of articles advancing atheism and denouncing religious faith between 1958 and 1985. Conferences were also convened on the critical cooperation between science and atheism. Journals, periodicals, newspaper articles, and public school curricula reflected the "conflict" between faith and science, emphasizing the superior intelligence of the materialistic world view and relegating the religious to one of ignorant superstition.

This period emphasized Darwinian evolution in order to counter religious ideas about origins and provide a platform for the advancement of anti-religious naturalism.

These innovations proved to be too subtle for the average citizen. *Pravda* warned that "religious prejudices" would not evaporate overnight simply because the roots of religious faith had been eliminated. It would require "daily efforts" to overcome them. The daily efforts would include scandalous, libelous assaults on clergy, especially activists; the mocking and derision of religious beliefs in the classroom, and defamatory cartoons and editorials in publications.

According to Dimitry V. Pospielovsky, professor of modern European and Russian History at the University of Western Ontario:

> Communist party cells at places of work or study, similar Komsomol branches, local sections of the Znanie (scientific) society, and trade-union branches appointed atheist members as personal tutors in atheism to known religious believers, in most cases workmates. They visited these believers at their homes and tried to convince them. If this did not work, they would bring it to the attention of their union or professional collectives, and these cases of "religious backwardness" or "obstinacy" were aired at public meetings. Should all these efforts prove fruitless, then followed the administrative harassment at work or school, usually culminating in lower-paid jobs, blocking of promotion, or expulsion from college if the believer was a student. The physical harassment of believing school children by their teachers was also common. There was a concerted campaign in the early 1960s to induce priests and theologians to defect to the atheist camp; this reaped a harvest of over 200 such defectors, including two theology professors, one priest, and one layman. These efforts, however, were soon abandoned after it was realized that the defections and their loud publicity had little effect on believers.[2]

The publication of editorial cartoons, especially in scientific journals, lampooned religious beliefs. Examples include depictions of Jesus and the disciples at the Last Supper playing cards; Jesus, wearing a crown of thorns, carrying his cross to the crucifixion and yelling "Porter!"; a parish priest greeting an unemployed man and holding forth a crucifix saying, "Are you unemployed? Well, pray to God, this will be your work."[3]

In addition, monasteries and convents, which served as essential spiritual centers for the Orthodox Christians of the Soviet Union, were subjected to official sanctions and forcibly consolidated and closed.

> To justify this process, it was accompanied by a massive anti-monastic campaign in the press, where monasteries were depicted as parasitic institutions, with fields and gardens tilled by exploited peasants while the monks and nuns were enjoying the proceeds. Monasteries were accused of black market operations, monastics of lechery with nuns and female pilgrims, and of drunkenness. Monastic administrators were accused of collaboration with the enemy during the war.[4]

> Articles inciting contempt and hatred for believers appeared in ever-growing numbers in the . . . Soviet press between 1959 and 1964 in particular, under such derogatory titles as "The Howls of the Obscurantists," "The Vultures," "The Wolfish Fangs of God's Harmless Creatures," "Swindlers in the Guise of Holy Fathers," "A Theologian Formenter," "Hysteria on the March." Believers were called "toadstools," "swindlers," "a hoard," "anti-Soviet sub-humans," "wicked enemy of all that lives," "the rot."[5]

> . . . The general attack on religion slanders the clergy and believing laity as lechers, drunks and parasites. . . . The lechery, luxury, pilfering, and accusations of materialistic greed are constantly repeated clichés in all such writings.

> . . . Assorted articles began to attack pilgrims and pilgrimages as charlatanism, clerical swindles to ex-

tract donations, distraction of people from socially useful work. . . . Among these one of the most vicious was Trubnikova's "Hysteria on the March," an ugly caricature of the traditional, centuries-old pilgrimage to an allegedly miraculous spring in a Kirov Diocese village, Velikoretskoe. . . . Trubnikova participated in the pilgrimage disguised as a humble pilgrim, spying on the genuine ones and depicting them as alcoholics, hysterical women falling into trances, hypocrites, and swindlers who simulate trances or disguise healthy persons as invalids, who after a dip in the spring shed their crutches and pretend to have received a sudden cure. . . . For Trubnikova, they are "a savage horde." The story ends with alleged robberies among the pilgrims, wild sexual orgies in cemetery woods, and a drunken murder.

In Trubnikova's writings we see the revival of the old Marxist-Leninist identification of religion with alcohol, crime, mental abnormality, and disease. Trubnikova was not an exception among anti-religious Soviet authors in this respect. . . . Countless articles appeared claiming that the rites of all religious faiths disseminated disease.

It is not objectivity and truth that the authors are after. Their purpose is to build up an image of believers, commonly called for the purpose "religious fanatics," disseminators of epidemics, social pests, or criminals, in order to justify their persecution to the public and to get approval for the destruction of pilgrimage centres, churches and monasteries.[6]

There is currently no American equivalent to the Communist conspiracy in the old Soviet Union. There, the Marxist atheists had exclusive political control, not only over the government and law enforcement agencies but also over the media, education, and the courts. Indeed, only Communists were permitted into any of these institutions, at least at the higher levels. Technically, politically, legally, the door remains open in America for Christians to participate in their government, in education, and in the media.

We have thus far, however, considered some of the ominous trends in the American cultural establishment as they impinge upon conscientious Christians who publicly practice their faith. These trends emerge from an underlying consensus, rather than conspiracy, and serve as harbingers of a potential persecution of Christians that may result from the growing intolerance toward the public practice of religious faith in secularist society. In order to understand the consequences of anti-Christian bias in the popular culture, we must consider the steps that have ultimately led to persecution at other times and in other places. These steps will be helpful in determining what the eventual outcome of the contemporary maltreatment of believers might be.

I have identified five steps that ultimately lead to all-out persecution. These five steps are identifiable in the notorious Nazi persecutions of the Jews and the Communist persecution of Christians. They are really universal—not confined to any specific time period or place—but appear in some form wherever persecutions have taken place.

Persecuting people is not an easy undertaking, as the Communists discovered. In spite of widespread indifference, which seems to be at epidemic levels in modern America, a significant proportion of the population still has a propensity to support the underdog. Our compassion as people and our Judeo-Christian "memory," as Francis Schaeffer called it, instills in us the ideal of the Good Samaritan. When we come across an opportunity to perform the civic and humane responsibility of the Samaritan, and we fail to follow through, due to fear or selfishness or some other reason, we're nagged by a conscience formed in part by the memory of the Judeo-Christian ethic, and we wind up feeling lousy because we know we should have "done something" better.

Since this is the case, and we don't normally abuse our neighbors, nor for that matter our fellow citizens, and we generally believe we should treat people kindly and fairly, getting to the stage of persecuting them would seem almost impossible, if for no other reason, because of our inertia, our lack of personal motivation to do so. After all, persecuting is not only unpleasant, it is, judging from the great persecutions of the past and the persecutions that go on in other places, an enormous amount of work. Just thinking about the logistics involved makes your head spin. So, even if one is utterly indifferent (which is quite likely the case in our age of self-centeredness), persecuting others is probably too big of a task, even for them.

So then, how does persecution occur?

While it may be too difficult for many, it is too easy for some. And that is just the problem. Widespread indifference has been taken as an invitation and as tacit permission to persecute by those whose ends it would serve. Inevitably, persecution has to do with power. Those who strive for power and control become sorely tempted to use "every available means" to secure their positions and suppress their opposition. This has been done since the dawn of civilization and before. It has occurred in virtually every imaginable context: between individuals, within tribes and nations and cultures. Persecution has occurred within generations, ethnic groups, ideologies and religions, and especially political rivals.

The first step in the progression toward the persecution of persons is identification. The second is marginalization; the third, vilification; the fourth, criminalization; and, finally, persecution. First, we will review each of these steps in detail. Then we will consider the ramifications of them at work in contemporary, secularist American culture.

The twisted, evil road to persecution begins with the identification of the persons or people that are targeted for the assault. The dictionary defines the term *to persecute* as "to harass in a manner designed to injure, grieve or afflict; specifically, to cause to suffer because of belief," and *persecution* is defined as "the act or practice of persecuting, especially those who differ in origin, religion or social outlook."[7]

Persecution, then, is composed of malicious acts perpetrated against people who are of a different belief, religion, or "social outlook," in a word, those who *differ* culturally from their persecutors. The persecutors exaggerate the characteristics that distinguish the persecuted from other members of the community. When people are being discriminated against, it is often personal traits—such as skin color, facial characteristics, economic status, cultural expression, or other distinguishing features—that are typically exaggerated and lampooned, thus creating a stereotype.

Stereotype has been defined as "a preconceived (i.e., not based on experience), standardized, group-shared idea about the alleged essential nature of those making up a whole category of persons, the most significant of such group-shared ideals being without regard to individual differences among those making up the category and being an emotion-charged, negative evaluation (but note that stereotypes are not invariably negative—e.g., that of the medical doctor.)"

Furthermore, "stereotypes often represent institutionalized misinformation, distorted information, and caricatured ideas of places, peoples, and things; and . . . stereotypes have profound influence on the formation of attitudes pertaining to these areas of experience."[8]

The stereotype is an easy subject of bigotry and a target of abuse. It is not a real person. It is a caricature, a cartoon. This is precisely why a member of a persecuted political, racial, ethnic, or religious group often reports hearing, "You're not like other _____s" or "I have a _____ friend, and he's not at all like all the other _____s." The image in that person's mind is not of real people who share those characteristics but of malignant cartoons, false images drawn up by bigots as clay targets of their prejudices.

According to *The Baker Encyclopedia of Psychology*:

> Psychologists have maintained that even though stereotypes may have a kernel of truth, they often produce a number of negative consequences. First, they result in an overestimation of differences between groups. Although the beliefs, values, and other characteristics of groups may be similar, stereotypes may result in those groups being viewed as vastly different. Second, stereotyping may result in an underestimation of the variations within groups. Individuals are prejudged on the basis of their category membership, and a large number of distinguishable persons may be treated as equivalent. Third, stereotypes typically have not only descriptive but evaluative content. They are . . . judgments by which members of their groups are evaluated on the basis of local

standards. As negative generalizations, stereotypes may be used as a justification for hostility and oppression, thereby providing a major mechanism by which prejudice is sustained.[9]

According to the *Encyclopedia of Psychology*,

Donald T. Campbell (1965) pointed out that the most pernicious fault with stereotypes lies not so much in their fallacious elements, as in the causal explanation we make for an inadequacy on the basis of a stereotype—for example that X's are "lazy." Thus, if X's are poor employees because they have not been properly trained, one can arrange to train them, but if they are "lazy," nothing can be done.

Another danger inherent in stereotypes lies in the human tendency to use them as "self-fulfilling prophecies." If we believe, stereotypically, that X's are inadequate or lazy, our interactions with them will take the form of "scenarios," "scripted" to entice them into actions that are likely to cause them to fail and that thus will "prove" the validity of our stereotypes.[10]

For Americans of African descent, stereotypes were promoted by slaveholders to suppress slaves and their natural inclination toward freedom, by segregationists to bolster a platform of racial separation and privilege, by racists to support their contention of supremacy, and by the entertainment industry to play off popular fears and prejudices. Even today, stereotypes of persons of color still prevail—especially those of urban blacks as drug dealers and pimps, gang members and "homeboys," and talented singers, dancers, and athletes. This is the way African-Americans are still viewed by a large segment of Americans of European descent, although these "typical" media images represent only a small percentage of the African-American population.

Anti-Semitic images proliferated in the first half of the twentieth century, but in part as a result of the work of organizations such as the anti-defamation League of B'nai B'rith, those stereotypes were exposed and thus declined considerably in the last fifty years. Regretfully, anti-Semitic acts of vandalism and violence are currently on the rise again in many American cities. The defamatory caricature of the Jew as an avaricious, scheming, unscrupulous profiteer is still prevalent in many places.

The prevalence of stereotype rises during times of national stress, such as economic hard times, war, and cultural upheaval. People use stereotypes to conveniently identify somebody on which to place the blame for the current troubles that defy solutions. This then grows into a community-wide usage of stereotype. Eventually, the members of a society identify and isolate other members—and the employment of exaggerated images and misrepresentations makes it easy to assign blame without proving the claims against the accused. Communities sometimes stereotype each other, exacerbating even further the rifts between people of different races or cultures.

In the case of Christians, it is their beliefs, their moral standards, ritual expressions, and practices, rather than physical characteristics, that distinguish them from nominal, non-religious, irreligious, secular, and atheistic members of the community. This is not to infer that members of other faiths should be regarded as "non-religious." It is, rather, the degree of conscientiousness and fervency with which many Catholics, evangelical, and fundamental Christians express their faith that sets them apart in a given community.

Christian emphasis on personal morality—such as modesty in style, chastity before marriage, disapprobation of divorce, delight in large families, sexual restraint, disapproval of habits such as drinking alcoholic beverages and smoking, discrimination in entertainment, and opposition to some forms of birth control and to abortion and homosexuality—has made these distinguishing characteristics the target of stereotyping. Christian practices associated with their moral conservatism are exaggerated and made to look ridiculous, impractical, and oppressive. Christian emphasis on family life is twisted and turned into a dangerous form of bondage, contributing to wife-beating, child abuse, incest, denial of children's rights, and to gay-bashing. In the end, the Christian esteem for sexual fidelity and for family is blamed for all manner of evil in the world, including oppression, discrimination, over-population, pollution, the destruction of the ozone layer, and global warming!

The fact that conscientious Christians worship a transcendent and personal Creator-God is enough to separate them from the members of the cultural establishment that subscribe to the false consensus and specialize in the doctrines of Darwinism and evolution. As we have seen, the creationist views of Bible-believing Christians have marked them in the eyes of many of the members of the academic elite as ignorant, uneducated, superstitious, and unscientific.

Christians believe that God has communicated to human beings in written form and that he is a universal potentate that has imposed a moral law on creation, to which he requires obedience. This conviction has delineated between the immutable moral law that governs the believer and the mutable laws of man. In the quest for total personal liberation, secularism has denied the existence of a transcendent moral or natural law that supersedes human legislative prerogatives. The result has been an isolation of the follower of Divine Torah from the liberal law establishment that does not recognize any "higher law" than that which is created in the legislative process.

Christians believe that they have an obligation and a duty to proclaim and spread the gospel and to work toward the conversion of their neighbors. This mandate distinguishes them from the militant separationists who fear any form of proselytizing in the public square and would deny publicly owned and supported forums to any person or group that would engage in such "offensive" activity. Assertive religious expression has been taken as a threat to a religiously "neutral" society. It must be contained, restricted, and controlled.

The moral standards that Christians believe ought to be practiced, not only by themselves, but by everybody else, standards that impinge on the most private aspects of human life, specifically human sexuality, offend the hedonism so widely embraced and practiced by the Hollywood elite. In an attempt to negate the power of the message of moral purity preached by Christians, Hollywood has maligned and libled the message and the messenger.

That Christians perpetuate the "neurosis" that is endemic in religious belief separates them from the followers of Freud.

Unfortunately, the stereotype of Christians is in large part an invention of the contemporary media, which has declared itself the ideological and pragmatic opponent of traditional religion. It is a travesty of the modern age of technology and communications that the broadcast and entertainment industries, namely music, television, and films, have fostered Christian stereotypes in their numerous slanderous depictions of people of faith.

According to the PBS film critic Michael Medved: "In the ongoing war on traditional values, the assault on organized faith represents the front to which the entertainment industry has most clearly committed itself."[11]

The entertainment/news establishment has popularized a stereotype of Christians that has been promulgated by the educational establishment, which in turn has been influenced by the anti-religious sentiments of Enlightenment philosophers, the nihilists, existentialists, materialists, and Marxist-Leninists. In addition, the Freudian theory of religion as neurosis has fueled the propaganda that depicts Christians as intellectually deficient and mentally impaired.

The negative stereotype of the conscientious Christian then has identified him as abnormal and has instilled in the community a suspicion about him. He is unusual enough not to be trusted, because his religious faith could be a cover-up for immoral, criminal, even deadly aspirations or activities. His presumed hypocrisy is repulsive, making him even more undesirable as a friend or neighbor. Even if he himself is assumed relatively harmless, his religious leaders are scoundrels and charlatans, who may very well use him as a dupe to prey on his friends and neighbors. His unrealistic and uncompromising moralizing makes him an impediment to social progress and contributes to the spread of sexually transmitted diseases, unwanted pregnancies, and perpetuates the threat of the deadly AIDS virus. His misguided ethical standards would deny the compassionate assistance of physicians in the suicides of their terminally ill patients, thus multiplying their suffering in their final days and denying them the dignity of a "good death." Furthermore, he would prohibit scientific experimentation on unborn children, thus preventing the victims of Alzheimer's and Parkinson's diseases from being cured. He demands control over women's most private decisions regarding reproduction and denies equality to them and happiness to homosexuals.

In a modern and "enlightened" society that is striving to liberate everybody to the maximum of personal freedom and autonomy, the conscientious Christian is a throwback to an old order that enslaved women and children and discriminated against people on the basis of their "sexual orientation."

The second step, then, on the way to persecution, is the effective marginalization of the stereotyped group. One of the first anti-Jewish laws of Nazi Germany expelled Jews from government positions and denied them civil service jobs. A Jew could not be a member of the party. And once the party was in power, one had to be a member of it to participate in government. The same conditions were imposed upon Christians in Communist countries. As we have already seen, communism in the Soviet Union insisted on atheism. A Christian is, by definition, not an atheist. The Christian's belief in God, the supernatural, and a law higher than Marxist-Leninism prevented him from being a Communist. Only Communists could participate in government and enjoy any place of influence in the community. Under communism Christians were often denied higher education and gainful employment and were always denied any civil service other than the military. Although the opportunity to participate in government still exists for the Christian in America, the secularist-New Left coalition, aided by the entertainment/news media, academia, and the liberal legal establishment, is postulating a position that would effectively try to deny Christians a place of influence that would lead to participation in governing.

The *New York Times* columnist Anna Quindlen expressed the concern of the false consensus that traditional Christians stay out of the arena of public policy when she attacked John Cardinal O'Conner for endorsing the ouster of the controversial New York Public Schools chancellor, Joseph Fernandez.

"The cardinal succeeded in doing what he has done consistently since he became the head of the New York archdiocese—he blurred the lines between politics and religion, church and state," Quindlen wrote.

This is a sentiment widely felt among the cultural elite. According to the false consensus, the "separation of church and state" means the exclusion of Christians from not merely influencing public policy but even from commenting on it!

By pushing Christians to the margins and out of the mainstream of the culture and the community, the false consensus makes them vulnerable to further prejudice, discrimination, and persecution. A recent public television documentary on the Holocaust stated that the evidence proves that the German people were unequivocally aware of the existence of the more than three hundred concentration, slave-labor, and extermination camps. But they simply "didn't care." They didn't care because German anti-Semitism had effectively pushed the Jews to the margins. In the margins, they were the easy targets of bigots and hatemongers, and, eventually, of their persecutors.

The use of derogatory imagery in news reporting and editorializing further stigmatizes religious believers and, especially, practicing Christians. Two recent syndicated editorial cartoons crossed the line of legitimate criticism when they employed ugly and malicious depictions of religionists.

MacNelly of the *Chicago Tribune* published a cartoon, carried in major American newspapers, that contained seven crazed, sinister-looking vultures perched on a gnarled tree branch leering down at unseen prey. Each vulture is called by a particular religion: Islam, Christian, Hindu, Sikh, Jewish, Protestant, and Catholic, followed by the word *loonies*. Together the scavengers shriek, "LET US PREY!"

More pernicious prejudice is exhibited in a Universal Press Syndicate cartoon by the ubiquitous Pat Oliphant. In a caricature horribly reminiscent of Nazi propaganda portrayals of Jews as vermin, Christians are depicted as sewer rats, viciously dragging the G.O.P. elephant into an infested storefront. Hanging over the door is a shingle bearing a cross with the words "Jesus Saves" and "Fundamentalist Christian Mission."

These illustrate the third step on the road to persecution: the vilification of the victims. A whole group, on the basis of their beliefs, and practices, are made out to be villains, and uncivilized, dangerous miscreants who, if unchecked, will pose a serious threat to the rest of the community. According to Pospielovsky, at the height of the post–World War II Soviet anti-religious campaign, the Soviet press continuously accused "the believers of duplicity and hypocrisy, blaming their behavior on religious teaching." Nazi anti-Jewish propaganda depicted Jews as vermin, as sleazy, grimy, salacious types unscrupulously seeking out illicit profits.

Recent studies of the holocaust of the Jews have begun to focus not on the deranged, anti-Semitic obsessions of the upper echelon of Nazi leadership but rather on the normal, "healthy" majority of Europeans who allowed the round-ups of their neighbors and fellow countrymen, who permitted the train transports to proceed uninterrupted and excused the gas chambers and crematoria, claiming ignorance or helplessness.

These studies have concluded that the horror and devastation of the Holocaust could not have occurred without the tacit complicity of innumerable citizens who were not depraved, homicidal mass-murderers but only indifferent and ignorant. They either did not care to know, or simply did not care, about what was happening to the Jews.

The reasons given by the historians, sociologists, and psychologists for the persecution and genocide of the Jews are numerous. But one thing is common to most of the theories. The Jews of Europe had been victimized by prejudice, having been made the scapegoats of a nation that had suffered a humiliating defeat in World War I, had more recently endured a severe economic depression, and that was experiencing uncertainty about its government and fear of a Bolshevik revolution.

At the vortex of this national tumult in Germany was the Jew. The Jews of pre-Nazi Germany amounted to less than 1 percent of the total population. Yet, in spite of their small numbers, they had achieved a level of visibility and notoriety in business, professions, and politics. Jews comprised about

25 percent of the work force in retail dry goods. They owned 20 percent of the banks and held 80 percent of the top positions in the stock exchange. A huge percentage of the doctors, lawyers, journalists, and professors were Jewish, ranging between 10 and 25 percent. And 10 percent of the Marxist Social Democratic party, the largest party in the Reichstag, were Jews.

For a generation, German Jews had enjoyed religious and political freedom in Germany, including the right to vote and to participate in government. It was the extent of freedom accorded the Jews at the turn of the century that attracted large numbers of eastern European Jews, many fleeing pogroms, to Germany. It was this freedom that allowed them to play a significant role in German politics and culture.

The smoldering embers of anti-Semitism had been burning, however, for fifty years in the German states. Anti-Semitic propaganda had circulated for more than thirty years, but it was to take on new dimensions after the signing of the Treaty of Versailles, which dictated the terms of the armistice to the battered and vanquished nation. Once the dominant military power of Europe, the country was forced to divest itself of most of its weaponry, including all of its offensive systems. In addition, it was forced to cede land to its former enemies and to pay an unrealistically huge amount of gold for reparations.

The result was a severe strain on Germany's economy. To pay back the bonds that had been sold to finance the war, more and more money was printed, causing a vast devaluation of the mark and skyrocketing inflation.

Germans began blaming the governing party, the Social Democrats, and, in particular, its more "visible" Jewish members, for treachery and conspiracy with, variously, socialists and capitalists. Jews, already stereotyped by anti-Semitic propaganda, were increasingly being held culpable for Germany's economic woes. Vilified in popular propaganda as subversive, they were set up for their subsequent persecution.

So effective was the propaganda that, in the wake of Kristallnacht, the night of violence perpetrated by the newly dominant Nazi party, "neither the leaders of the Christian churches nor the generals nor any other representatives of the 'good Germany' spoke out at once in open protest."[12]

These images, which in both the Communist and Nazi cases led to indifference toward and prejudice against Christian and Jewish believers, were ultimately instrumental in creating a cultural context tolerant of vicious and genocidal persecution. The vilification of conscientious, practicing religionists, and especially traditional Christians, threatens a similarly grave eventuality in a secularized state increasingly intolerant of religious dissent.

Something ominously similar to this is beginning to shape up on the shores of secular America. As the secularist-New Left-sexual revolutionaries grasp power, they're using "every available means" to silence the opposition. The most aggressive play yet has been Hollywood as the most significant tool of propaganda for the anti-religionists of the secularist-New Left coalition.

"Infotainment" shows, talk shows, and television magazines have been a relentless and unrepentant source of propaganda presenting conscientious believers as villains. In March 1993 virtually all the major network news programs, newspapers, magazines, and talk shows focused on what was, for the false consensus, a trilogy of evil religious fanaticism: the murder of Dr. David Gunn, the bombing of the Twin Trade Towers by an obscure group of Islamic extremists, and the fifty-one day stand-off mass suicide of the Branch Davidians in Waco, Texas. There is no question that these dramatic events were newsworthy and that the news reporting, with the exception of the Gunn murder, was relatively fair. However, the accretionary effect of the detailed reporting of such dramatic aberrations with the more subtle, year-round deprecation of believers is an unmistakable image of deeply religious persons as villains.

The relegation of Christian faith to the category of ignorant, unscientific superstition further depicts Christians as intellectual robber barons who would stealthily convert American children by taking over the nation's schools. In contrast to "supernaturalism, mysticism, and miraculism," declared the National Council of Teachers of English, "Humanism offers the reasoned view that human beings alone shape their destinies, leaving to scientific inquiry the probing of nature's unknowns." The opposite of reasoned? Unreasoned (unreasonable). Some synonyms for unreasonable? absurd; crackbrained; crackpot; extreme; immoderate; inappropriate; insane; irrational; perverse; radical; rabid; rash.

The second to the last was the choice of one officer of the court. Arguing on behalf of the New York attorney general against a tiny group of pro-life pickets consisting of two women, an African-American minister, and two Jews, the attorney described the Christians as "rabid."

"These people, Your Honor," he told the federal judge hearing the motion ". . . are rabid Christians." Some synonyms of *rabid*? Fanatical; fierce; furious; insane; raging; rampant; virulent; violent. The secularist propaganda has had a promotive effect on anti-Christian bigotry, advancing the misconception that serious religionists should be widely suspected of villainy.

The fourth step is the criminalization of religious practices. The increasingly widespread judicial restrictions on religious rites, including public preaching, prayers, litanies and liturgy, hymn singing, caroling, and colportage, are a precursor to more permanent legislation that would restrict and even ban worship and evangelism. Thus far, as was the case with communism in the old Soviet Union, legislation restricting religious practices has been confined mostly to matters of policy, such as in education, taxation, and protest. Bureaucrats and judges have for the most part been responsible for imposing restrictive policies on Christians.

Elected officials, especially legislators, are too much aware of the important place religious faith holds for the American voter to do as New York Attorney General Abrams has done, and that is to state that religion "serves the community only in the eyes of its adherents" and that it yields no benefits for anybody other than the believers. It should be noted that there is a statute in New York criminalizing public behaviors that are "offensive" and "serve no redeeming public purpose." While New York's courts have permitted women to bare their breasts on public lands, the attorney general would criminalize the display of a film on Christian parenting!

The fifth and final stage is the persecution of the be-

liever. Persecution entails officially sanctioned actions employed against religious believers and includes harassment,
the denial of civil and constitutional rights, false accusations,
arrests and detention, intimidation, imprisonment, torture,
and death. The Jewish and other victims of the Nazi Holocaust and the Christians under communism suffered these
lengths. Their eventual exterminations, however, were not
implemented overnight. This is never the case. Despite the
essentially sinful nature of man—as the rabbis call it in Hebrew, the *yetzer ha ra*, the "bent towards evil"—modern human society is not ready instantaneously to countenance the
mass mistreatment of even its most ignoble members. This
takes time and requires a slow, deliberate, incremental isolation of the victims.

We see this process as we review the steps that led to the
genocide of the Jews. The German culture was world renowned for its intellectual, artistic, and religious achieve-
ments. Although Germanic lands were host to centuries-old
anti-Semitism, by the time of the Weimar republic, Jews held
prominent places and played strategic roles in the professions of law, medicine, and the arts and were well represented in government. German Jewish culture flourished
and was the dominant expression of Judaism in the West.
Yet, by slowly fanning the anti-Semitic embers and fueling
bigotry and prejudice through the deliberate use of defamatory stereotype, Jews were separated from the so-called Aryan
Germans. The vilification of the Jews granted the Nazis
permission to begin enacting laws depriving Jews of citizenship and restricting their participation, even their residing,
in the community. By the time they were being forcefully
deported to the camps, few Germans, comparatively, cared
enough to protest. The Jews were no longer considered
productive members of German society, and therefore their
fate was of no concern to the average German.

Jews and Christians shared about equally in the sufferings under the Nazis and the Communists, respectively, but
in opposite proportion. The Jews formed the main target of
the Nazis, but many Christians were persecuted by Hitler as
well; the Christians formed the main target of the Communists, while many Jews and Moslems suffered also. The "sepa-

ration of church and state" as it was referred to in the old
Soviet system, was originally conceived of by Lenin to secure
a secular state for the advancement of Communist ideals.
Many Christians testify that under Lenin they enjoyed relative religious freedom. Yet over the course of time, the
forced imposition of atheism was seen by the Communists as
essential if they would see progress toward a complete Communist state. Christianity, as with all religion, was considered
the antithesis of communism and therefore had to be stamped
out. "Religious prejudices" crippled the Soviet peoples, and
it was the job of all conscientious Soviet citizens to eradicate
those primitive prejudices.

As a result of this, the church was identified as anti-social
(and anti-Socialist) in propaganda inspired, but not necessarily always approved of, by the governmental authorities. In
contrast to popular belief, the Soviet constitution always
guaranteed religious freedom. It was the public practice of
religious faith that met with increasing opposition. This was
especially true of any effort to evangelize or convert others,
which met with particularly severe punishment.

I am not suggesting that anything close to the Nazi ideological dominance over Germany in the 1930s and 1940s,
nor the political and social monopoly of the Communists in
the old Soviet Union, exists in America today. Rather, I hope
to send the opposite message: That the political and religious freedom of the United States today affords the Church,
and all conscientious citizens, the opportunity, indeed the
imperative, to confront malicious anti-religious bigotry and
prejudice before it leads to persecution, and to restore the
respect, deference, and dignity that America has historically
given to the worship of Almighty God.

NINE

Securing the Sacred

———————— | ————————

Just after Rebecca and I were married, we moved into a rather ramshackle apartment. It was located in an all-white enclave of second generation immigrant European families in a fusty old section of Buffalo called Riverside. Our first house guests were a black Canadian minister, his Caucasian wife, and their three children. We had no sooner said farewell to them as they left for Toronto when a knock came on the door. It was just a moment after their departure, so I assumed they had returned for something they had left behind. But to my surprise, when I opened the door, our landlord and his sister were standing in the stairwell.

"Who were those people?" she asked.

"Friends, a colleague in ministry," I replied.

Then she blurted out, "Colored people haven't darkened the door of this house in sixty years!"

"Years ago, the neighbors' cross the street had some colored move in. It wasn't long before they burned the house down," he added.

I stood there incredulous and speechless, frustrated with myself for not being able to come up with a quick rejoinder. As I stared at the two of them, wondering what to say, they then informed me, "You've got thirty days to pack your things and get out. Find yourselves another place." Then they turned on their heels and left.

Neither my wife nor I had ever had a confrontation with such blatant racial prejudice and discrimination. We were bewildered as to where we would go (and we had very little financial resources since I was working for a small Christian ministry at the time), but we both agreed that we didn't want to stay in that kind of environment. Yet we believed we had to fight our eviction, hoping to bring our landlords out of the past and into reality.

We appealed to the municipal housing authority and won a terribly uncomfortable thirty-day extension. Because we were unfamiliar with civil rights litigation at the time, however, we decided to drop any further proceedings.

Christians are not the only victims of bigotry, defamation, and discrimination in America; regrettably, Christians too often are the perpetrators of it. Nor are they the only ones whose views have been censored and suppressed. Throughout our nation's history blacks, women, immigrants, and innumerable other religious and socially active groups have been denied the unrestricted freedoms guaranteed by the Bill of Rights, sometimes by people who appear very religious.

On the other hand, the twentieth century has been witness to the emancipation of many such groups. The first half of the twentieth century saw major strides in the conferral of civil liberties to African-Americans, including the outlawing of Jim Crow laws and segregation. It also saw the implementation of voting rights and civil rights acts. Women received the right to vote, and significant progress was made in granting women equal opportunity in government and business. Minorities no longer were barred from meaningful roles in government or commerce. However, these accomplishments were tempered by the continuing reality that prejudice and discrimination still lingered, affecting many individuals in their pursuit of social and economic justice.

It cannot be denied that the advances in civil rights in the twentieth century were due, to a great extent, to the conscientious efforts of religious people. In particular, Christians had been protesting against moral evil for more than one hundred years. The abolition of slavery in America came about in large part because of the incessant protestations of Christians. These men and women were deeply committed to the belief that slavery, as it was practiced in the eighteenth and nineteenth centuries, was a terrible sin for which God would judge the nation. Christians vigorously preached, published, and protested against the institution of slavery. At times, radical Christians like William Lloyd Garrison and Theodore Weld upset the majority of churchgoers with their uncompromising assault on this sinful institution. Brave men such as Garrison and Weld were often denounced in the pulpit, maligned in the press, charged in the courts, harassed, jailed, stoned, and sometimes killed for their relentless pursuit of righteousness.

Anabaptism,[1] evangelicalism, and revivalism were particularly associated with the abolitionist cause. Famous Christians like the evangelist Charles Grandison Finney and the novelist Harriet Beecher Stowe maintained that it was not possible to be a true Christian and to endorse slavery. Sojourner Truth, an emancipated slave from New York, became a renowned prophetess as she "traveled up an' down the land, showin' the people their sins and bein' a sign unto them." In the end, this minority of conscientious Christians saw their labors and sufferings vindicated when slavery was abolished by Abraham Lincoln and the Fourteenth Amendment was passed.

The abolitionist movement was fertile soil for Christians committed to the dignity and equality of all people created in the image of God. Abolitionist women, like the Grimke sisters, insisted on not only emancipating blacks but women too. The Quakers Lucretia Mott and Susan B. Anthony were also associated with both the abolitionist and women's rights movements. The famous women's rights leader, Lucy Stone, attended Oberlin College where Finney was president. Oberlin was the first college in the United States to admit women. There she became acquainted with Antoinette Brown, the first ordained woman minister in America.[2]

These forbearers of equal rights were inseparably linked to the evangelical and pietistic movements.[3] Their testimony of faith demonstrates that commitment to biblical Christianity is not equivalent to racism or sexism. Rather, the opposite is true. The abolitionists and suffragists drew their philosophy from the Scriptures. In the Bible they saw that there is neither "slave nor free, male nor female; . . . all . . . are one in Christ Jesus."[4]

The Christian women and men of the women's rights

movement were also criticized and censored for their public advocacy of women's equality:

> For example, at the third National Woman's Rights Convention held in Syracuse, New York, in 1852, a group of belligerent ministers came to disrupt the convention. When a woman delegate proposed a resolution claiming that the Bible recognized women's equality with men, these ministers read out loud passages to disprove women's equality.[5]

Modern feminism, for the most part, asserts that traditional Christianity denies women the right of self-determination, economic independence, and leadership. Joycelyn Elders, director of the Arkansas Department of Health and the Clinton administration nominee for surgeon general, expressed this notion at a pro-abortion rally celebrating the nineteenth anniversary of *Roe v. Wade*. After castigating prolifers for their "love affair with the fetus," the good doctor explained that the "celibate, male clergy" and medical profession were responsible for controlling women and opposing abortion.

In contrast we find that the nineteenth-century pioneers of women's rights, were predominantly religious, moral crusaders. Serious Christian reflection on women's issues led Elizabeth Cady Stanton to publish the *Woman's Bible* in the 1890s. "Neither [Matilda Joselyn] Gage nor Elizabeth Cady Stanton regarded herself as irreligious nor her works as attacks on religion itself. Rather, they attacked the perverse side of religion that degraded women and converted religious traditions like Judaism and Christianity into weapons of oppression to be used against women."[6]

We find that Susan B. Anthony was not motivated by a negative, critical agitation for equality but by a spiritual ideal of the equality of men and women. As a Quaker she was familiar with the role of Quaker women in the religious community. Since there were no formal ordained clergy among Quakers, women as well as men were permitted and encouraged to share from Scripture, and to testify and preach at Quaker meetings.

Susan B. Anthony and the suffragists were women and

men of strong moral conviction. Not only did they work for the abolition of slavery and alcohol (which they viewed as a destroyer of family life) but also the abolition of prostitution and promiscuous sexuality. These early leaders in women's rights actively rescued women who had been forced into prostitution by widowhood or divorce, shared the gospel with them, and built "Magdalene Homes" for shelter and rehabilitation.

We further note that one of the first public appeals for women's suffrage came in 1848 during a convention held in a Seneca Falls, New York, Wesleyan church. The Wesleyans believed in a literal interpretation of the Bible, evangelical preaching, and strict standards of a "holy" lifestyle.

As the women's movement progressed, and the nineteenth century came to a close, another religious movement was born. That movement, known today as Pentecostalism, grew out of the pietistic and "inner light" movements, as well as the Wesleyan-Holiness movement. Pentecostalism, then, had much in common, religiously and culturally, with the women's suffrage movement.

Since its inception, Pentecostalism has admitted women into every rank of ministry, albeit tentatively. The Church of God and the Assemblies of God have ordained women for over sixty years. The Assemblies of God today ranks second of any organized Christian body in the number of ordained women in its ranks. Only the Salvation Army has more. A cursory reading of Pentecostal history will reveal such names as Florence Louise Crawford, the founder of the Apostolic Faith Church and erstwhile partner with the black holiness leader, William J. Seymour; Marie Woodworth-Etter, the pioneer woman pastor and famed nineteenth-century healing evangelist; Aimee Semple McPherson, the most famous woman preacher of all time, who was originally ordained through the Assemblies of God; and the Christian healer, Kathryn Khulmann, an ordained Holiness-Methodist minister.

Blacks and whites had a unique parity and shared unprecedented fellowship in those early days of the revivalistic and Pentecostal movements. Throughout the South, Midwest, and the Old South, the black bishops William J. Seymour and C. H. Mason laid hands upon and ordained white evangelists and pastors. In those days of strict segregation, that was a dramatic and sometimes dangerous break from the pervasive prejudice in American churches. Revivals were conducted in desegregated tents, where black and white believers sang, prayed, waited in "prayer lines," and walked "the sawdust trail" together. Photographs of the great revival meetings of the period 1906-1946 display what are likely to be the most integrated audiences anywhere in America during that time.

Remarkably, not only have evangelicalism and Pentecostalism had an unprecedented impact on women and blacks but also on Asians and Hispanics as well. In the period 1969-1982, for instance, Baptists and Pentecostals together experienced a nearly 100 percent increase in adherents in both Korea and Singapore. The largest evangelical congregations in the world are now found in Korea.[7] As early as 1962 *Time* magazine referred to Pentecostalism in Latin America as "the fastest growing church in the hemisphere." Although the vast majority of Hispanics continue to be Roman Catholics, evangelicalism and Pentecostalism are experiencing unabated growth in South and Central America as well as among Hispanics.[8]

The last decade has witnessed the emergence of a regenerated pro-life movement, most noted for its nationwide Operation Rescue campaign. While Operation Rescue has been portrayed by pro-abortion organizations such as the National Organization of Women (NOW) and Planned Parenthood as a "male-dominated woman-hating" movement, nothing could be further from the truth.

To date a large segment of the participants in the rescue movement have been Pentecostal or charismatic Christians of various ethnic orientations. Randall Terry, widely regarded as the founder of the rescue movement, is a graduate of Elim Bible Institute in Lima, New York. Elim is one of the oldest Pentecostal institutions in the world and has ordained women ministers for over sixty-five years. Terry, who is white, has three black foster children.

Concerning women in the rescue movement, "rescues" have involved far more female participants than male. One

of the most outstanding personalities in the rescue movement is Joan Andrews Bell, who as a forty-five-year-old Catholic
newlywed and the mother of a newborn child, spent two-
and-one-half years of a five-year sentence in a Florida penitentiary for her rescue activities. Another woman at the
forefront of the effort to save the lives of the preborn has
been Mother Teresa of Calcutta. A Noble laureate and one
of the world's most admired women, Mother Teresa has
said, "Every abortion kills two—the child and the conscience
of the mother."

We also see that the leaders and participants in the civil
rights movement were predominantly Christian. Martin
Luther King, Jr., was an ordained Baptist minister, as were
Adam Clayton Powell, Andrew Young, Jesse Jackson, and
Dr. E. V. Hill, now of Los Angeles. Church services, religious
rallies, and public prayer gatherings figured prominently in
the early protests against racial segregation and discrimination. Dr. King inextricably linked the African-American
struggle for equality and justice to Christian and biblical
ideals, as does Archbishop Desmond Tutu in South Africa
today. In his book, *Strength to Love*, Dr. King wrote, "Like the
early Christians, we move into a sometimes hostile world
armed with the revolutionary gospel of Jesus Christ. With
this powerful gospel we shall boldly challenge the status quo
and unjust mores and thereby speed the day when 'every
valley shall be exalted, and every mountain and hill shall be
made low: and the crooked shall be made straight, and the
rough places plain: and the glory of the Lord shall be revealed.'

"Our hard challenge and our sublime opportunity is to
bear witness to the spirit of Christ in fashioning a truly
Christian world."[9] Many white spokespersons for civil rights
issues were also Christian clergy.

When Operation Rescue conducted its anti-abortion
campaign during the Democratic National Convention in
Atlanta in 1988, the ABC news magazine "20/20" featured
the protests. I was present and interacted often with the
crew that was covering the events. I noticed, and then pointed
out to others, that whenever a woman or black pro-life leader
addressed the audience, the klieg lights and cameras were

almost immediately turned off. After the pattern became
apparent to me, I brought it to the attention of the on-site
producer. He expressed surprise at my observation and assured me it was not intentional. However, when the final
product was aired, it was quite apparent to everybody that
virtually all the members of the movement who were not
Anglo-Saxon males were given short spots or were cut out
altogether. The media chose to focus on a decidedly
unrepresentative southern white, overweight, and heavily
jowled middle-aged male who fit their "fundamentalist"
stereotype. This misrepresentation is demonstrated by the
fact that while 46 percent of white Americans consider themselves born-again Christians, that number rises to a whopping 52 percent for African-Americans. Among Hispanics,
the overwhelming majority are traditional Catholics, who
believe that large families are a gift from God and follow
their Church's prohibition on artificial birth control and
abortion. As was noted earlier, Baptists, Evangelicals, and
Pentecostals make up a large minority of Hispanics throughout the world.

A study conducted for the Christian Coalition by the
Marketing Research Institute (MRI) surveyed 1,529 American voters and profiled that segment of the Christian population identified as "churchgoing." The results contrasted
dramatically with the image of Christian believers projected
by the false consensus. The news media has inferred that
Christians with socially and morally conservative beliefs are
a minority of disenfranchised, male-dominated whites whose
opinions are largely exaggerated. The MRI study showed
that churchgoers (defined as attending worship services twice
or more weekly) make up the largest single block of the
electorate, a whopping 39 percent, with women being the
highest percentage within that figure. The research further
revealed that:

> Contrary to popular stereotypes, churchgoing Ameri-
> cans are well-educated (with 66% having attended col-
> lege or having earned a graduate degree). They are
> primarily employed in professional, white collar occu-
> pations with a $40,000 median household income.

61% of all church-going Americans are women; 39% are men. Fifty percent of all churchgoing women work outside the home. Among women sixty years or younger, 67% have careers.

The profile of Christian America that emerges from the survey is of a career-oriented, baby-boomer woman with children whose political attitudes are largely shaped by concerns for the welfare of her children and family.[10]

Furthermore, according to a study conducted by the Barna Research Group among black Americans, religion is

strong and significant. Most believe that marriage is still a relevant concept for our society; that getting legally married is important to providing a stable family; and that God intended for marriage to be once and for all.

They have a strong sense that community is important and that a strong society requires networks of supportive relationships, but they do not believe that the key relationships involve only the nuclear family. They are just as likely to perceive an extended family as being the core of a strong society.[11]

Hispanic adults . . . tend to preserve the family traditions that make up their heritage [and] . . . are predominantly Catholic[s]. . . . Eight out of ten believe that God intended marriage to last a lifetime. . . . They are more likely to perceive family to be a core element in life, one that is best pursued at the earliest possible time. Finances, housing, relationships, and all other lifestyle factors all follow from the needs of the family. . . . Given the higher priority Hispanics place upon marriage and family, it is not surprising to learn that the divorce rate among Hispanics is lower than the white population.

Considering the strategic role religion has played among diverse ethnic groups and among women in America, it is surprising that the oft heard chant of the secularist-New Left coalition—"Racist, sexist, anti-gay, born-again bigots go away!"—has received such wide play. How is it then that sincere and conscientious religious believers who span the racial, ethnic, and gender spectrum have become equated, in the eyes and ears of the watching and listening public, with hatred, bigotry, and prejudice?

There are perhaps several explanations. Christians tend to be conservative when it comes to cultural innovations, and understandably so. They recognize in the present popular culture the denial of divine authority and the idolization of self. Much of what passes for "rights" is in reality the elevation of selfishness at the expense of moral obligation to God and to others. Social liberals confuse "civil rights" with self-indulgence and a libertarianism that maximizes personal autonomy and minimizes personal accountability. Therefore, Christians have often failed to differentiate between the libertine agenda of the sexual revolution and legitimate agendas for social justice. As a result, many conscientious Christians have rejected much of the civil-rights agenda, throwing the proverbial baby out with the bath water. This is particularly true in regard to the modern women's rights movement due to its intimate association with a radical feminism that tends to denigrate marriage, motherhood, and domestic devotion while endorsing the abortion industry.

Black civil rights leaders are viewed by many conservative Christians as cohorts of the secularist-New Left coalition, which they rightly perceive to be anti-Christian. Because much of the "old guard" civil rights representatives are politically cooperative and often sponsored by liberal groups that traditionally oppose Christian concerns, the involvement of Christians with civil rights issues has been minimal at best.

Yet, while this is true, Supreme Court Justice Clarence Thomas offers another explanation for the apparent lack of involvement by political conservatives in civil rights issues. In an article in the October 1992 edition of *Dimensions* magazine, Thomas wrote, "I often felt that the media assumed that to be black, one had to espouse leftist ideas and Democratic politics. Any black who deviated from the ideological litany of requisites was an oddity and was to be cut

from the herd and attacked. Hence, any disagreement we
had with black Democrats or those on the Left was exaggerated. Our character and motives were impugned and challenged by the same reporters who supposedly were writing
objective stories."[12]

Here is the omnipresent entertainment/news establishment projecting personalities through the cracked lens of
the false consensus. Justice Thomas (who was raised Roman
Catholic and who currently, according to most reports, at-
tends a charismatic Episcopalian church, which is, according
to *Newsweek*, "active in the anti-abortion movement") goes on
to explain that conservatives are concerned with protecting
and extending civil rights. "According to our higher law
tradition, men must acknowledge each other's freedom and
govern only by the consent of others. . . . Natural law of this
form is indispensable to decent politics. This approach allows us to reassert the primacy of the individual and estab-
lishes our inherent equality as a God given right. This inherent equality is the basis for aggressive enforcement of civil
rights laws and equal employment opportunity laws."[13]

Another reason that Christians tend to avoid or reject
civil liberties issues is the widespread belief among them that
social and political involvement is worldly. Temporal resolutions to what are arguably spiritual problems, often requiring a large measure of compromise, are seen as untrustworthy.
Even when Christians do not hold these views about public
policy or service, decades of isolation from the political arena
and public policy have left them ignorant of how to address
or participate in devising resolutions to social and political
problems. As a result, conservative Christians tend to focus
on the life and health of a local church that may already be
racially integrated or at least racially tolerant, one that provides meaningful roles to women, ministers to the poor, and
nurtures children. Christians see success in their own congregations in these areas while left-wingers look to government for solutions.

The last reason that I will mention is eschatological.[14]
The emphasis on the imminent return of Jesus Christ has de-
emphasized in the minds of some Christians their responsibility to the world in which they live. Not all believers in the

Second Coming of Christ abandon their civic responsibilities; indeed, many are among the most active citizens in the community. But the emphasis on the return of Christ makes earthly industry, especially politics, seem unworthy of investment. Many Christians view societal disintegration, political corruption, anti-religious discrimination, immorality, and soaring crime as the fulfillment of prophecies. The Bible describes the last days as "terrible times" when "people will be lovers of themselves, lovers of money, boastful, proud, abusive, disobedient to their parents, ungrateful, unholy, without love, unforgiving, slanderous, without self-control, brutal, not lovers of the good, treacherous, rash, conceited, lovers of pleasure rather than lovers of God."[15] Can Christians be blamed for seeing such Scriptures as being fulfilled in the daily news?

The Bible does clearly teach that the end of history will include great evils on a gargantuan scale. Therefore, the depth of mankind's present wickedness does not surprise the believer. The prophet Jeremiah said, "The heart is deceitful above all things and beyond cure. Who can understand it?"[16] It is the humanist, who adheres to a doctrine of man's inherent goodness, and not the religionist who is baffled by the depth of man's depravity.

Yet knowing that the world must grow tenebrous before the ineffable light of Christ's return does not excuse us from seeking righteousness on earth. Jesus, in his high priestly prayer, petitioned his Father: "My prayer is not that you take them out of the world but that you protect them from the evil one. . . . As you have sent me into the world, I have sent them into the world."[17] Furthermore, Jesus taught his disciples to "occupy until I come,"[18] and that "night is coming, when no one can work."[19]

The Christian has a responsibility to work for justice and righteousness on the earth, even though he recognizes that perfect justice will not be realized until Jesus returns. The disciple of Christ is a witness to some things and a witness against some things. He is a witness to the love, grace, and mercy of God. As such, the Christian must "put on tender mercies, kindness, humility, meekness, long-suffering," and furthermore, Christians must "bear with one another, and forgive one another, and if anyone has a complaint against another, even as Christ forgave, so you also must." The Apostle Paul concludes, "But above all these things put on love, which is the bond of perfection."[20] The humble love of Christ is "the true mark of the Christian" according to the philosopher Francis Schaeffer.

But the Christian is also a witness against sin, evil, and injustice. "Therefore, put on the full armor of God, so that when the day of evil comes, you may be able to stand your ground, and after you have done everything, to stand. Stand firm then, with the belt of truth buckled around your waist, with the breastplate of righteousness in place, and with your feet fitted with the readiness that comes from the gospel of peace. In addition to all this, take up the shield of faith, with which you can extinguish all the flaming arrows of the evil one."[21]

Conscientious Christians will seek not only to "make every effort to live in peace with all men and to be holy,"[22] but will also "struggle against sin"[23] and "encourage and rebuke with all authority."[24]

The exercise of this spiritual and moral authority is dependent upon the personal integrity of the individual believer. *Integrity* is defined in the dictionary as: (1) The quality or state of being complete, entire, unbroken; (2) The entire, unimpaired state or quality of anything; (3) The quality or state of being of sound, moral principle, upright, honest, sincere.

"Let me not be put to shame" cries the Psalmist, "for I take refuge in you. May integrity and uprightness protect me."[25]

For the Christian, *integrity* means being spiritually whole, having all the parts of the Christian life in their proper place and order. *Integrity* comes from the word "integer," which is defined as "a whole and complete number, as distinguished from a fraction." So an *integer*, or integrity, is "not a fraction." *Fraction* is defined as: (1) The act of breaking, the state of being broken apart; (2) A small part, amount, fragmentary.

The book of James insists that "perseverance must finish its work" in the Christian life "so that you may be mature and complete, not lacking anything."[26] This is another reference to having all the components of the Christian life in order. *Teleois*, the Greek noun here translated "mature," refers to the "fulfilled end" and "realized goal of a thing." *Hololderoi*, which is translated here as "complete," means "whole, having all its parts; sound; perfect." This Greek word comes from *holos*, or "whole," and *kleros*, meaning "parts." Therefore, James urges Christians to have all the parts of their lives perfectly or soundly in order, in other words, to have integrity.

The New English Bible translates this verse as "if you give fortitude full play, you'll go on to a completed, balanced character, that will fall short in nothing." The Amplified Bible offers "let endurance and steadfastness and patience have full play and do a thorough work, so that you may be people perfectly and fully developed, with no defects, lacking in nothing." Finally, the Catholic Westminster Version renders it "full grown in every part, nothing lacking."

In chemistry, "to fraction" refers to "any of the processes used to separate the constituent parts of a mixture by taking advantage of the boiling points." The measure of our integrity is tested, not when the temperature is even or the weather is fair; our integrity is tested at the boiling points of our lives. Boiling is a process that separates dross. Certain precious metals are brought to boil in order to separate the scum and purify the substance.

The opposite of spiritual integrity is spiritual fragmentation. Parts of the Christian life are missing, out of place, or deformed, stunted, and exaggerated. We say one thing and do something else. This is a characteristic of immaturity. James has "maturity" and "integrity" as synonymous in the Christian life. The healthy Christian is marked as *teleos kai holokleroi*, "mature and having integrity."

In his fascinating book on human evil, *People of the Lie*, the psychologist M. Scott Peck writes: "The truly good are they who in time of stress do not desert their integrity, their maturity, nor their sensitivity. Nobility might be defined as the capacity not to regress in response to degradation, not to become blunted in the face of pain, to tolerate the agonizing and remain intact."[27]

Secularist anti-Christian hatred, bigotry, and defamation are bringing a great deal of stress upon believers. Bias in the media, discrimination in schools and other institutions, and prejudice in the courts press modern Christians to the limits of their spirituality. In the face of this assault, Christians may become cynical, bitter, and vindictive. This current situation threatens to inculcate bigotry and prejudice in the believer toward his tormentors. It also threatens to separate believers from the larger concerns of social justice in their communities.

Christianity and bigotry are mutually exclusive. They are incompatible and antithetical as well as inexcusable. While there may be explanations for ignoring social injustice or harboring prejudice, there are no legitimate excuses for it. Attitudes of prejudice and stereotype held by believers only fuels prejudice against them. It is reciprocal. It is a case of sowing and reaping.

Once, when speaking at a Christian business association meeting, I was approached by a woman after my talk. As she rubbed her banker's fingers together at their tips, she said, "I really enjoyed your talk tonight. You're not like other Jews—you know the ones that are always after the money." Her inability to comprehend the depth of offense she had caused me by invoking the stereotype astounded me. To a modern Jew, her ignorant prejudice had an ancient sound to it, like somebody making reference to the world's being flat or man's not being created to fly. I found myself in wonderment at where a contemporary American would have caught this disease. To me, she was as unusual as somebody who had contracted the bubonic plague. Another time, my brother, who is also an ordained minister and a missionary, was attending a denominational missions conference where several thousand missionaries had gathered. The speaker was an old veteran, now retired, but revered for his many decades of service abroad. In the course of his speech, he referred to his being on the first flight to China after Nixon had opened up relations with the Communists. Also on the flight, he reported to his listeners, were a "group of New York Jews" that, he added, although they were "God's chosen people, are not my chosen people."

The presence of racial prejudice among Christians is deplorable. Epithetical jokes and slander told about people of other racial, ethnic, or religious groups is sinful. By them the Christian is debased and the Lord is scandalized. "Now you must rid yourselves of all such things as these: anger, rage, malice, slander, and filthy language from your lips. Do not lie to each other, since you have taken off your old self with its practices and have put on the new self, which is being renewed in the image of its Creator."[28]

Of all people, Christians should not use stereotype. First, the Christian has no right to complain about others stereotyping him if he is willing to stereotype others. Second, stereotyping is very close to an operational lie. If we think honestly, we can always identify someone, perhaps even a majority of people, who do not fit the stereotype. Third, stereotyping is inherently unfair and thereby undermines the integrity, credibility, and the witness of the believer.

This is true of Christian thought regarding women, people of color, ethnic groups, and other subcultures. It doesn't serve the Christian end of evangelizing and delivering a homosexual from his bondage to stereotype him as a limp-wristed, effeminate, lisping "homo." Nor does it serve the Kingdom of God to misrepresent urban blacks as uneducated, anti-social welfare cheats. It does not further the gospel of Christ when we lampoon women as blond "bimbos" or bad drivers or obsessed shoppers. These stereotypes only undermine the receptivity of others to the truth of the Gospel. The Jewish sacred Scriptures command, "Do not spread false reports."[29] It is not essential to exaggerate characteristics and deride behaviors in order to oppose sin. If Christians are to stand up against the evils of bigotry and prejudice, then they must not only be "hearers" of the Word but "doers" of the Word also. They must "do to others what you would have them do to you."[30] In the words of Clarence Darrow, we can effectively "hate the sin but love the sinner."

The horror of Northern Ireland, the devastation of Beirut, and the abomination of the civil war in Bosnia graphically illustrate the curse of religious hatred. Religious inclination can be the fertile garden of the fruit of God's Spirit or a stygian bog of the works of sinful human nature.

"The entire law is summed up in a single command-ment," the Scripture says. "Love your neighbor as yourself. If you keep on biting and devouring each other, watch out or you will be destroyed by each other."[31]

If we Christians expect to be heard in our complaint about our own treatment by the makers of popular culture, we must be very careful to avoid the temptations of stereo-type and to give every man and woman created in the image of God the same dignity, respect, and charity we ask for ourselves. "If anyone considers himself religious and yet does not keep a tight rein on his tongue, he deceives himself and his religion is worthless."[32] "Nor should there be obscen-ity, foolish talk, or coarse joking, which are out of place."[33] "Even angels, although they are stronger and more power-ful, do not bring slanderous accusations."[34]

Heaven Help Us

—————————— | ——————————

On 8 April 1945, a truck containing a handful of prisoners drove up to a small schoolhouse in a forested area in the little village of Schonberg in Bavaria. The school had been temporarily converted into a military jail. The men inside the van were herded out and into the schoolhouse. It was the first Sunday after Easter, and several of the prisoners asked the only clergyman among them, Pastor Dietrich Bonhoeffer, to conduct a service. After leading them in prayer, he then shared a meditation from the words of the prophet Isaiah: "By his stripes we are healed." One of the inmates, a British intelligence officer named Payne Best, recalled, "He reached the hearts of all, finding just the right words to express the spirit of our imprisonment, and the thoughts and resolutions which it had brought."

Before the benediction, they were interrupted by two Gestapo officers dressed in plain clothes, who ordered Bonhoeffer to come with them. The pastor took a few moments to bid each of his fellow prisoners farewell. He took the British officer aside and asked him to convey a message to the Bishop of Chichester: "This is the end—for me, the beginning of life."

Bonhoeffer was taken to a stark, rectangular shed, about twenty by thirty feet, that was erected in a clearing and surrounded by an eight-foot high concrete wall. There, early the next morning, he was escorted with other prisoners to an area where a small array of gallows had been constructed. Before reaching the place of death, he paused for a moment of silent prayer. Then again, on the platform, before the hanging rope was fitted around his neck, he prayed.

A prison doctor who witnessed the thirty seven-year-old pastor's execution later remarked, "In the almost fifty years I have worked as a doctor, I have hardly ever seen a man die so entirely submissive to the will of God."

The life and death of Dietrich Bonhoeffer was a remarkable example of Christian devotion. He was far from the image of the tranquilized, stoical submissive who unquestioningly followed the divine mandate even to his own demise. Bonhoeffer loved living and enjoyed his family and friends. He was engaged to Maria von Wedemeyer, the daughter of his parents' friends, with whom he had fallen in love during visits to her home in 1942. She was almost twenty years younger than he was. During his imprisonment, he wrote to her that she was the one who gave him reason to persevere. The young Bonhoeffer was no hermit. He had wrestled through the most vexing issues of his modern existence. In his less than forty years, Dietrich Bonhoeffer was a brilliant intellectual that won his doctoral degree before he was twenty-one years old. He had published several renowned books, was a university professor, traveled extensively, lectured in the United States, served as a secretary of the World Council of Churches, led a schism in his denomination, founded an illegal seminary, and joined a conspiracy to assassinate Hitler.

One could suggest that Bonhoeffer did not fit the description of a martyr at all. He was arrested and hanged as a traitor to his nation. He had conspired, with certain members of the Abwer, or German intelligence agency, to kill Hitler and then capitulate to the Allied demands for surrender. Exploits like that are not typical of the stories of Christian suffering. The common description of martyrdom would leave all of that out and have the pastor falsely accused and killed for simply "preaching" the gospel. But that was just the point. Dietrich Bonhoeffer did the things he did because he believed that to preach the Gospel of Christ required living out the Gospel of Christ. To live out the Gospel of Christ is to aid the suffering and the oppressed, to speak up for the downtrodden and deliver those unjustly condemned to death.

"Only those who cry out for the Jews," he once wrote, "may also sing the Gregorian chants."

The passage of history, and its revelation of the inscrutable evil of Nazism, leaves contemporary Christians with no comprehension of what Bonhoeffer and the innumerable other conscientious Christian dissidents suffered. At the other side of history, it is simply too easy to imagine the glorious adventure of being a witness of moral righteousness, godliness, and humble obedience to the will of God in the face of such abject evil. We imagine how exhilarating it must have been to take a stand against such an obviously demonic power and to live, and even die, in contrast to such unmitigated malevolence. In the naivete of our own comfort and security, we yearn to experience such saintliness.

Yet we have no understanding and cannot grasp what it was like to refuse to go with the flow, to stand against the tide of "destiny," and to be branded a "traitor." We have no identification with the indignities of being silenced by governmental authorities, investigated by the police, prohibited from performing ministry, subjected to official harassment and detention, and finally, to be put to death for actions that derive from our deepest convictions.

No matter how morally right the Christian life may be, there is an inescapable sensation of shame that accompanies ostracism. Very few people on earth, whether religious or not, can live disconnected and detached from companionship and community. As human beings, we begin our lives attached—from the singular umbilicus that connected us to the nourishment of our mother's womb, to the cradling arms of our parents, grandparents, and siblings, to the reception of the community and connections to the world, we enjoy fellowship.

To be forcibly severed from those earthly attachments as Bonhoeffer was, and to be made into a criminal and a traitor, and finally subjected to an ignominious death—followed by the desecration of the corpse—is unfathomable to most modern American Christians. That, however, is the minimal meaning of martyrdom.

The real suffering of the persecuted is not in being punished for doing what is right or what is good—or for being someone different from others. The real suffering of the martyr is in the side effects of persecution; it is being remembered as a trouble maker, a liar, a thief, a contagion. That is how it is to experience the sufferings of persecution.

"If the world hates you," Jesus taught his disciples in John 15:18, "keep in mind it hated me first. . . . Remember the words I spoke to you: No servant is greater than his master. If they persecuted me, they will persecute you also." The serious follower of Christ must expect to receive persecution. The disciple of Christ recalls that the Master "came to that which was his own, but his own did not receive him." The conscientious Christian cannot expect commendation and prestige for his abandonment to Christ. The normal experience for the true believer is suffering at the hands of the world:

"Remember those earlier days after you had received the light, when you stood your ground in a great contest in the face of suffering. Sometimes you were publicly exposed to insult and persecution; at other times you stood side by side with those who were so treated. You sympathized with those in prison and joyfully accepted the confiscation of your property, because you knew that you yourselves had better and lasting possessions."[1]

That was the situation that the early Christians found themselves in. For three centuries the Church endured waves of persecution that surged or subsided with each new Roman emperor who would rise and fall from power. Over the centuries, Christians suffered persecution and martyrdom on almost every continent and in every country. Conscientious Christians even suffered sometimes at the hands of their own co-religionists, as happened to the Waldenses, the Anabaptists, and the Puritans in medieval, Renaissance, and Reformation Europe.

The first Christians did not resent their persecutions. They knew the teachings of their Lord when he said to them in the Sermon on the Mount, "Blessed are you when people insult you, persecute you and falsely say all kinds of evil against you because of me."[2] They remembered him telling them, "All men will hate you because of me,"[3] and when he warned, "Woe to you when all men speak well of you."[4] When Saul the Pharisee was converted and Ananias was sent by God to announce to him his apostolate to the Gentiles, God showed him "how much he must suffer for my name."[5]

Suffering, therefore, was not incongruous to the primitive Christian's understanding of his calling. Although there were Christians in "Caesar's household," the early church also knew that ostracism, persecution, and death awaited many of them. The glorious testimonies of the martyrs show that those believers accepted their mistreatment as the imitation of Christ. St. Peter wrote, "If you suffer for doing good and you endure it, this is commendable before God."[6]

If then, the apostolic Christians both expected and endured persecution in obedience to Jesus' teachings, and in imitation of his life and death, why should Christians in America respond any differently today? Should not Christians refrain from complaining about any mistreatment that they might receive from their culture, any injustice or prejudice? Are not these the marks of true discipleship, and if so, should they not be accepted and endured without protest?

The answer is no. Persecution cannot be cultivated, nor can it be contrived. Some sincere Christians may be misled into searching out persecution, or to succumbing too soon to secular pressures and labeling them "persecution." The persecutor must be proven and exposed. It can only be considered persecution when it has been given every opportunity to relent or mitigate. An example of this can be found in the arrest of the Apostle Paul in Acts 22:22-29.

> The crowd listened to Paul until he said this. Then they raised their voices and shouted "Rid the earth of him! He's not fit to live!"
>
> As they were shouting and throwing off their cloaks and flinging dust into the air, the commander ordered Paul to be taken into the barracks. He directed that he be flogged and questioned in order to find out why the people were shouting at him like this. As they stretched him out to flog him, Paul said to the

centurion standing there, "Is it legal for you to flog a Roman citizen who hasn't been found guilty?"

When the centurion heard this, he went to the commander and reported it. "What are you going to do?" he asked. "This man is a Roman citizen."

The commander went to Paul and asked, "Tell me, are you a Roman citizen?"

"Yes, I am," he answered.

Then the commander said, "I had to pay a big price for my citizenship."

"But I was born a citizen," Paul replied.

Those who were about to question him withdrew immediately. The commander himself was alarmed when he realized that he had put Paul, a Roman citizen, in chains.

The next day . . . he released him.

Some commentators have merely excused Paul for invoking his rights of citizenship when he was about to be beaten. After all, he was in great danger, and it was only natural that Paul would be tempted to save his skin in any way he could.

But this was not the case. Paul was an intelligent, accomplished, and cosmopolitan man. He was an orthodox Jew, "of the people of Israel, of the tribe of Benjamin, a Hebrew of Hebrews; in regard to the Law, a Pharisee."[7] He was fluent in Greek and was thoroughly versed in Hellenistic culture. He was also a citizen of Rome, an important status that conveyed upon him the rights of a Roman, which included a sort of due process of law.

Despite the notice given him by Ananias of the sufferings he must endure for Christ, Paul held the authorities that were persecuting him accountable to their own laws. This is an important lesson for American Christians in the face of a rising tide of militant secularistic aggression. Christians must hold their government and fellow citizens accountable to their laws and covenants. Those laws have traditionally advanced and exalted the worship of Almighty God and of godliness. The founders of the United States and the framers of the Constitution never intended to create a secular nation that would be hostile to religious beliefs or practices.

The current wave of anti-religious bias, prejudice, defamation, and discrimination is not the product of the philosophy of the nation's founders. Neither is it essential to a multicultural pluralism. It is a manifestation of anti-Christian ideologies that have permeated the cultural institutions of America. According to the Constitution, the United States remains a nation committed by law and tradition to the advancement of religious freedom. But the establishment clause of the First Amendment, intended by its drafters to protect religious faith and practice from government oppression, has been turned into the weapon of choice by militant secularism.

A federal appeals judge in Chicago complained that the nation was drifting dangerously close to requiring that private citizens prove that their religious actions comported with the current interpretation of the Constitution. His was an ominous warning that the establishment clause cases were generating hostility and general disdain for religious expression. What the judge failed to notice, though, in his stinging dissent, was that such hostility is part and parcel of the secularism that has taken root in the cultural establishment.

Yet, although the secularist consensus has indeed taken root in the cultural establishment, it does not mean that it has taken root in the consciences of ordinary Americans. As we have already demonstrated, the vast majority of Americans still believe in the Judeo-Christian tradition. The Constitution has been misread and misinterpreted by some as being antagonistic to the peoples' faith. Correctly understood, it still preserves the religious liberty so cherished by its authors. Therefore, Christians have the right, indeed the duty, to hold the government accountable to its covenants and its constitution. American government only exists by the consent of the governed. The religious citizen must protest the injustice of anti-religious defamation and prejudice. If, after he has done everything to expose that defamation and to confront prejudice, the persecution persists, then let him endure it, knowing he has "better and lasting possessions."

Another point should be raised here: that the Christian citizen has the duty to do his utmost to rectify his nation and to mend its faults. In spite of attempts to push Christians out of the election process, our democratic form of government still affords us the invitation and responsibility to work for good representation in government. Our free market economic system still affords us the opportunity to engage in business and commerce, including the business of news and entertainment, that will encourage and enhance religious traditions. Academic freedom still allows us to form schools, to teach, and to train teachers that will respect religious faith and heritage. It is incumbent upon believers to engage in each of these occupations, to act as salt and light in the world and to redeem the cultural institutions of American society.

The false consensus that prevails in those institutions does so in large part because of the negligence of the church. As Christians abandoned the cultural institutions, in favor of a highly privatized piety, those institutions fell to secularist-New Left exploitation and were used as instruments of its propaganda. At this stage, it is the absence of Christians in the fields of entertainment and news, in academia, and in law, and not their presence, that contributes to the anti-Christian bias within them. What then, must be the response of conscientious Christians to defamation in secular American culture?

First, the defamation must be exposed. This can be done by calling attention to the unfair use of stereotype when depicting Christians, as we have done throughout this book. The general public must be made aware that discriminatory images are deliberately being used in the media, in the classroom, and in the courtroom to stigmatize Christians as well as other believers—making them more vulnerable to assaults by their secularist opponents.

Let's take, for instance, the accusation on the part of the Left that "conservative," "fundamentalist," and "Catholic"

Christians are racists and sexists. Setting aside the unfortunate reality that there are many people in American society that consider themselves to be Christians who still hold personal prejudices against people of other colors, religions, ethnic or cultural heritage, or gender, the body of Christ is not corporately or constitutionally racist or sexist. The Church is made up of members that are literally from "every tribe and tongue and people and nation." The Church is present on virtually every continent, and is made up of every race and ethnic group. The depiction of Christians as racist bigots can be easily proven false.

Destroying stereotypes is one mission we have taken very seriously. One time, we were invited by our local newspaper, the *Buffalo News*, to meet with their editorial board. The *News* considers itself a liberal publication and takes every opportunity to champion civil rights. In both its editorials and its stories, the paper demonstrates its belief in a classless, discrimination free society.

We received the invitation through Karen Swallow Prior, a pro-life activist rescuer. Prior is an intelligent, articulate high-school teacher and college professor who was, at that time, working on her doctoral degree in literature. We agreed that Prior should act as our representative in the meeting. We were told that no more than four leaders should attend, and so we arranged for the Reverend David Anderson, a pro-life activist, graduate of Jerry Falwell's Liberty University, and pastor of a fundamental Baptist church, to accompany us. The pastor Anderson is also a registered Choctaw Indian. We also asked a prominent African-American clergyman, who was a pro-life supporter and served as the chaplain of the county jail, where many pro-life demonstrators were often incarcerated, to be there. I was in the meeting, too, and am known by the *News* as a "Jewish convert" to Christianity.

So there we were, a "rainbow coalition." A professional woman in the field of higher education, a Native American, an African-American, and a Jewish Christian, representing what was consistently depicted to be a racist, sexist, white-male-dominated Eurocentricist movement. As we sat and waited for the editors of this supposed "liberal" publication,

I could not help being amused by what I predicted we were about to encounter. I just had a sixth sense that we represented the racial-ethnic-gender ideal that our liberal critics had likely failed to achieve themselves.

As each of the editors filed into the all-glass conference room, my suspicions were confirmed. Out of some eleven people, there was only one black and one woman. All of the rest were white, Anglo-Saxon, middle-aged males (who had a distinctly middle-class appearance). Their response was visceral, and it appeared to me that the senior editor who chaired the meeting was slightly embarrassed by it all!

· Another time I was asked to address a combined audience from the departments of sociology and anthropology at a local college. We had a new baby then, just six or seven months old. My wife was teaching school one day a week, and it was my responsibility to care for the baby during school hours. The lecture was scheduled on the particular day that Becky was teaching and I decided that I would take the baby along with me to the college.

I dressed in jeans and dock shoes, a casual shirt, and a tweed sport coat. I slung the baby in a denim front-pack and carried the well-equipped diaper bag over my shoulder. When I arrived, I was ushered into the lecture hall, which accommodated about three or four hundred students. About half that number of pupils were in attendance. In full view of the audience, just before I was introduced, I sought for a couple of volunteers that would care for the baby and administer her bottle while I spoke. I had no problems finding takers. It was a powerful display and I believe very effectively dismantled the Neanderthal caricature of pro-life Christians.

Protests and boycotts have proved to be successful avenues of exposing anti-religious bigotry in the media and government. The blasphemous film *The Last Temptation of Christ* was stymied when tens of thousands of Christians, along with Jews and Moslems, protested its release en masse at Universal Studios in Hollywood and at theaters all over the country. The abortion industry was dealt a lasting blow as tens of thousands of conscientious believers, again accompanied by traditional Jews and in a few rare cases, Moslems, some atheists, and pro-life feminists, took to the streets during the 1980s and early 1990s. Over seventy thousand arrests were made as protesters conducted sit-ins called "rescues," picketed, distributed literature and held rallies in support of the protection of the unborn. President Clinton's executive order permitting homosexuals to serve in the military was slowed to a crawl when thousands of ordinary Americans, many of them Christians, telephoned, faxed, and telegraphed their opposition to the White House.

Even with the defamation exposed and the stereotypes countered, a lot more work remains. Christians must work together to reclaim the bastions of American culture. We can no longer afford to ignore the immense importance of the media, television and motion pictures and to neglect them. Christian people of means with money to invest need to come together with other talented Christians to create marketable entertainment that encourages traditional family values. We must graduate from the negative strategies of protests and boycotts to the positive strategies of investment and creativity. In other words, we must learn from the enemies of Christianity who have so successfully pushed Christians out of the mainstream of culture. We must prayerfully and carefully position ourselves so that we can positively exploit the media for the edification, rather than the degradation of American culture.

The war against Christianity must be seen for what it truly is: a war against God. I asked public television critic Michael Medved how he would describe the anti-religious consensus in Hollywood. His reply was, "It's simple, isn't it? It's a hatred for God." Christians swear allegiance to a Lord other than self, to a law other than survival of the fittest, to a kingdom other than selfish satisfaction, and to a life beyond the grave. This is enough to infuriate the devil and to stir up opposition to the people of God. Throughout history, spirits of Antichrist have warred against God, and against his Christ:

> For all that is in the world—the lust of the flesh, the lust of the eyes, and the pride of life—is not of the Father but is of the world.

And the world is passing away, and the lust of it; but he who does the will of God abides forever.

Little children, it is the last hour; and as you have heard that the Antichrist is coming, even now many antichrists have come, by which we know that it is the last hour.

They went out from us, but they were not of us; for if they had been of us, they would have continued with us; but they went out that they might be made manifest, that none of them were of us.

But you have an anointing from the Holy One, and you know all things.

I have not written to you because you do not know the truth, but because you know it, and that no lie is of the truth.

Who is a liar, but he who denies that Jesus is the Christ? He is the antichrist who denies the Father and the Son.[8]

The spirit behind the bias, the defamation, and the discrimination against Christians in popular American culture is the spirit of Antichrist. It is a spirit that wars against Lordship and against accountability. It is a spirit that resents being told that there is a God who demands allegiance. It is a spirit that denies that Jesus is the Christ.

This is not to say that all non-believers are of Antichrist. Indeed, the Bible itself declares rather plainly: "[F]or when Gentiles, who do not have the law, by nature do the things contained in the law, these, although not having the law, are a law to themselves.

"Who show the work of the law written in their hearts, their conscience also bearing witness, and between themselves their thoughts accusing or else excusing them in the day when God will judge the secrets of men by Jesus Christ, according to my gospel."[9]

Jesus also taught his disciples, "For whoever is not against us is for us."[10] This truth is demonstrated in a growing number of non-Christians who are becoming alarmed about the rise in anti-Christian defamation. People like Nat Hentoff, a liberal atheist, Michael Medved and Don Feder, practicing Jews, as well as some agnostics and nominal Christians.

Christianity has been considered to be the dominant religion in America by the secularist elite. Therefore, it is the biggest target for anti-religious prejudice. Judaism and Islam are seen as minority religions that pose no threat to the monopoly that secularism holds on popular culture. The New Age religions basically pose no threat at all to liberalism since they adhere to no specific tenets and no absolute moral standards. That is the reason why they are so popular among the entertainment crowd. But Christianity is viewed as the enemy of elitist culture.

Epilogue

---|---

By Rev. Robert L. Schenck

Two significant events happened for me on Monday, 19 April 1993. One was my being sentenced to nine months in a county penitentiary for kneeling to pray on public property outside an abortion facility. The other was the cataclysmic demise of the heretical Branch Davidian sect in Waco, Texas. The two episodes had nothing to do with each other, except for their timing. Still, their convergence had meaning to me. The one seemed a harbinger of things to come; the other an excuse to be sure they did.

My sentence came after a long trial in which I was found guilty of disorderly conduct and resisting arrest. The charges stemmed from an incident during the previous spring, when I was arrested during a large pro-life demonstration outside an abortion business in Amherst, New York, a highbrow Buffalo suburb near where I live.

Though I had many times before engaged in acts of civil disobedience in order to voice my dissent from our nation's abortion policies, that day I determined not to risk arrest. It had been a very intense two weeks of public confrontation, and I was physically and emotionally drained.

When I arrived at the scene, there were already hundreds of pro-life and pro-abortion demonstrators there. The pro-lifers were, for the most part, gathered in one place, holding signs and singing. Others had gone to the doors of the facility to sit-in. The police had cordoned off a wide area, leaving an easement for themselves, the demonstrators, and the three dozen or so reporters who were covering the event.

Looking from across the street, I could see the pro-lifers in a prayer circle. I knew them to be largely Evangelical and Catholic Christians. Many of them had never participated in such public manifestations before and were quite beleaguered by the verbal and mild physical assaults they received from the "pro-choice" side. I decided to go over and encourage them with a pastoral prayer.

My wife, Cheryl, accompanied me as I crossed the street with the help of a police escort. When I arrived on the other side, the pro-abortion activists reacted vehemently. Recognizing my face and clerical collar, they began chanting, "Buffalo has a Schenck-er sore! Buffalo has a Schenck-er sore!"

Then, several broke off from their group and formed a human wall, preventing me from making contact with the pro-life contingent. I attempted without success to maneuver around them. A young woman spit in my face; another repeatedly shouted obscenities at me; and a puckish-looking man in his early twenties angrily shook his fist inches from my nose. Their rage was escalating, so I dropped to my knees and began to pray. As I tucked my head into my chest to protect my glasses from being damaged, someone grabbed me in a headlock with his knees.

At that, I heard someone call out, "They're beating up on the Reverend!"

Moments later a voice from behind my right shoulder asked, "What are you doing, Reverend?"

I answered, "I'm trying to get to my people to pray."

With that I felt someone grab me under the arm and heard the same voice announce, "I'll take you to your people." I was hoisted up, lifted over a police barricade, turned face down on the ground, handcuffed, and carried to a waiting police bus, where I was photographed and charged with criminal trespass in the third degree and resisting arrest.

When I arrived at police headquarters, I asked an officer, "Why did they arrest me and not my assailants?"

"Reverend," he explained in a lowered voice, "strictly off the record, when there's going to be a riot, they can arrest anybody. And you people come in here like ladies and gentlemen.

"When the abortion people come in here, they're kicking and cursing and biting, and these officers don't know whether or not they've got AIDS. Who would you arrest?"

I thanked him for the compliment and was placed in a cell. Shortly afterwards I was joined by another minister and a physicist who worked for the defense department in Washington. Both had been arrested while sitting in at the doors of the abortion facility.

We were arraigned with scores of others at an abandoned museum that had been commandeered by the town court. I met my attorney, John Broderick, a volunteer from Long Island, for the first time as I stood before the judge. Because they had earlier confiscated my eyeglasses, without which I felt functionally blind, I couldn't see much of what was going on. What I could see was a blurred form in a black robe, seated behind what I took to be a metal desk.

"OK, Robert Schenck. Disorderly conduct and resisting arrest," the form curtly declared. I wondered when they had smartened up and changed the charge.

"Yes, Your Honor," a fuzzy prosecutor responded. "The district attorney's office is asking for $1,000 in bail."

My attorney leaned over and asked where I lived and what I did. I told him I was a minister in the community, that my church and home were less than three miles from the courthouse, and that I maintained a family and many responsibilities in the area. Mr. Broderick repeated those things to the judge and asked for $500 bail, arguing that I posed a very small risk of flight.

"I know who he is," the robed form replied. "The court doesn't live in a vacuum. $2,500."

Everyone seemed stunned. I was taken back into custody and later transported to the basement of the National Guard Armory, which had been transformed into a temporary jail during the protests. Two days later a couple from our church posted my bail.

I was to be a codefendant with twenty-four others. Trial was scheduled for August of 1992. By now I knew the judge to be Sherwood Bestry, a blustery, miserable, and sometimes eccentric man about whom few people had good words.

In the period leading up to the trial, someone brought

to our attention the fact that Judge Bestry's wife and two daughters had contributed money to have their names listed with hundreds of others on a two-page advertisement in the Buffalo newspaper calling for the pro-lifers to be driven out of the area. The ad was sponsored by the Pro-Choice Network, a front organization that had sued us successfully in federal court for passing out New Testaments and tracts in front of another abortion business in the city.

"Look, Reverend Schenck," he told me. "I'm not with you on this. I'm pro-choice. But I believe everyone's entitled to a fair trial, and you're just not gonna get one. I've been in this guy's house, and I know just how he feels about all you people, and especially you and your brother. And it's not flattering. And I'm willing to testify to all this under oath."

I informed our attorneys, who then motioned for the judge to recuse himself or step aside, on the basis that his personal interest could get in the way of his objectivity. With cavalier disregard for our arguments, he denied the motion and insisted on a trial.

It seemed an eternity, but the first day of hearing eventually got under way. By then I was being represented by William Ostrowski, a retired New York State Supreme Court judge who had volunteered to defend my brother and me in a previous pro-life case. John Broderick remained the attorney for the other twenty-four defendants.

Before he was even seated on the bench, Judge Bestry issued his order banning all forms of what he called "religious demonstrations," including prayer, singing, and Bible reading. When my attorney challenged the constitutionality of such an edict, Judge Bestry responded in what would become a familiar diatribe, insisting that he meant "mass praying" or "mass demonstrations."

A number of us took that to mean that we were free to engage in private, individual prayer, which we did. During a break, two of us, myself and another man, knelt to pray at our seats. The judge, his clerks, the prosecutors, and our attorneys were in conference in chambers. The courtroom was noisy as prospective jurors, spectators, and family and friends to the defendants milled about, talking and laughing.

I had been on my knees only seconds when I heard the courtroom door open and the judge's voice boom, "All right! Go ahead; defy me! Thirty days in the holding center! Take him away."

I stood up to surrender, then I saw the guards pass by me and arrest the other man. Noticing that they had grabbed the wrong person, I called to the judge, "Your Honor, are you speaking about me?"

He turned and with a scowl, pointed his draped finger at me, and barked, "Take him too!"

The two of us were taken into custody and stripped of shoes and belts; my glasses were also removed. Then, we were placed in tiny holding cells in the back of the courthouse. Minutes later I watched in dismay as they paraded my brother in handcuffs through the holding area and off to a different cell block. I was completely bewildered; Paul was not a defendant in this case and hadn't even been in the courtroom when all this had taken place. Why could they have possibly arrested him?

It was much later when I learned that he had entered the courtroom after the episode, was told what had happened, and had opened his Bible to begin reading quietly to a small group of the defendants. A court officer reported it to Judge Bestry, who demanded that Paul be brought to his chambers, where he was warned that if he were to so much as bow his head, or open the Bible, he would be in contempt and summarily sentenced to thirty days in jail.

My brother, emulating Daniel and other courageous servants of God, refused to close his Bible but instead knelt on the floor and prayed for the judge. He was immediately arrested and sentenced to thirty days as well.

The account of our arrests hit the news media like a bombshell. Twenty-four hours later a county judge granted us an emergency stay of sentence, and we were released pending appeal. A special term supreme court judge agreed to hear us and eventually overturned the order, effectively rebuking Judge Bestry for his actions.

The victory was a mixed blessing. I still had to face this man for trial, now with the added burden of having publicly

exposed his anti-religious bias. This wouldn't make the or-
deal any easier.

The trial was long and complicated. The prosecutor's
performance was very good, but the evidence he had to work
with was heavily slanted in our favor. At the eleventh hour
though, he cooked up an ingenious scenario, suggesting that
I had deliberately instigated the melee in front of the abortion clinic in order to capture it on videotape and use it for
fund-raising. In the climate created by an extremely hostile
media, combined with the judge's antics, some of which
bordered on blatant manipulation, the jury bought it. They
returned a verdict of guilty, but only after several hours of
deliberation and a 2:30 A.M. threat by the judge to sequester
them and send police officers to notify their family members.

State law mandates that the county probation department prepare a pre-sentence investigation, after which they
make a recommendation to the judge on what they believe
to be an appropriate penalty. In my case they recommended
a fine and a conditional discharge—in other words a warning
not to get involved in another similar activity upon pain of
incarceration. Judge Bestry ignored the report and slapped
me with nine months in jail and a $1,000 fine.

Several hundred supporters had turned out to pray, and
they, together with my family, sat and wept in stunned silence. I had just enough time to kiss my wife and kids before
being taken off into custody. Later on I was joined by Rev.
Paul Koehn, a Lutheran minister, who, unknown to me, had
also been arrested that day and was sentenced separately
from the other group because of an illness. We had wonderful fellowship, singing, praying, and reading the Scriptures
together. Late that night we were transported to the Erie
County Holding Center, an overcrowded way station for
prisoners en route to permanent detention units.

Handcuffed to a long line of prisoners, we sat uncom-
fortably in the well-secured transport van. As we barreled
along the streets late at night, one of the prisoners began
asking what everybody got from the judge.

"Whatju' get?" he kept asking.

"Ten days," "Thirty days," "Ninety days," came the replies.

"Preacher, wha'd he give you?" he asked, turning toward me.

"Nine months."

"Nine months! S——, Reverend, when I do drug deals I get ninety days!" he pronounced incredulously. "And I plan those for the winter!"

The rest of the men laughed. One said sarcastically, "Just stay away from prayin' man. Just do your drugs!"

By now we had arrived at the holding center. In another ironic twist, the intake officer on duty was a member of one of our sister churches, where I had preached many times. He wagged his head in absolute disbelief. "I can't believe it," he kept saying to himself. "They don't send hard-core criminals in here anymore because of the crowding. And they sent a preacher? What is this world coming to?"

Indeed. His exasperated question haunts all of us. What is the world coming to? Some of the elements of my trial will clue us in to an answer, but more on that later.

I was eventually released on yet another emergency stay, but not before posting an additional $2,500, bringing my total bail to $5,000.

Five thousand-dollar bail, nine months in jail, and a $1,000 fine seemed awfully steep for just praying. But as we shall see, it may only be the beginning.

I summed up my analysis of the trial in a statement I made while addressing the judge prior to sentencing. In New York state a convicted criminal has the right to be heard by the court before he is sentenced. I took my full liberty, delivering what I now call my "Sermon to Pharaoh." Never had I felt so confident about delivering the Word of the Lord.

"What I was guilty of in this court, Your Honor," I offered respectfully, "was not a violation of the New York penal code, but a violation of the spirit of our times."

That became my apologia—my formal defense of my actions. In fact, the very demeanor of the jury toward me was one of disdain, as if to say, "He's the troublemaker; he oughta just stay out of other people's business. Let him get what's coming to him."

From what they saw on videotape and heard from wit-nesses, it would have been impossible for them to find me guilty of disorderly conduct and resisting arrest. There was not one shred of evidence to support those allegations. Quite the contrary—what they saw utterly contradicted the asser-tions of the prosecutor. But we (that is, those conscientious Christians who refused to contain their sentiments in a frus-trated conscience but instead brought them out into the open) had been sufficiently vilified that these six men and women felt justified in convicting me of being what the prosecutor said—a rabble-rouser who dared raise his voice in the hearing of the public.

During the course of the trial, the prosecutor had actu-ally suggested that I knew my presence, and especially my praying, would agitate the crowd, so I just should have stayed home. I guess I had never thought that the victim of a crime could be considered the perpetrator because he knew that his presence might upset somebody to the point of violence!

The most disturbing thing about my experience, how-ever, is that it is not an isolated case. Account after account bears out the fact that conscientious Christians are suffering similar and worse fates in police stations and courtrooms across the country. Pro-lifers have been beaten, kicked, and run down by horses. They have had their faces pushed into burning hot asphalt, mace sprayed in their eyes, and their limbs broken, as occurred in Los Angeles. A group of pro-life women in Pittsburgh, Pennsylvania, were sexually mo-lested by police officers, who pulled the victims' shirts and bras up over their faces while they kicked them down flights of stairs. And these acts have not resulted simply in the wake of trespass activity. Some of these things happened to indi-viduals who were arrested for aiding and abetting, but not actually participating in, any civil disobedience. In several recent federal contempt cases, the alleged contemners, all outspoken Christians, have been prosecuted, fined, and even jailed at federal prisons for doing nothing more than speak-ing out against abortion in public meetings.

These are all precisely the steps that occurred in Russia

following the Bolshevik revolution and in Eastern Europe before it was annexed by the Soviet Union.

Many Christians naively believe that the worldwide persecution predicted in Scripture will occur overnight, that somehow on one day we are perfectly free to worship the Lord and speak about him as we wish and the next day it will be illegal to be a Christian. That's not how it works. It is hard to imagine any government system that could act so swiftly on such a sacrosanct matter. No, it is far more insidious than that. Restrictions on faith must be incremental. Like the age-old analogy of boiling the frog, it must happen so slowly that no one really notices until it is too late. Keep in mind, it has never been illegal to be a Christian in Communist China. In fact, the constitution of the People's Republic of China guarantees freedom of religion. A Chinese citizen is free to believe anything he wants to—so long as he keeps it to himself. And to be sure that he does, the government has a sophisticated department of religious affairs that is charged with licensing and maintaining churches and ministers. This was accomplished by slowly "restricting" and "removing" the rights of religious people.

This is why the second event involving the Branch Davidians seemed strangely linked to my tribulation in the Amherst court that day.

The fiasco in Waco was a long time in the making. For fifty-one days the cult leader, David Koresh, a.k.a. Vernon Howell, had held off federal, state, and local law enforcement personnel in a dramatic, sometimes entertaining, stand-off. The heart of the matter, though, was anything but amusing.

The Branch Davidians were a sect that splintered from the Seventh Day Adventist Church back in the early 1920s. The group went through several metamorphoses, some of them violent, until it came under the bizarre leadership of Koresh.

Headquartered in a farm-like compound, one hundred or so men, women, and children practiced communal self-sufficiency. They also stockpiled weapons. When agents from the United States Bureau of Alcohol, Tobacco, and Firearms attempted to serve a search warrant on Koresh, they were fired at as they entered the property. Four of the agents were killed. The siege began.

In the nearly eight weeks that followed, the Texas Rangers, FBI, ATF, and the United States Department of Justice played a game of cat and mouse with Koresh and the cult members. There were a few humorous interludes, but it was mostly a tense, frustrating, and volatile stand-off. Several times Koresh promised to give himself up but he reneged in each instance.

According to subsequent accounts given by federal authorities, the long days of standing vigil began to wear on the officers. Finally, on 19 April the order was given to assault the compound using tanks equipped with non-incendiary tear gas. As their cannons punched holes in the walls of the main building, the gas was pumped inside. According to ATF and FBI commanders, the women in the compound were expected to remove the children to safety, presumably surrendering in the process. They didn't. In fact, all the children, who were repeatedly referred to by the same federal agents as "hostages," perished in a sweeping inferno that engulfed the entire complex, burning it utterly to the ground before fire-fighting equipment could be moved in. An independent investigator concluded that cult members started the blaze. The chief pathologist charged with examining the bodies exhumed from the debris also found that some of the victims had died of gunshot wounds presumably inflicted by fellow cult members.

There is no excusing the murderous machinations of David Koresh and his accomplices; but the reactions of the responsible law enforcement personnel also provoked serious questions. It was during subsequent congressional hearings on the debacle that U.S. Attorney General Janet Reno was asked a disturbing series of questions by members of the House Subcommittee on Crime and Criminal Justice.

George Sangmeister, a Democratic congressman from Illinois, gushed with adulation for the new Justice czar, after which this dialogue took place:

MR. SANGMEISTER: I've been told that there are these types of cults all throughout the United States and that this may be opening up Pandora's box as to how we're going to control these things. There are many people who would say, "Ya' know, these are all religious fanatics. Under the first amendment they have the right to worship as they see fit and that, uh, and that we should not be getting involved at all into this area." Do you have any thoughts about that, as to where we are proceeding?

MISS RENO: I think if a person or group has not violated the law that we certainly shouldn't get involved, and I think that we should take a measured response based on the evidence in the law when we have evidence that they've violated the law and take appropriate precaution, number one, to effect a prosecution and to effect, to the extent humanly possible based on the seriousness of the case, an appropriate response to secure their apprehension. . . .

MR. SANGMEISTER: Well obviously you're referring to the cache of arms that was there, but ya know, there's a lot of people that will tell you in this country, there's a lot, there's enough NRA advocates that would tell you that you can go into a lot of people's homes and find caches of arms that are very close to what you found here and wonder if that should be the deciding factor as to whether we should go into the compounds, but that's all I have and I yield to balance out my time.

Later on, Mr. Xavier Becerra from California seemed to pick up where Mr. Sangmeister had left off:

MR. BECERRA: Given your strong support for preventative approaches to resolve problems, and I'm pleased in the chances I've had to discuss this with you that you seem to focus so much on prevention versus trying to remediate a problem, what do you think that we will glean from this that will help in terms of preventing a situation like this from occurring, and perhaps you can expand a bit on what your philosophy is of prevention of this type of criminal activity?

MISS RENO: Well, having been in situations where I've never met a person who was a victim of a crime who wouldn't have rather had it prevented, I've gotten into the habit over the last fifteen years of looking at prevention and what could be done, and I think my meeting with Congressman Hughes *was a good step in* trying to explore what we can do with respect to cults where children are involved to address the issue of child abuse and the problems associated with that—in abuse in all of its forms, because some of the information that comes back to us is that after a child is in a cult situation for any length of time there may be a permanent damage to that person. We've got to work through it, understand it. The mysteries of the human mind in all sorts of forensic issues have been one of the great puzzles of the last ten years as we have learned more about it. And what I want to do is again try to talk to every expert that we can through the process that we will develop, that we develop, to make sure that we have as much information as we can. . . .

MR. BECERRA: Your response raises another question in my mind. Do we know how many of the individuals were beyond, say, perhaps the age of forty, in the compound?

MISS RENO: They . . . the FBI, may have that information. I'm sorry Congressman, I don't.

MR. BECERRA: It seems that most of the individuals were either of a younger age, or what might be considered young adult and not yet past a particular age, forty or so, and I don't know if it's worth examining, but it seems to me, along the lines of what you just said, there might be something to that, that a lot of young minds are being influenced in negative ways, and perhaps it is important to us to be there to provide resources to young people, children, at an early stage, rather than to wait till we find that their minds are polluted with a lot of information that causes things like this to occur.

MISS RENO: [With a smile] Absolutely.[1]

These questions and their attendant answers would not be so disturbing if it were not for the political backdrop of the Clinton presidency and its ever more driven social-change agenda. There is no question that the Clinton camp identified conservative/orthodox Christians as serious political enemies early on in their campaign for the White House. Such Christians are particularly despised by the aggressive pro-abortion and pro-homosexual lobbies, to whom Clinton owes so much, but there is more. The extreme left wing of the Democratic party—coalesced in organizations such as the American Civil Liberties Union, People for the American Way, Planned Parenthood, and the National Abortion Rights Action League—has been the primary force militating against everything from school prayer to abstinence-based school health curricula.

They know that to fully have their way without facing what is more and more commonly referred to as "psychological and conscientious impediments" to a hedonistic lifestyle, they are going to have to eradicate "the lunatic Christian fringe." Making subtle associations between biblical Christians, extremists, and terrorists, as Congressmen Sangmeister and Becerra did, suits this purpose quite well. The liberal news media and academia have also joined in. In a cover article published in the 3 May 1993 issue of *Newsweek* magazine, the reporter Kenneth Woodward quoted Edward Shorter, a specialist in the historical development of the family at the University of Toronto, on the failure of mothers to aid their children in escaping the deadly Waco fire. In his analysis of their negligence, Shorter said they "were typical of Bible-belt parents," who, he opined, "feel a responsibility to guarantee eternal life for their children and a mandate to keep them from the hands of Satan."

This kind of caricaturing is included in more and more attacks on such notable personalities and organizations as Pat Robertson and the Christian Broadcasting Network, who already have been subjects of government harassment and wiretapping; Dr. James Dobson and his Focus on the Family organization, who have received escalating media criticism, threats of lawsuits, and picketing by homosexual groups; Don Wildman of the American Family Association, who is repeatedly maligned in the press; and a host of others.

Given the current trends in culture and public policy, it will not be long before "official" measures are taken to curb the influence of these and many other leading ministries. Government regulation from "human rights commissions," like those already in place in some provinces of Canada, will be given the authority to control what religious spokespersons say, beginning with radio and television, then moving to print and ultimately into the pulpit.

For example, once homosexuals and women seeking abortions are classified as protected minorities, and certain forms of speech are defined as "hate crimes," then the government can move in to protect such groups under the ruse of "compelling interest." Even a reference to homosexual behavior or abortion as "sin" will soon be determined to be an act of animus toward a select minority. After all, the reasoning will go, what is more hateful than suggesting that God does not approve of a person's values or lifestyle choices?

The strategy becomes even more expansive once certain "civil rights" are accorded. Should abortion be legislatively guaranteed as a constitutional right under the proposed Freedom of Choice Act, anything construed to be an attempt to dissuade a young mother from ending the life of her pre-born child will become an obstruction to enjoying that unfettered "right," and the individuals responsible for erecting such an obstruction will be punished under federal law.

The scenario becomes even more frightening in the arena of "homosexual rights." Once homosexuals become a "protected class" of citizens, they will be entitled not only to special treatment but also to "extraordinary rights." One such "right" will be a quasi-constitutional guarantee of legal marriage. The Supreme Court of Hawaii has already ruled that that state's ban on same sex marriages "probably violates" the state's constitutional guarantees against sex discrimination. It will not take long before other state courts, and eventually the federal courts, fall in step. When this

happens, the ramifications for clergy of conservative, orthodox, and evangelical churches will be enormous.

Again, if current trends are not thwarted, I predict federal policy, initiated in the executive branch and ratified in
the courts, will coerce states into sanctioning homosexual
unions and granting them traditional spousal rights. Clergy
who refuse to solemnize such unions will be denounced as
hateful and bigoted. They may even be required to cooperate with such entitlements through mandatory licensing or
face punitive measures. Innumerable "illegal" clergy in the
former Soviet Union and the current People's Republic of
China have suffered civil penalties, incarceration, exile, and
even execution for non-cooperation with such compulsory
measures.

Except for our nation's traditional stand for righteousness and its acknowledgment of the sovereignty of the one
true God over the affairs of state and individuals, there is no
biblical rationale for believing that God will bless our land.
History is replete with examples of those nations who once
professed fidelity to God and his Word, enjoying prosperity
as they did, only to abrogate that covenant and be relegated
to impotence. Witness the once great "Christian" nations of
Europe, who, having lost their first love, now abide in an
anxious social, economic, and spiritual malaise.

During a recent preaching tour of the newly freed Russian republic, I met a state school administrator who earnestly adjured me to deliver a warning to the people of
America.

"Please," she implored. "Go back to your country and
tell the American people not to forget God. We are like
those lost in the forest without a compass. For seventy-four
long and terrible years, the government would not allow us
to hear about God. Now our young people do not know
what is right or wrong, good or bad, truth or a lie.

"Please," she begged in tears. "Tell your people they do
not want to be where we have been."

I told her I would. I hope we have.

Notes

—————— I ——————

Introduction

1. Francis Schaeffer, *A Christian Manifesto*, (Westchester, IL: Crossway Books, 1981), 17.
2. 1 John 5:5 (NKJV)
3. *Webster's Ninth New Collegiate Dictionary* , s.v. "secularism"
4. Kenneth L. woodward et al., "A Search for Limits,"*Newsweek (22 February 1993)*.

Chapter One

1. Galatians 3:28.
2. Leviticus 24:22: "You shall have one manner of law, as well for the stranger, as for one of your own country: for I am the Lord your God." The Hebrew word here translated "stranger" is *ger* and can be applied to members of another race.
3. Ephesians 5:22-31; 6:1-4.
4. 1 Timothy 3:4-5.
5. Writing in *Congress Monthly*, the magazine of the American Jewish Congress, the New York University law professor Burt Neuborne writes that "the Establishment clause requires us to be suspicious of religion, even hostile to it. . . . One clause says that religion is something to be cherished, while the other says that religion is something to be feared" (quoted by Richard John Neuhaus in *First Things First: A Journal of Religion in Public Life*).
6. Keith A. Fournier, "In Defense of Liberty" (Virginia Beach, VA: American Center for Law and Justice).

Chapter Two

1. Hannah Arendt, *Eichmann in Jerusalem: A Report on the Banality of Evil* (New York: Viking Press, 1963).
2. Hans Askenasy, *Are We All Nazis?* (Secaucus, NJ: Lyle Stuart, 1978), 28.
3. Douglas Popora, *How Holocausts Happen: The United States in Central America* (Philadelphia: Temple University Press, 1990), 26.
4. William S. Sahakian, *History of Philosophy* (New York: Harper and Row, 1968), 251; quoted in Josh McDowell and Don Stewart, *Understanding Secular Religions: Handbook of Today's Religions* (San Bernardino, CA: Here's Life Publishers, Inc., 1982), 56.

5. Ibid., 57.

6. Dinesh D'Souza, *Illiberal Education–The Politics of Race and Sex on Campus* (New York: The Free Press, 1991); cited by Charles Sykes, *Prof Scam* (Washington, DC: Regnery-Gateway, 1988).

7. Mortimer Adler and Charles Van Doren, eds., *A Treasury of Western Thought* (New York: R.R. Bowker Co., 1977).

8. Jeremy Rifkin, *Algeny* (New York: Viking Press, 1983), 113.

9. Karl Stern, *The Flight From Women*, (New York: Farrar, Straus and Giroux, 1965), 290 quoted by Rifkin, *Algeny*, 114.

10. *Existentialism* is defined as "a chiefly twentieth century philosophical movement embracing diverse doctrines but centering on analysis of individual existence in an unfathomable universe and the plight of the individual who must assume ultimate responsibility for his acts of free will without any certain knowledge of what is right or wrong or good or bad" (*Webster's Ninth New Collegiate Dictionary* (Springfield, MA: Merriam-Webster Inc., 1984).
Nihilism: a viewpoint that traditional values and beliefs are unfounded and that existence is senseless and useless. Nihilism denies any objective ground of truth and especially of moral truths, and maintains that a society is so bad as to make destruction desirable for its own sake, independent of any constructive program or possibility (adapted from *Webster's Ninth New Collegiate Dictionary*).
Hedonism: "The doctrine that pleasure or happiness is the sole or chief good in life" (*Webster's Ninth New Collegiate Dictionary*).

11. 1 John 2:18-19.

12. "Schools, group dispute right to distribute anti-abortion leaflets," *Buffalo News* (n.d.).

13. Let me offer the following point of clarification. During a picket outside a Buffalo abortion clinic, Dr. Barnett Slepian emerged from his car after the car had been stopped by a group sitting in the street, including myself. I approached the doctor and told him that a "physician who kills instead of heals is as unclean as a pig. You, Dr. Slepian–are a pig." I confess it was not the most effective tactic, and if I had to do it over again, I would probably choose different terms.

14. Dana Oakes, "Double Standards Mark Today's Political Correctness," *The Christian New Yorker* (January 1993); published by the Christian Coalition of New York.

15. Ken Sidey, "*Scientific American* drops Christian Writer with Creationist Beliefs," *Christianity Today* (19 November 1990).

16. St. John 8:32.

Chapter Three

1. Rudolf Hess, *Death Dealer: The Memoirs of the S.S. Kommandant at Auschwitz*, ed. Steven Paskuly, Jr., and Andrew Pollinger (Buffalo: Prometheus Books, 1992), 141.

2. Paul Johnson, *Modern Times: The World from the Twenties to the Nineties*, rev. ed., (New York: Harper Collins, 1991), 413.

3. William L. Shirer, *The Rise and Fall of the Third Reich–A History of Nazi Germany* (New York: Simon ad Schuster, 1960), 430-31.

4. Ibid., 432.

5. Ibid.

6. Ibid., 434.

7. Ibid.

8. Eloise Salholz et al., "The Death of Dr. Gun," *Newsweek* (22 March 1993).
9. "Two Parallel Lines Collided in Slaying at Clinic," *The Buffalo News* (14 March 1993).
10. David Shaw, "Abortion Bias Seeps into News—A comprehensive study finds that the press often favors abortion rights in its coverage, even though journalists say they make every effort to be fair," *The Los Angeles Times* (1 July 1990).
11. Ibid.
12. Pat Robertson, "Pat Robertson's Perspective—a special report to members of the 700 Club" (November-December 1992).
13. Henry M. Morris, Ph.D., *The Long War Against God-The History and Impact of the Creation/Evolution Conflict* (Grand Rapids, MI: Baker Book House, 1989), 197.
14. Harold Lindsell, *The New Paganism* (San Francisco: Harper and Row, 1987), 120.
15. William J. Bennett, *The Devaluing of America-The Fight for Our Culture and Our Children* (New York: Summit Book, 1992), 206.

Chapter Four

1. "Press 1 for the Christian Right," *Newsweek* (8 February 1993): 15. See also Franky Schaeffer, *A Time for Anger* (Wheaton, IL: Crossway Books, 1982), 15.
2. Sharon Boone, "No Leap of Faith," *Cable Guide* (December 1992): 8.
3. Michael Medved, *Hollywood vs. America: Popular Culture and the War on Traditional Values* (New York: Harper Collins/Zondervan, 1992), 80-81.
4. Ibid., 81.
5. Sharon Boone, "God and TV," *Cable Guide* (December 1992).
6. David Shaw, "Abortion Bias Seeps into News," *Los Angeles Times* (1 July 1990).
7. Ibid.
8. Ibid.

Chapter Five

1. Michael Medved, *Hollywood vs. America: Popular Culture and the War on Traditional Values* (New York: Harper Collins/Zondervan, 1992), 52-60.
2. Michael Rubinoff, 1992. *AFA Journal* (April 1992): 16.
3. Alan Dean Foster, *Alien 3* (novelization, based on a screenplay by David Giler, Walter Hill, and Larry Ferguson; story by Vincent Ward; New York: Warner Books, 1992), 64.

Chapter Six

1. Nat Hentoff, *Free Speech for Me but Not for Thee* (New York: Harper Collins, 1992), 10.
2. Dinesh D'Souza, *Illiberal Education: The Politics of Race and Sex on Campus* (New York: The Free Press, 1991), 9.
3. Gerard V. Bradley, "Dogma-tomachy—a 'privatization' theory of religious clause cases," *St. Louis University Law Journal* (March 1986): 275-330.
4. From Justice Jackson's decision in *Emerson v. Board of Education* (1974)
5. From the majority opinion, *Lemon v. Kurtzman* 403 U.S. 602 (1971).
6. Bradley, "Dogmatomachy," 297.
7. On 19 March 1993, Justice White announced he would retire at the end of the term.

Chapter Seven

1. Dinesh D'Souza, *Illiberal Education: The Politics of Sex and Race on Campus* (New York: The Free Press, 1991), 229.

2. *Lamb's Chapel and John Steigerwald, Petitioners, v. Center Moriches Union Free School District, et al.*; transcript at 35 at 5,6.

3. Ibid., 36 at 18-24.

4. Ibid., 47 at 1-10.

5. William J. Bennett, *The Devaluing of America—The Fight for our Culture and Our Children* (New York: Summit Books, 1992), 205.

6. Stephen Jay Gould, *Wonderful Life* (New York: W.W. Norton and Company, 1989), 40, 44, 291, 318.

7. "High Court: The day God and Darwin collided," *U.S. News & World Report* (29 June 1987):12.

8. Carl Sagan, *Broca's Brain* (New York: Random House, 1979), 284.

9. William F. Allman, "Cooking the paleontological books? U.S. News & World Reports (8 May 1989): 61.

10. Peter Huidekoper, Jr., "My Turn," *Newsweek* (2 April 1984): 17.

11. Source for 1970-1978: Testimony before U.S. Senate Committee on Labor and Human Resources, 31 March 1981, presenting data from the National Center for Health Statistics, U.S. Department of Health and Human Services, U.S. Bureau of the Census, and the Alan Guttmacher Institute; figures for 1979-1981 from the National Center for Health Statistics and the Alan Guttmacher Institute.

12. Douglas R. Scott, *Inside Planned Parenthood* (Falls Church, VA: CAC Publications, 1990), 25.

13. "AFA Law Center Sues in Behalf of Civil Rights of Christians,"*AFA Journal* (February 1992): 17.

Chapter Eight

1. Dimitry V. Pospielovsky, *A History of Marxist-Leninist Atheism and Soviet Anti-religious Policies*, vol. 1 of *A History of Soviet Atheism in Theory and Practice, and the Believer* (New York: St. Martins Press, 1987), 75.

2. Ibid., 78.

3. Dimitry V. Pospielovsky, *Soviet Anti-religious Campaigns and Persecutions*, vol. 2 of *A History of Soviet Atheism in Theory and Practice, and the Believer* (New York: St. Martins Press, 1988), 100.

4. Ibid., vol. 1, 90.

5. Ibid., vol. 2, 101f.

6. Ibid., 102-107.

7. *Webster's Ninth New Collegiate Dictionary* , s.v. "persecution."

8. *Dictionary of Modern Sociology*, prep. Thomas Ford Hoult (Totowa, NJ: Littlefield, Adams & Co., 1969), 319.

9. *Baker Encyclopedia of Psychology*, ed. David G. Benner (Grand Rapids, MI: Baker Book House, 1985), 1118.

10. *Encyclopedia of Psychology*, ed. Raymond J. Corsini (New York: John Wiley & Sons, 1984), 367.

11. Michael Medved, *Hollywood vs. America: Popular Culture and the War on Traditional Values* (New York: Harper Collins/Zondervan, 1992), 50.

12. William I. Schirer, *The Rise and Fall of the Third Reich: A History of Nazi Germany* (New York: Simon and Schuster, 1960), 435.

Chapter Nine

1. *Webster's Ninth New Collegiate Dictoionary,* s.v. "Anabaptism."
2. Pamela J. Milne, "Feminist Interpretations of the Bible: Then and Now," *Bible Review* (October 1992):39.
3. *Webster's Ninth New Collegiate Dictionary,* s.v. "pietism."
4. Galatians 3:28 (NIV)
5. Milne, "Feminist Interpretations," 38.
6. Ibid., 42.
7. *The Dictionary of Pentecostal and Charismatic Movements,* ed. Stanley M. Burges, Gary B. McGee, and Patrick H. Alexander (Grand Rapids, MI: Zondervan, 1988).
8. Ibid.
9. Martin Luther King, Jr., *Strength to Love* (Philadelphia, PA: Fortress Press, 1963).
10. "National Survey of Churchgoing Voters" conducted by the Marketing Research Institute for the Christian Coalition (February 1993).
11. George Barna, *The Future of the American Family* (Chicago: Moody Press, 1993), 166.
12. Clarence Thomas, "A Political Pariah," *Dimensions Magazine* (October 1992).
13. Ibid.
14. Having to do with the end times.
15. 2 Timothy 3:1-4.
16. Jeremiah 17:9 (NIV).
17. St. John 17:15,18 (NIV).
18. St. Luke 9:13 (KJV).
19. St. John 9:4 (NKJV).
20. Colossians 3:14 (NKJV).
21. Ephesians 6:13-16 (NIV).
22. Hebrews 12:14 (NIV).
23. Hebrews 12:4 (NIV).
24. Titus 2:15b (NIV).
25. Psalm 25:20-21 (NIV).
26. St. James 1:4.
27. M. Scott Peck, M.D., *People of the Lie* (New York: Simon and Schuster, 1983), 222.
28. Colossians 3:8-11 (NIV).
29. Exodus 23:1 (NIV).
30. St. Matthew 7:12 (NIV).
31. Galatians 5:14b,15 (NIV).
32. St. James 1:26 (NIV).
33. Ephesians 5:4 (NIV).
34. 2 Peter 2:11 (NIV).

Chapter Ten

1. Hebrews 10:32-34 (NIV).
2. St. Matthew 5:11 (NIV).
3. St. Matthew 10:22 (NIV).
4. St. Luke 6:26 (NIV).
5. Acts 9:16 (NIV).
6. 1 Peter 2:20 (NIV).

7. Philippians 3:5 (NIV).
8. 1 John.2:16-22 (NKJV).
9. Romans 2:14-16 (NKJV).
10. St. Mark 9:40 (NIV).

Epilogue

1. U.S. Congress, House Committee on the Judiciary. Hearing on the Branch Davidian Cult Standoff. 103d Congress, 28 April 1993.

ORDER THESE HUNTINGTON HOUSE BOOKS !

_____	America Betrayed—Marlin Maddoux	$6.99 _____
_____	Angel Vision (A Novel)—Jim Carroll with Jay Gaines	5.99 _____
_____	Battle Plan: Equipping the Church for the 90s—Chris Stanton	7.99 _____
_____	Blessings of Liberty—Charles C. Heath	8.99 _____
_____	*Christ Returns to the Soviets—Greg Gulley/Kim Parker	9.99 _____
_____	Deadly Deception: Freemasonry—Tom McKenney	8.99 _____
_____	The Delicate Balance—John Zajac	8.99 _____
_____	Dinosaurs and the Bible—Dave Unfred	12.99 _____
_____	*Don't Touch That Dial—Barbara Hattemer & Robert Showers	9.99/19.99 _____
_____	En Route to Global Occupation—Gary Kah	9.99 _____
_____	Exposing the AIDS Scandal—Dr. Paul Cameron	7.99 _____
_____	Face the Wind—Gloria Delaney	9.99 _____
_____	False Security—Jerry Parks	9.99 _____
_____	From Rock to Rock—Eric Barger	8.99 _____
_____	*Gays & Guns—John Eidsmoe	7.99/14.99 _____
_____	*A Generation Betrayed—Randy Kirk	9.99 _____
_____	*Heresy Hunters—Jim Spencer	9.99 _____
_____	Hidden Dangers of the Rainbow—Constance Cumbey	9.99 _____
_____	*Hitler and the New Age—Bob Rosio	9.99 _____
_____	Inside the New Age Nightmare—Randall Baer	9.99 _____
_____	*A Jewish Conservative Looks at Pagan America—Don Feder	9.99/19.99 _____
_____	Journey Into Darkness—Stephen Arrington	9.99 _____
_____	Kinsey, Sex and Fraud—Dr. Judith A. Reisman/ Edward Eichel	10.99 _____
_____	Legend of the Holy Lance (A Novel)—William T. Still	8.99/16.99 _____
_____	*Loyal Opposition—John Eidsmoe	8.99 _____
_____	New World Order—William T. Still	9.99 _____
_____	One Year to a College Degree—Lynette Long/Eileen Hershberger	9.99 _____
_____	Political Correctness—David Thibodaux	9.99 _____
_____	*Prescription Death—Dr. Reed Bell/Frank York	9.99 _____
_____	*Real Men—Dr. Harold Voth	9.99 _____
_____	"Soft Porn" Plays Hardball—Dr. Judith A. Reisman	8.99/16.95 _____
_____	*Subtle Serpent—Darylann Whitemarsh & Bill Reisman	9.99 _____
_____	To Grow By Storybook Readers—Janet Friend	44.95 per set _____
_____	*Trojan Horse—Brenda Scott & Samantha Smith	9.99 _____
_____	Twisted Cross—Joseph Carr	9.99 _____
_____	*When the Wicked Seize a City—Chuck & Donna McIlhenny/Frank York	9.99 _____
_____	*Why Does a Nice Guy Like Me Keep Getting Thrown in Jail—Randall Terry	8.95 _____
_____	You Hit Like a Girl—Elsa Houtz & William J. Ferkile	9.99 _____

* _New Title_   **Total** _____

Shipping and Handling _____

Enclosed is $_____ including postage.

VISA/MASTERCARD#_____ Exp. Date_____

Name_____ Phone: ( )_____

Address_____

City, State, Zip_____